"This accessible and engaging text is a must read for anyone with an interest in Children and Young People's Mental Health. This book is full of practical advice grounded in many years of expert practice and leadership. The authors' absolute belief in the essential role of parents and carers, coupled with the explanation of how networks of care are structured, will build parents' and carers' confidence as they navigate complex systems. Professionals from all agencies will appreciate the balanced and thoughtful demonstration of how their contribution sits within the system of wider support for those in difficulty and areas they may like to improve. It will be particularly helpful to commissioners and policy makers as they seek to improve outcomes and a truly integrated approach. By identifying key principles and weaving case studies throughout, the authors create a compelling narrative that gives hope whilst being realistic about challenges that cannot always be overcome even with our best efforts. But by giving our children, young people and those who care for them, agency, input as equals into developing a choice of what, who, when and where help is provided, building system-wide collaboration and clear leadership with expert training and supervision, whilst monitoring and reflecting on outcomes with curiosity, honesty and humility, we can make a real difference."

Kathryn Pugh, *MBE and former Deputy Head of Mental Health in NHS England, leading the Children and Young People's Mental Health Community Transformation Programme*

"Following a decade of implementation of the THRIVE Framework for system change, this timely and compassionate book offers an evidence-informed approach to helping children and young people with mental health needs that recognises the importance of clinical intervention where indicated, whilst challenging the idea that therapy alone is sufficient.

With clarity and warmth, it illustrates the ways in which adverse conditions amplify risks and hinder recovery, highlighting the powerful roles of families, schools and communities in supporting young people alongside professionals, attending to their life context, and drawing on trusted relationships to create psychologically safe environments where children live their everyday lives.

Clear, accessible and hopeful, it promotes a practical approach to supporting children and young people where mental health and wellbeing is everyone's responsibility through a robust, collaborative and effective 'helping system' to meet rising mental health needs."

Dr Rachel James, *Director of Clinical Services, Tavistock & Portman NHS Foundation Trust*

"This book is an invaluable text for anyone concerned about child and adolescent mental health, and for anyone supporting children and young people in a personal or professional capacity. Based on their extensive clinical, academic and policy experience, and illustrated sensitively with reference to the lived experiences of families, the authors communicate their confidence in the ability of the many different people who are present in children and young people's lives to work together to support them. By providing opportunities, empowerment and support, the clear principles provided here outline how this wider system can contribute, in complementary ways, to positive outcomes for children and young people."

Professor Cathy Creswell, *University of Oxford*

"This book offers an excellent exploration of the concept of 'Help' through the experiences of six young individuals.

Using the THRIVE Framework as an organising structure, 'Helping Children' serves as an accessible and practical guide to better understand children's mental health and the diverse range of experiences associated with it. It emphasises the need for a varied support system around each child to effectively meet their unique needs.

This book reminds us of our collective responsibility to support children's mental health by strengthening resources within the community and families. It encourages us to engage in shared decision-making, involving young people in the design of support services, which promotes their participation and improves the effectiveness of the help provided."

Rose McCarthy, *Senior Organisational Consultant and National i-THRIVE Programme Lead at Tavistock Consulting*

"For all of us working with young people who are trying to cope with their mental health challenges, this is an important and accessible book on how to best help such young people by really listening to their stories and needs. Based upon the principle that it is not just direct work that is needed, but effective engagement and support with family and wider networks, this book will really help professionals and carers in supporting such young people and their networks."

Brian Littlechild, *Professor Emeritus, University of Hertfordshire*

"Significant and much-needed progress has been made over the past decade to radically rethink the way that child and adolescent mental health services are delivered. Despite this progress, ongoing variation in and fragmentation of delivery persists, impacting the lives of many children and young people. This book brings together many of the foundations for developing an exciting new model for all child and adolescent mental health services, from crucial insights into how services should be configured, how they can best engage, intervene and include young people in their care, to emphasising the importance of measuring change, supporting safe care and ensuring that all those in contact with children, young people and families have a responsibility to consider and provide for their emotional health and well-being. It brings together learning from a wide range of sources to provide a practical framework for delivering services that are responsive to and co-constructed with children, young people and their families, following individual young person stories throughout to eloquently illustrate the importance of adopting a new paradigm for care. Set in the context of the innovative THRIVE Framework for system change, this ambitious book is a key text to be read by practitioners, managers, commissioners, strategic decision-makers and service users alike."

Dr Paul Wallis, *Director of Psychological Services – MFT CAMHS, Chief Psychological Professions Officer MFT, GM i-THRIVE/CAMHS Workforce Lead, Manchester University Hospitals NHS Foundation Trust*

"This is an important and timely book. One that invites professional experts and system organisers to engage humbly with the awkward fact that despite over an hundred years of research and development into what works for whom in the treatment of children and adolescents with mental health needs (a project both authors have long and intimate experience of), 'we' have signally failed to create systems of help commensurate with the burdens that epidemiology shows us as prevalent across the world.

Our best evidence-based treatments help only a proportion of the children and young people they are directed at and are insufficient to bridge the 'treatment gap' by orders of magnitude. Even the evidence that strict fidelity to evidence-based models of specialist therapies offers more than marginal gains in terms of outcomes is weak at best; meanwhile, the impact of systemic, social and cultural factors is consistently underestimated. This book invites us to consider a significant rebalancing of the nature of professional help and the part that it might play *alongside* the necessary acknowledgement, active engagement with and scaffolding of those 'extant helping systems' (albeit often fragile, and perhaps even actively harmful) that inevitably exist around all children and young people. These are the informal real-world networks that professionals can only hope to join, rather than to (re)build from scratch. As the saying goes, 'Culture eats strategy for breakfast', and this is relevant especially if by 'strategy' we mean decades of effort to develop evidence-based interventions and the systems to target and deliver these efficiently. Through the use of well-worked case examples that illustrate six core principles centred on the nature of the helping process itself (emphasising collaboration between professional and non-professional helpers, active participation by young people and families, outcome measurement, safety and whole-system approaches), this book makes a powerful argument for a more systemically (and, if truth be told, *reality*-) rooted approach that – without in any way dismissing the value of technical professional expertise – invites it into a profoundly new relationship, one less managerial and power-suffused and instead more *grounded*, in and with the worlds which our patients inhabit. I thoroughly recommend this book to anyone embarking on a career in the 'helping professions', to service planners and managers, and even, dare I say it, to the politicians who hold the power to direct the energy and financial resources intended for their constituents' future wellbeing."

Dr Dickon Bevington, MA, MBBS, MRCPsych, PGCert, *Consultant in Child and Adolescent Psychiatry, Medical Director, Anna Freud*

Helping Children

Children and young people's mental health is now recognised as one of society's most pressing challenges. Rates of distress and disorder have risen sharply while services struggle to keep pace. Long waiting lists and public concern highlight the growing gap between what children need and what professional systems can deliver. Yet, there remains an expectation that therapy alone should provide the answer.

This book argues that the mental health needs of children cannot be met by specialist services in isolation. Instead, it calls for a new approach that brings together parents, teachers, peers and communities alongside mental health professionals, each playing an equal part in supporting children's well-being. Drawing on research, policy and practice experience, this book identifies six principles of effective help: the active involvement of parents and carers; the importance of listening to children's own wishes; creating environments of psychological safety; recognising that help can come from many sources; embedding support within everyday community life; and building a culture where caring for children's mental health becomes everyone's shared responsibility.

Written by leading figures in child mental health, this book offers a powerful new framework for rethinking how society responds to young people's distress. It speaks to professionals, educators, parents and policymakers alike, showing how families, schools and communities can work together to nurture resilience and belonging, reducing dependence on overstretched specialist services.

Peter Fuggle has been a clinical psychologist working with children since 1984. He was the clinical director at NHS Islington Child Mental Health Service and then at Anna Freud. He contributed to the development of child-IAPT, the Thrive Approach, Community Wellbeing Practitioners and Educational Mental Health Practitioners. With Dickon Bevington, he co-developed the AMBIT Programme for young people with multiple needs.

Peter Fonagy, CBE, is a Professor of Contemporary Psychoanalysis and Developmental Science and Head of the Division for Psychology and Language Sciences, UCL. He is also Senior National Clinical Adviser for NHS England on Children and Young People's Mental Health. He was the Chief Executive of Anna Freud for over 20 years.

Anna Freud: Key Ideas and Best Practice

Series Editors: Chloe Campbell & Elizabeth Allison

The Anna Freud centre has long been a centre of both research and clinical innovation. Each book in the Routledge/AFC series explores a different area of cutting-edge thinking in mental health and its treatment, with a strong but not exclusive focus on children and families. Accessible and clearly written, these books will range from clinical practice through to research and implementation issues and will be of interest to a wide audience of those concerned with mental health and the latest thinking on prevention and treatment as well as understanding more about the experience of psychological difficulties and their development.

Titles in the series:

High-Conflict Parenting Post-Separation: The Making and Breaking of Family Ties
By Eia Asen and Emma Morris

Improving Mental Health Therapies for Autistic Children and Young People: Promoting Self-agency, Curiosity and Collaboration
Edited by Georgia Pavlopoulou, Laura Crane, Russell Hurn and Damian Milton

Helping Children: Principles of Good Practice in Child Mental Health
By Peter Fuggle and Peter Fonagy

For more information about this series please visit: https://www.routledge.com/Anna-Freud/book-series/BSEAFBP

Helping Children

Principles of Good Practice in Child Mental Health

Peter Fuggle and Peter Fonagy

Routledge
Taylor & Francis Group
LONDON AND NEW YORK

Designed cover image: Getty Images

First published 2027
by Routledge
4 Park Square, Milton Park, Abingdon, Oxon OX14 4RN

and by Routledge
605 Third Avenue, New York, NY 10158

Routledge is an imprint of the Taylor & Francis Group, an informa business

British Library Cataloguing-in-Publication Data
A catalogue record for this book is available from the British Library

ISBN: 978-0-367-70293-9 (hbk)
ISBN: 978-0-367-70291-5 (pbk)
ISBN: 978-1-003-14552-3 (ebk)

DOI: 10.4324/9781003145523

Typeset in Times New Roman
by codeMantra

Contents

Chapter 1

Children and Young People

Introduction

This book outlines principles of good practice in helping children and young people with mental health needs. At its core, effective practice involves collaboration between specialist mental health professionals and families. Both play crucial roles in helping children and young people manage distress and cope better with such challenges. For some, professional services may be more central; for others, family support may be paramount. In this book, we will propose rebalancing this collaboration to give greater emphasis to the contributions of families and their communities alongside the role played by professionals and services.

Child mental health resembles a kaleidoscope, viewed through various lenses. Some focus on the nature of mental health issues affecting children and young people; others concentrate on available treatments or the necessary training for professionals providing such interventions. In this book, our guiding lens is the concept of help—how help takes place between children, young people and the adult world responsible for their care. Professional treatment for child mental health is part of this broader concept of help and, for many children, a key aspect of the help they need. Our inclusive definition of help encompasses various forms of help beyond therapy or health treatments, highlighting the vital roles of parents, carers, family members, community projects, schools, teachers, social workers, peers and many others. The starting point is recognising the contributions of many caring and responsible adults and young people in the helping process. We term this inclusive help. A key theme is understanding how different components of this inclusive helping system collaborate to enable a child or young person to overcome the needs and challenges that they face.

This book is also a collaboration between two authors. Peter Fonagy works at UCL and is an expert on child mental health, deeply involved in research and service initiatives in the UK and internationally. Peter Fuggle is a clinical psychologist who has held various roles in NHS services, including Clinical Director of the NHS Islington Mental Health Service and Clinical Director of

DOI: 10.4324/9781003145523-1

the Anna Freud Centre. In these roles he has adopted a pragmatic approach to helping children, believing that the fundamental task is for children to receive help that makes sense to them. This is more important than whether help is what adults think they should get.

We aim to integrate the narratives of children, young people and their families with those of services, therapies and research. To achieve this, we will weave the stories of six children and young people alongside discussions of helping processes, treatments, therapies and services. These six stories are based on young people seen by Peter Fuggle over many years, with details altered and combined to ensure anonymity. These individual narratives will counterpoint general descriptions of how services should be organised and the practice standards that they should follow. These descriptions run the risk of being simplifications compared to the complicated realities of helping individual children, potentially misleading us into thinking such ideas are true in ways that they are not. So the intention is to describe core principles of good practice while staying close to real-life stories in order to 'keep us honest' and avoid overconfidence in the ideas we advocate. These principles are guides, not absolute truths and good practice must be rooted in the realities of children and carers' experiences of help. Their stories will include both ups and downs, reflecting the journey young people undertake through their difficulties and distress and are intended to provide a reference point from which we invite the reader to gauge the value of our suggestions. We now provide a brief introduction to the lives of these children and young people, each with very different types of mental health needs.

Children and Young People with Mental Health Needs

Jacqui, a 14-year-old Black African young person, lived with her birth parents. At 12, her grandmother, who had cared for her in her early life, died unexpectedly, coinciding with Jacqui's transition to a new secondary school at Year 8 which separated her from primary school friends. She increasingly withdrew into herself both at home and school, complained of being unwell and stopped attending classes. Although she did not call it this herself, she became depressed and irritable, straining relationships with her parents through frequent rows and emotional storms. Her mother consulted their GP, leading to a referral to the local child mental health service, where Jacqui was offered individual therapy. Despite initial reluctance, she connected well with her therapist, and over time, her mood improved. She gradually resumed regular school attendance. The therapy included joint sessions with her mother, who was eager to better support her at home.

Martin, an 11-year-old White British boy, lived with Sandra, his foster carer for two years. In early life, he was cared for by Maisie, his birth mother, who had a long-term addiction problem. Martin frequently clashed with his foster carer and with staff at school. Two years previously, he had been diagnosed with attention deficit hyperactivity disorder (ADHD) and took daily medication, but this had not improved his concentration or behaviour. At psychiatric appointments, he was usually silent and clearly disliked attending. The special needs team at his primary school collaborated closely with Sandra to develop an adapted school curriculum for him, leading to Martin becoming more settled in school over the past year.

Abdul, an 8-year-old from a British Asian family, was diagnosed with Autistic Spectrum Disorder at six and attended his local primary school. Considered 'high functioning', he managed the school curriculum but struggled with changes in school routines and was often overwhelmed by sensory stimulation. He experienced 'behavioural storms', becoming very distressed, covering his ears and banging his head, taking a long time to calm down. Initially, the school would always call his mother during these episodes. He had a health and education support plan, which included help for these outbursts. As part of this, Abdul attended the local child mental health service with his mother to help him to learn coping strategies when he became stressed and anxious.

Simone, a 4-year-old from a White European family, moved to the UK shortly after her birth. Before starting school, she was cared for by her mother and grandmother and was generally happy and developing well. The transition to primary school was extremely stressful for Simone and her parents, Brigitte and Patrick, who were unfamiliar with the British education system and became very anxious about how she would settle. Simone experienced severe separation anxiety, screaming uncontrollably when parted from her parents. The school referred the family to the Early Help team, who developed a graded approach to support Simone's school attendance. Progress was slow, and the team sought advice from the mental health team. After six months, Simone was attending school nearly every day, with occasional setbacks, particularly after weekends or holidays.

Daniel, a 16-year-old White British boy, lived with his mother, Judith, who was divorced from his father. He attended his local secondary school and did okay academically. He hated his body image and was convinced he needed cosmetic surgery and made detailed plans as to the surgery he would have when he was an adult. He rejected the label of body dysmorphic disorder which he did not believe applied to him. Acutely sensitive to rejection, Daniel experienced intense anxiety and low moods, which he sometimes relieved by cutting himself or by using cannabis. He regularly isolated himself in his room, engrossed in computer games and social media. He worried about his mother, who was stressed by work and relied on medication to cope; on weekends, he sometimes had to care for her when she remained in bed. Daniel found support in an online chat room, where interactions with peers in this forum led him to join an extreme exercise group, and he began to feel better in himself as he became involved with this.

Teresa, a 17-year-old White Irish young person, was part of a large family that had moved to London during her early childhood. Although impulsive, her early life had been reasonably settled. In secondary school, she began experiencing severe rages, becoming violent towards peers and family members. At 15, she assaulted a teacher and was permanently excluded from school. At 16, she attempted suicide with a large paracetamol overdose, leading to a period of inpatient care. She was believed to be engaging in risky sexual behaviour with strangers, posing a risk to herself and others. After her hospital admission, she was passed to the local outreach team and gradually developed trust in Molly, a community nurse who she met in community settings such as cafes and parks because Teresa hated clinics. Molly focused on building trust in her relationship with Teresa and supported her to engage with sexual health services and to enrol at college.

Jacqui, Martin, Abdul, Simone, Daniel and Teresa all had what are defined as mental health needs, despite differences in age, circumstances and the help they received. Five of them had contact with mental health services at some point, but this was not their only source of support. They and their families had their own ideas about their problems and opinions about the help they wanted—or didn't want—from others. Not unusually, the young people were more hesitant than their parents or carers about seeking professional help. They experienced help in different ways from their family, peers, school, mental health professionals, their community (e.g., faith groups) or emotional partners. The mental health treatment provided by mental health professionals was part of this broader system of help and support, as illustrated by the stories of these six young people.

In including these six young people as the core thread of this book, we will not limit our descriptions to their interactions with mental health services. All six had lives extending beyond their mental health issues: they formed and broke friendships, played games, watched films, took part in education, discovered things about the world, were close (or not) with their parents or carers, engaged in social media, developed future aspirations, worried about climate change and were excited by football. Jacqui was talented at football. Martin spent Saturday mornings at the local urban farm, helping to clean out the stables. Abdul had an encyclopaedic knowledge of anime cards. Despite her general anxiety, Simone loved swimming and appeared fearless in the sea. Daniel found that extreme exercise provided respite from his self-image worries. Teresa found a loyal and supportive boyfriend, despite her meltdowns and low moods. For these young people, their lives included the common triumphs and disasters of childhood and adolescence. And these took place within family circumstances also subject to adverse and fortuitous events. There were times when their parents argued, lost jobs or found better ones; when a grandparent became ill and needed constant care; when their house was burgled; or when the family's football team won the league or was relegated. These fluctuating events impact all families. By including this wider perspective on their lives, we do not imply that their difficulties were merely common childhood dramas. Mental health problems are much more severe than that, being extremely distressing for both the child and the family and often leading to enduring negative states of mind that may affect their future life as adults.

Helping Systems for Children and Young People with Mental Health Needs

Support for children and young people with mental health needs varies widely so that sometimes specialist mental health services are central; other times, they play a lesser role. This depends on factors such as the views of the child, the resources of the service, beliefs of the parents/carers, the degree that the school is involved, the friends that they have and the life events that they have either endured or celebrated. In multiple varying combinations, each child or young person has a different set of helping relationships that may support them well, falter or temporarily collapse altogether. Effective help involves enabling this helping system to function well so that families, professionals, schools and communities collaborate to enable a child to find their way through the challenges that they face.

But these support systems do not operate on an even playing field, but in a landscape marked by social inequality, discrimination and injustice. Throughout this book, we acknowledge the destructive impacts of racism, poverty, social disadvantage, invalidation of sexual and cultural identities and the oppression faced by vulnerable groups like refugees and asylum seekers. Mental health challenges don't arise in isolation; these adverse conditions amplify risks and hinder recovery. Addressing children's mental health involves supporting the individual and attending to their life context, and our task is to explore how society can best support children like Jacqui, Martin, Abdul, Simone, Daniel and Teresa.

A common response to this challenge is to hand over this task entirely to professional mental health services, advocating for increased resources to ensure greater availability of professional help. While adequate resourcing is essential, we suggest this is not the sole or even best solution. We need to think not only about helping services but also about helping systems as being central to effective help. Beyond specialist services and professional treatment, families, children, young people, schools and communities play crucial roles in these helping systems. Focusing solely on professional care risks overlooking the significant contributions of these crucial parts of each child's wider helping system.

For instance, Jacqui's access to professional help was crucially supported by the role played by her family in overcoming her reluctance to receive professional help and in supporting her after her return to school. Abdul's development was significantly influenced by the support the family received from their faith community. Martin experienced an accepting and beneficial relationship from Polly and Brian, who fostered his love of animals. Teresa had a pattern of disrupting supportive relationships but somehow her relationship with her boyfriend Sean survived. In the support systems around these six children, specialist practitioners were sometimes central as was Teresa's outreach nurse, Molly, while for Martin, his relationship with his psychiatrist was more peripheral. In emphasising the importance of family, school and community relationships to mental health support, we're not proposing something new but advocating for a narrative that gives greater prominence to the non-specialist parts of existing support systems, which may often (and crucially) require specialist professionals to assist and guide them. We cannot do without mental health professionals, but they cannot meet these needs alone. Currently, there's a risk of overburdening the professional services with expectations to fix mental health difficulties single-handedly. This book articulates a rebalancing that we see as crucial for effectively supporting children and young people with mental health needs. By recognising and strengthening these collaborations, we can create more robust support systems for children and young people facing mental health challenges. Inclusive help, seeing the value in multiple contributions to supporting and helping children and young people, provides a balanced narrative that gives due prominence to all parts of the helping system. Specialist mental health professionals are essential, but they cannot meet such needs alone, and over-reliance on them may lead to undermining the crucial contributions of many others. This is what we mean by rebalancing our approach so that the vital roles played by families, schools and communities can provide more effective support for children and young people with mental health needs.

Plan for the Book

In the upcoming chapters, we will first examine the significant challenges currently confronting specialist mental health services in their efforts to provide effective help, followed by an exploration of similar difficulties faced by parents and families. These discussions will lay the groundwork for addressing the issues that the remainder of the book aims to tackle. To structure our analysis, we will employ the THRIVE Framework, developed by Professor Miranda Wolpert and colleagues approximately a decade ago which emphasised the need to support multiple methods of help for children and young people and to ensure that they played an active role in designing their own help. Using this framework, we will outline six principles that focus on enhancing helping systems rather than solely relying on services. This will be followed by proposing how these principles can be applied to key aspects of mental health support. Throughout this journey, the experiences of young people will serve as the backbone of our discussion, ensuring that our ideas remain relevant to their needs.

The narratives of these six young individuals are not universally positive (not all get better) but are intended to be consistent with general observations about outcomes for children and young people. We aim to use accessible language and will minimise academic references within the text. Each chapter will be accompanied by endnotes providing references to support our claims. Additionally, at the conclusion of each chapter, we will include an additional story about a child or parent aimed to illustrate the variability of the helping process in practice. These stories are drawn from families where the core issues are portrayed honestly but specific life details have been changed. These narratives are also not universally positive, as presenting them as such would be misleading. We strive to respect the children and families we describe, acknowledging that our understanding has been shaped through our relationships with them. Our overarching vision is that by recognising the contributions of various individuals to effective helping systems, we can improve how we alleviate the suffering of young people. This optimistic narrative is dedicated to all the young people we have endeavoured to help, who have, in turn, taught us how effective helping systems may actually work.

Chapter 2

Providing Help

The Problems for Mental Health Services

Introduction

Improvements in child mental health in the UK cannot rely solely on specialist services, yet these services are often expected to do just that. Addressing the needs of children and young people involves both professional help and strengthening family and community resources towards the same end. As we have already seen in the stories of the six young people, it is essential to include the roles of non-specialist professionals, family members, schools and the community in supporting children and young people with these difficulties. The largest workforce in child mental health in the UK are undoubtedly parents and carers, who often provide the most substantial share of help when major needs emerge. This chapter focuses on the nature and problems of specialist professional services in meeting these needs. The following chapter will examine the challenges for families and communities.

The Value of Professional Mental Health Treatment

Modern industrial digital societies employ many people to help others. Regarding mental health needs, long ago, this role was primarily filled by priests and doctors. In post-industrial societies, the provision of help for those with mental health needs has proliferated, along with our evolving understanding of these needs, especially in the way that social conditions play such a big part in creating them. Help has become professionalised, requiring demanding and lengthy specialist training to become a qualified practitioner. These include child and adolescent psychiatrists, clinical and educational psychologists, social workers, family therapists, specialist teachers, speech and language therapists, occupational therapists, psychiatric nurses, youth workers and child psychotherapists. The assumption is that the help they offer can only be provided by professionals who have undergone such training. Specific methods of help become exclusive to that profession. In many instances, this makes sense and protects clients from receiving help that could be ineffective

DOI: 10.4324/9781003145523-2

or even harmful. Obvious examples include prescribing medication, which can only be done by qualified doctors. Similarly, specialist therapeutic methods, such as treating trauma, require properly trained therapists. These developments have significantly benefited many children and young people who receive such treatments. Such treatments work particularly well when the child or young person trusts the help they are receiving and has only one main problem, not complicated by simultaneous intersecting difficulties, notably, for example, problems in family relationships, substance misuse or bullying. Specialist treatments emphasise that the expertise of the helper is crucial in relieving the young person's distress. As others do not have this expertise, this may invalidate their role in providing help for the child or young person with this need. This dilemma is well recognised by those who offer such treatments and is not intended here as a criticism but as a consequence that expertise brings. Many expert treatments fully embrace the possibility that expert treatment may not be necessary in all cases. For example, for children exposed to traumatic events (war, earthquakes, terrorist attacks), the first line of help is to encourage them to communicate with trusted adults, usually parents.

Not all children affected by traumatic events will require therapy with professional therapists.[1] Many will not suffer traumatic reactions, and communication with trusted adults can provide crucial support. Non-judgemental curiosity about a child's distress and experiences from trusted adults can be as beneficial as professional help. However, for some, due to the severity of their distress or lack of informal support, professional treatment becomes essential. Traumatic distress involves re-experiencing traumatic events and requires carefully created conditions to create a change, including the expertise of a therapist. The example of trauma illustrates that specialist expertise may not be needed for all children and that, for some, effective help may be more about maintaining or re-establishing trusting relationships within the child's life in the face of new emotional challenges. The skills needed to help a child or young person with such difficulties may be closer to familiar helping processes such as love, encouragement, kindness and the availability of a trusted helper than specialist psychological techniques. While the professionalisation of help and the development of mental health treatments provided by highly trained specialists have clearly brought significant benefits,[2] they may lead to the belief that all children with mental health needs require specialist direct help. From the broader perspective of helping systems, this idea may not be helpful.

In the UK, child mental health services often face criticism, may be described as 'creaking' or 'broken', with long waiting lists[3] and a significant proportion of children not accessing professional services for their mental health needs.[4] Less attention is given to the number of children who improve or recover under their care. The dominant narrative is that distress in children is exacerbated by insufficient service capacity. Despite considerable government investment (often unacknowledged) in health provision for children and young people over the last 20 years, pressure on waiting lists remains high. We will briefly consider five problems contributing to this and why relying solely on professional services alone to fix these difficulties may not be the best approach.

Problem 1: Large Numbers of Children and Young People Have Mental Health Needs

Jacqui, Martin, Abdul, Simone, Daniel and Teresa are not alone. In the UK, over a million children face probable mental health problems, approximately two to three per classroom.[5] These needs fall into three categories: emotional problems, behavioural problems and developmental disorders. Factors such as adverse childhood experiences,[6] early trauma, poverty, parental substance misuse and domestic violence significantly increase the risk of these mental health needs. However, effectively mitigating these factors remains complex. For instance, while it's evident that domestic violence heightens the risk of mental health needs for children being cared for in such environments, this is not the same as knowing how to reduce its occurrence. Few dispute that reducing the impact of parental substance misuse on children's lives would be beneficial for children, but altering parent behaviour around this is extremely hard. Martin was cared for in early life by Maisie, his birth mother, who was unable to provide adequate care despite efforts to support her in this role.

Not only are mental health needs very frequent, but they are also increasing although the reasons for this are unclear and there is unlikely to be a single reason for this. For example, the prevalence of attention-related problems has surged in the past two decades.[7] Diagnoses of Attention Deficit Hyperactivity Disorder (ADHD) have increased significantly since 2000. Similarly, diagnoses of Autistic Spectrum Disorder (ASD) have shown a substantial rise over a similar period. The exact reasons for this increase are unclear, but criteria for what constitutes these mental health conditions have become broader over this time. Children who would previously not have received a diagnosis now do so. These increases may be due to broader diagnostic criteria, leading to more children receiving these diagnoses. Additionally, a diagnosis of ADHD or ASD can provide access to enhanced educational support or medication. From our six children, Martin was diagnosed with ADHD and exhibited restlessness, distractibility and difficulty focusing on tasks requiring sustained attention. He was prescribed methylphenidate from the age of eight, which modestly reduced his impulsivity at school. However, the effects were limited, and much of the support for his attentional challenges fell to his teacher, Fatima, and his foster carer, Sandra. Both Sandra and his social worker, Matt, were unenthusiastic about medication, believing some of Martin's difficulties to be related to his early care experiences. Such differing views on medication are common and often based on misunderstandings. An ADHD diagnosis doesn't imply the problem is solely intrinsic or 'biological'; adverse experiences can contribute to attentional issues, and medication can be an appropriate treatment. In Martin's case, since the medication had little effect, it was discontinued. But the overall impact of these changes has been a sharp increase in demand and pressure on specialist mental health services. Referral rates have risen significantly, outpacing investment and making it difficult for services to keep up.[8] The emphasis on diagnosing psychiatric conditions has reinforced the belief that only specialist mental health services have the necessary expertise to help children and young people. This is both unhelpful and misleading, as addressing children's needs almost always requires collaboration between professionals, families and communities.

For Martin, the opportunity to experience himself as calm and stable came not from professional intervention but from his Saturday mornings at the urban farm with Polly and Brian. Abdul's educational and social progress relied heavily on the patience and dedication of his mother, Aisha, and her partnership with Fenulla, his teacher, in developing tailored strategies to help him to anticipate changes in the routines of his day which he found so disorientating. But Aisha's approach was not simply based on her own ideas and feelings about how to be a mother but was shaped by what she had learnt both from the assessment that led to Abdul's diagnosis and from sessions with Rachel, the clinical psychologist that Abdul saw in the clinic, where she learned how best to communicate with and support him at home. While these therapeutic sessions did not eliminate Abdul's distressing outbursts at school, Aisha valued Rachel's guidance and found it crucial in improving her ability to support her son both at home and in the classroom.

Rising mental health needs among children and young people cannot be attributed solely to diagnostic practices. Societal factors, such as the Covid pandemic, have also contributed to increased anxiety and distress for many children. However, environmental and relational stressors do not automatically lead to mental health problems, and it remains unclear whether these recent increases will persist over time. Many children exposed to significant adversity do not go on to develop mental health difficulties, highlighting the importance of understanding resilience. Why some children cope well in difficult circumstances while others struggle remains a central question in developing effective support systems.

Nonetheless, the sheer scale of identified need presents the most urgent challenge for professional services.

Problem 2: Treatment Isn't as Effective as We Would Like

Help provided by mental health professionals generally involves treatments that have been researched and evaluated for their effectiveness.[9] This is known as evidence-based practice and relies on precisely defining a condition or disorder and then offering the best course of treatment for such a condition. Extensive research has examined the mental health needs of children and young people, working on the premise that by defining the problem (or condition), we will know what treatment to offer or how to provide help.[10] The nature of the treatment follows from this understanding. This powerful line of thinking has been very effective in radically improving treatments for many medical conditions, but progress in child mental health treatments has been less substantial. The difference in effectiveness between evidence-based treatments and other methods, while present, is smaller than might be hoped.[11] As a rule of thumb, across many different types of mental health conditions, evidence-based treatments result in reliable improvement for about 50–60% of children and young people who take part in them.[12] This does not mean that the remaining 40% do not benefit at all. Many families report that the support has been valuable, yet the primary issue for which they sought help has not altered that much. So, for a young person with eating difficulties treatment may have increased their understanding of their difficulties, may have repaired some of the ruptured relationships in the family and led to a shared appreciation of the young person's difficulties, but the core problem of eating and low weight continues relatively unchanged. Similarly, a young person with depression may experience positive changes in some areas of life but continue to struggle with persistent low mood. The fact that 30–40% do not experience the hoped-for improvement places considerable pressure on services, which must then determine how best to support these children when standard treatments have not been as effective as we would wish.

Evidence-based practice[13] is vital for improving the help available to children, but it follows a supply-side logic—defining "how we think we can best help you". When children and young people sufficiently agree with the approach that this offers them, then there is no question that this is the way to go. But not all want or respond to help in the same way. They have their own feelings about who they would like help from and what they believe will make a difference.[14] Their ideas may be vague and often children find it hard to know. But sadly, they may not be asked, and their views are often overlooked. Their engagement—or lack of it—may be apparent more by their behaviour than what they say. We know some like to talk, some hate to talk. Some wish to involve their parents; others prefer to keep them at a distance. Some believe the solution lies in having more enjoyable experiences, while others think the real issue is that their parents should change their behaviour (e.g. stop arguing), or that the teachers should stop picking on them. The range of ways which children find help is as varied as their difficulties. Rather than placing the problem itself at centre stage, we suggest that we need to both focus on problems children have and give attention to the many ways children and young people experience support as helpful. Even when the nature of a child's problem seems well understood, the most effective way to help may still be unclear.

Jacqui's experience could be understood as a form of depression or low mood following the loss of her grandmother and the simultaneous loss of friendships due to changing schools. But Jacqui didn't call her experience 'depression'. She thought the world was horrible, that she was 'useless', and that she just wanted to hide away. The idea of going to a mental health service only made her feel worse, as it seemed like another place where she would feel stupid and humiliated. It took a great deal of sensitive care from her family to help her see that treatment might actually help. What made the difference was a conversation with her father, Kande, about his own unhappiness as a child when he first arrived in the UK to live with his aunt. She had assumed his general aloofness meant he was critical of her 'weakness', so this revelation surprised her. She had also (just enough) trust in her mother, Chisomo, to try something she would otherwise have avoided without her support. But for Martin, specialist help reinforced the idea that he was the problem, and he hated that. But when he was at the farm, he wasn't a problem; he could be patient and persistent in ways he couldn't manage at school or, at times, at home. Feeling better came not from treatment, but from simply being allowed to spend time at the farm. Teresa would make friends fast. She would pour her heart out to new people without hesitation. She was exciting, wild and fun—but exhausting. Friendships were formed easily and ended just as fast, leaving her with feelings of rejection and despair. She received help, but it didn't last. Daniel's path to help was blocked by his anxiety about his mother.

For all six young people, their lives were shaped not just by their difficulties but by how they related to the help they felt was available to them, which was safe enough to accept. Help did not always lead to things getting better. Getting help is not the same as getting better, though it is often a necessary step towards progress. This raises one of the key questions of this book: can we improve the likelihood that different forms of help lead to improvement in the life of a child or family? We believe this is possible—not just by defining the problem but by focusing as much on the process of help itself. This leads to the next challenge for professional services as to its difficulties in supporting individualised help.

Problem 3: Individualised Help Is Hard to Do

The six stories of young people described so far make it clear that children and young people will experience help in many different ways. Rather than seeing this diversity as a problem, we see it as a necessary and essential part of the solution. There is no singular or correct approach to addressing any specific mental health need. A range of responses is not just unavoidable but necessary. While this idea is easy to state, putting it into practice is far more challenging.[15] We have never met anyone who is opposed to individualised help. No one argues that children and young people should simply accept the help they are given. Yet, in reality, individualised care is extremely difficult to do. It is disruptive for organisations, often clashing with efforts to address the problems already outlined: overwhelming demand, the reliance on professional help and the limited effectiveness of standard treatments that are routinely offered. On its own, individualised care seems simple. Within complex helping systems, it can feel like a service manager's worst nightmare.

Take the example of social anxiety. Many children experience some anxiety in social situations; this is a normal part of development. Young children often fear strangers or unfamiliar social settings, but for most, this passes with time. However, for some, social anxiety becomes extreme, severely limiting their life and opportunities. This is not just a minor difference in experience or something a child can simply 'get over'. It is more like a continuous terror, an overwhelming sense of dread and physical discomfort. As one young person put it, 'I would just love to have anxiety like everyone else has it, not like I have it.'

For these young people, avoiding school or not leaving their room or consuming large amounts of cannabis may become ways of managing their distress. There are now well-established evidence-based treatments for social anxiety, and these treatments are generally more effective than other forms of help although this difference is not always large and they do not help everyone. What may be crucial is that these approaches are adapted to fit the individual child and their family, considering the social or personal factors that contribute to their difficulties.

For example, for families who have been subject to ongoing and persistent discrimination and abuse either in the form of racism or other injustices, the meaning of social anxiety may be very different from that of families who have not faced such adversity. In these families, social anxiety may be an adaptive response to a hostile or threatening environment rather than a purely maladaptive condition. Supporting children and young people with social anxiety may need to be sensitively adapted to both their lived experiences and their circumstances in order to address the conditions that shape their distress. Anti-racism programmes in schools, for instance, may be a crucial part of addressing the root causes of anxiety for a young person whose distress is exacerbated by discrimination. This shifts the focus away from locating the 'problem' solely within the child and instead considers the broader conditions that sustain their difficulties. Without addressing these conditions, there is a risk that interventions are seen as irrelevant in a threatening environment where anxiety is a rational and adaptive response to ongoing threats. A similar need for adaptation applies to families who are part of faith communities with strong beliefs about the power of religion in alleviating suffering. Most mental health treatments have been developed within a secular framework, yet in practice, effective support may involve integrating psychological approaches with religious understandings. Social anxiety may carry very different meanings for a young person in a family with deep-rooted cultural traditions of collective worship, particularly if their anxiety affects their participation in religious gatherings. If a family believes that mental health difficulties are an indication of a broken relationship with God, they may see the appropriate 'treatment' as re-establishing that connection through prayer or other religious practices.[16] In such cases, families may seek guidance from faith leaders rather than turning to secular mental health services.

These examples reinforce the importance of diversity and inclusion in mental health support. A 'one size fits all' approach is insufficient. Strengthening relationships between faith communities and mental health services can help ensure that when these dilemmas arise, they are navigated with greater cultural and religious sensitivity. Forms of help must also accommodate important differences in personal identity. At present, this is particularly important in validating and supporting children and young people with diverse sexual identities. Young people who self-identify within the LGBTQ+ community[17] may well experience social anxiety in ways that differ significantly from those in dominant social and cultural groups. Humility is essential in recognising that it may not be appropriate for those with heterosexual identities to determine how support should be adapted to the needs of this group. As with communities subjected to racism, faith groups facing marginalisation, and those with non-dominant sexual identities, the role of power must be acknowledged in shaping effective help. Seeking help is a process that involves exposing personal vulnerability, which is far more precarious for those whose life conditions include ongoing conditions of threat or disadvantage.

It is crucial to recognise the necessity of adaptation in respecting diverse identities. Social anxiety may, in some cases, be an understandable adaptation to a society that remains, at best, ambiguous—and often hostile—towards certain identities. A central principle of this book is that diversity in approaches to helping children and young people is essential. This does not mean that anything goes. Well-tested methods should form the foundation for considering what may work well for children, young people and families in different social contexts. Recognising the needs of different social groups highlights the importance of social context in shaping effective support. But this is only the starting point. The experiences of Jacqui, Martin, Abdul, Simone, Daniel and Teresa illustrate that individualisation goes much further than simply recognising group identities. Help is a process of intimacy, shaped by the fine-grained details of a child or young person's life, which is inevitably unique. Recognising this uniqueness is crucial in building trust and making help effective. For example, Cognitive Behaviourial Therapy (CBT) approaches to social anxiety may be an effective evidence-based intervention, but if a young person unconsciously associates these sessions with past experiences of being told off—or worse—by their parents, the treatment may not work as intended. In such cases, creating space for the young person to express their feelings about authority and control may be necessary before they can fully engage with CBT strategies for improving social confidence.

While individualising help is an agreeable concept in theory, it presents major challenges for services under severe pressure to meet high referral demands. Setting limits on the number of treatment sessions is one way of managing this pressure, and this may work for many young people, such as Jacqui. But for those who establish trust with more difficulty (like Martin), who fear change (like Simone), whose difficulties are more visible to others than to themselves (like Abdul), who feel their distress is dismissed as 'not real' (like Daniel) or who struggle with impulsivity and inconsistency (like Teresa), standardised, short-term interventions may require more flexibility than they can manage. When children struggle to engage, they may be labelled as 'hard to reach' or 'unmotivated', when the difficulty may lie with the service's inability to adapt to their needs and the support networks already in place around them. This challenge may seem impossible to resolve—if help is viewed solely through the lens of services. But if helping services shift their focus from addressing the needs of the child in isolation and consider ways of strengthening the wider helping systems that already exist around a child, then there may be far greater opportunities for flexible and individualised support than may be apparent if services are constrained by fixed protocols of help.

Problem 4: It's Hard to Agree What Is the Best Type of Help

Young people with mental health problems often have other difficulties in their lives other than mental health needs. These may be closely related to, or even the cause of, their distress. They may have no money, no friends, hate going to school, find it hard to read, have no opportunities to make music or play football and be unsure of their sexuality. They may have family members who are unwell, in debt or out of work. They may feel overwhelmed by concerns about global warming, the impact of international wars and the horrible things they see on the internet. As previously highlighted, mental health problems rarely exist in isolation from a young person's broader life circumstances, family relationships or social environment.

Many children and young people experiencing mental health difficulties receive support from a range of different agencies and professionals.[18] At first sight, this may seem beneficial and that the young person is receiving help across the range of their needs. In some cases, this works well. For Jacqui, the school accommodated her therapy appointments during school hours, and both services worked effectively with her mother to support her return to school. Similarly, for Simone, the school, early help team and mental health services collaborated successfully to help her settle into school life. However, in many cases, having multiple sources of help does not work so well. Martin was supported by social care through his foster placement, by education for school-based support and by health for managing his hyperactivity. But everyone directly involved with caring, or teaching or supporting Martin was also involved in managing his behaviour. His foster carer would discuss Martin's behaviour with her supervising social worker on how best to respond when he was angry or oppositional. These approaches differed from the school's overall approach to managing behaviour, and this contrasted with the psychiatrist's recommendations. When Martin became angry and refused to follow instructions, he encountered different responses depending on the setting.

Such variation is common, but for Martin, it was highly ineffective. Each agency believed they had legitimate expertise in what would work best, but their lack of coordination resulted in inconsistency that left Martin without a clear or stable framework for support. Teresa's experience illustrates a similar issue. At 15, she struggled both in terms of her educational progress and in her ability to meet the social and behavioural expectations of her school. She was receiving additional educational support, but her behaviour was deteriorating, and she was at risk of being excluded from school. She had started using cannabis, and the local substance misuse team had successfully engaged her—she saw them as the only people who truly understood her. From the school's perspective, her exclusion was a necessary way of maintaining acceptable behaviour in the school context. Exclusion increased the likelihood of her continued substance use. Even partial school attendance could have helped maintain some structure in her life and supported efforts to reduce her cannabis use. A shared plan between services was needed—one that kept her in school while allowing her to continue engaging with the substance misuse team. But the school did not see her substance use as their responsibility. After another violent outburst, she was permanently excluded. She was offered short-term educational support at a Pupil Referral Unit, but her engagement with education declined further. She attended infrequently and formed a new friendship with another pupil, but this friendship revolved around shared cannabis use, reinforcing the very problem that services had been trying to address.

Similar contradictions can arise in many situations where children face disadvantage or threat. Young people exposed to situations of domestic violence may experience trauma and anxiety as a direct result of these circumstances. Mental health support for anxiety in this context should be closely coordinated with efforts to address the violence itself. Otherwise, offering support to a young person in isolation may unintentionally reinforce their belief that they are in some way responsible for the violence at home. Meanwhile, a team working with the adult experiencing abuse may encourage her to consider relocating for safety. However, this could mean the young person either moving schools (which she does not want) or staying with the other parent. These considerations and possible life changes may take place separately from the mental health support the child receives. Each service may be providing skilled and expert help, yet from the young person's perspective, the experience can feel confusing and fragmented.

The proposed solution to these challenges is integrated or collaborative care. As with individualised care, few would argue against this principle, yet it remains extremely difficult to implement. The fundamental support system for children consists of education, social care and health services, alongside voluntary sector initiatives. Aligning the perspectives of these key agencies is an ongoing challenge—not just in service planning but in constructing an effective helping system around an individual child. Professionals not only have differing views on what would be helpful for a child or family but may also disagree on how coordinated support should take place. The difficulty with integrated care[19] is not in its theory but in its execution. Despite service models and treatment guidelines promoting integrated practice, current systems struggle to achieve it. Past efforts have often focused on service reorganisation, but this has delivered only limited improvements. We argue that better integration will not come from restructuring services but from shifting the focus to the child and family as the central point of the helping system. This means explicitly asking and considering the child and family's ideas about what would be most helpful to them. Instead of merely attempting to join up interventions based on professional assessments of the child's best interests, a different approach is needed—one in which families play an active role in shaping their own support system. This, again, is a key theme of this book.

Problem 5: Immediate Needs Override Investment in Prevention

Prevention work in child mental health exists in various forms, such as mental health promotion, anti-bullying initiatives and anti-racism programmes. However, given what is known about the impact of negative environmental conditions on mental health needs, the scale of this work remains radically insufficient. While reducing child poverty falls within the realm of broader political agendas and beyond the resources of child mental health services, harnessing the support of peers, schools and communities is not. Despite strategic recognition of its importance, funding overwhelmingly prioritises immediate treatment needs. The focus of national debate is typically on reducing waiting times for professional services—an understandable but short-term concern that diverts attention from the longer-term potential of prevention. Effective prevention cannot be achieved by specialist services alone. If a national policy genuinely addresses social injustice, prevention must be built on collaboration with the communities it serves. Later chapters in this book will explore how this could be achieved.

Prevention and treatment, however, should not be seen as entirely separate. A strict division between the two risks oversimplifying the reality of how mental health support operates. In a sense, all support for young people like Jacqui, Martin, Abdul, Simone, Daniel and Teresa is aimed at preventing the likelihood of their adult lives being shaped by enduring mental health difficulties. Since most mental health problems have their roots in childhood, reducing their severity and impact early on is, by definition, a preventative measure. At the level of individual helping systems, prevention played a role in the experiences of the young people in this book. Jacqui's school received input from a Mental Health Support Team, and staff had access to mental health resources and ongoing training. Her Head of Year, Graham, although initially sceptical about depression in young people, had participated in training that encouraged a supportive rather than punitive response to Jacqui's school absences. Similarly, Abdul's therapeutic treatment focused on increasing his adaptability within a school environment, but his school worked hard to accommodate the specific needs of neurodiverse pupils. These approaches did not prevent the difficulties from arising but are likely to reduce their longer-term impact. Perhaps the clearest example is Simone. Her eventual ability to settle in school was critical for her longer-term social and educational development. Had she developed a pattern of persistent school absence from an early age, this would have posed a significant risk of escalating difficulties throughout childhood and into adulthood.

Summary and Conclusions

This chapter has outlined some of the key challenges facing specialist mental health services for children and young people. These services are a vital part of the overall support system for children and young people with mental health needs. However, the scale of need far exceeds what specialist services alone can meet. Effective support requires contributions from parents, families, schools and communities.

Current evidence suggests that specialist mental health treatments lead to meaningful improvement for approximately 50–60% of children who receive them. This, however, leaves a substantial proportion who do not experience significant improvement despite professional intervention. For these children, help often comes from family members, friends and their wider community. Many young people also have limited trust in professional services, and their mental health difficulties are frequently entangled with social, educational or relational issues. These complexities can lead to disagreements between young people and adults about what kind of help is most beneficial for them. Effective help usually involves collaboration between the child, their family, specialist services and their school. Yet, the role of parents in this process is not always given the prominence it deserves. While individualised care is widely promoted as a key approach for addressing complex needs, implementing multi-agency individualised support remains a major challenge. Achieving this requires a stronger joint agency approach to such needs.

These challenges indicate the need for greater investment in mental health services for children, young people and their families, but also highlight that professional services alone cannot meet all these needs. Support for children and young people is provided by a far wider group than the specialist mental health workforce. Parents, siblings, teachers, peers, youth workers and others play a critical role—sometimes in partnership with professionals, sometimes on their own. However, these individuals, particularly parents, face their own difficulties in how best to help children and young people. In the next chapter, we turn to them, recognising that while they are essential to children's mental health support, the responsibility cannot be handed back to them alone.

Key Practice Points

1 Specialist mental health services are a vital part of the overall helping system for children and young people with mental health needs but cannot address these needs alone.
2 Mental health difficulties are often intertwined with social, educational and relational issues, requiring collaboration between the child, their family, specialist mental health services, their school and other support networks.
3 Children with multiple needs, which include mental health needs, may encounter conflicting views on what type of help would be most beneficial, leading to disagreements over what the priorities should be.
4 Individualised care is widely promoted as a key approach for addressing multiple needs. However, implementing multi-agency, individualised support is challenging and requires far greater joint working between services than is currently standard practice.

A Family Life: Gavin

Gavin was a 16-year-old who struggled with depression and occasional suicidal thoughts, though he had no specific plans to act on them. When we first met, he was polite, apologetic and expressed deep feelings of hopelessness. He believed he had no friends and spent long hours alone on the internet in his room. His family consisted of his birth mother, Colleen, his stepfather, Dennis, and his 14-year-old sister, Sophie. He had been deeply affected by his parents' separation when he was eight. His birth father had moved abroad, and their contact was now infrequent. Initially, I worked with Gavin alone, focusing on his anxiety and depression. However, much of what he spoke about related to the ongoing conflict between his mother and stepfather, so we moved to having sessions with the whole family who agreed to participate. In one session, I invited them to reflect on how decisions were made in their household, asking each member to consider this from another family member's perspective. Sophie surprised and helped everyone by talking sympathetically about Dennis, noting how difficult it must be for him to navigate his role as a stepfather in their family. This became a turning point. The family became more engaged in working through their difficulties, experimenting with new ways of making decisions together and would try things out between sessions. Over time, tensions between Colleen and Dennis eased, and Gavin felt more able to express his feelings at home. By the end of the family sessions, his sense of despair had lifted, and he no longer felt the need for further individual professional help.

Notes

1 **Children exposed to traumatic events.** Several key studies have reported the prevalence of post-traumatic stress disorder (PTSD) among children exposed to traumatic events. The National Comorbidity Survey-Adolescent Supplement (NCS-A)

reported a prevalence among adolescents aged 13–18 of 6.3% who met the criteria for PTSD in the past year (Merikangas, K. R., He, J. P., Burstein, M., Swanson, S. A., Avenevoli, S., Cui, L.,… & Swendsen, J. (2010). Lifetime prevalence of mental disorders in US adolescents: Results from the National Comorbidity Survey Replication–Adolescent Supplement (NCS-A). *Journal of the American Academy of Child & Adolescent Psychiatry, 49*(10), 980–989). The Longitudinal Study of Child Maltreatment and Neurodevelopment (2017) reported higher rates for children who experienced severe physical abuse where up to 50% developed PTSD (Busso, D. S., McLaughlin, K. A., Brueck, S., Peverill, M., Gold, A. L., & Sheridan, M. A. (2017). Child abuse, neural structure, and adolescent psychopathology: A longitudinal study. *Journal of the American Academy of Child & Adolescent Psychiatry, 56*(4), 321–328). The Pediatric PTSD Study (2010) reported that among children who had experienced a natural disaster (e.g., hurricanes), around 30% of those exposed met the criteria for PTSD (De Bellis, M. D., Hooper, S. R., Woolley, D. P., & Shenk, C. E. (2010). Demographic, maltreatment, and neurobiological correlates of PTSD symptoms in children and adolescents. *Journal of Pediatric Psychology, 35*(5), 570–577). In summary, around 10–20% of children exposed to a traumatic event will develop PTSD, with variations depending on the type and severity of the trauma. Children exposed to severe forms of trauma (such as abuse, neglect or witnessing violence) may experience higher rates, with estimates ranging from 25% to 50% depending on the context.

2 **Effectiveness of PTSD treatment in children.** There are several effective treatments for PTSD in children including Trauma-focused Cognitive Behaviourial Therapy (TF-CBT), child-parent psychotherapy, Eye Movement Desensitization and Reprocessing (EMDR). The most effective treatment is TF-CBT which reports reductions in PTSD symptoms in 60–80% of cases. (Thielemann, J. F. B., Kasparik, B., König, J., Unterhitzenberger, J., & Rosner, R. (2022). A systematic review and meta-analysis of trauma-focused cognitive behavioral therapy for children and adolescents. *Child Abuse & Neglect, 134*, 105899).

3 **Waiting times for NHS mental health treatments for children and young people in the UK.** In the UK, there has been widespread concern about access to mental health services. For example, the Children's Commissioner produced an annual report on children and young people which included information about waiting times for children for NHS services. This reported that the average waiting time for a first appointment was about three months but there was wide variability so that some children were reported to be waiting more than two years for treatment. (Children's Commissioner for England. (2023). *Children's mental health services 2022–23.* www.childrenscommissioner.gov.uk/resource/childrens-mental-health-services-2022-23/). These types of figures are often quoted in the media and heightened public concern.

4 **Many children and young people who meet criteria for mental health problems do not come to mental health services for treatment.** In the UK, 66% of children and young people aged 5–19 with a mental health disorder have had contact with a professional service in the past year, and only 32% of children and young people referred to mental health services received support (*Children's commissioner for England, annual report and accounts 2022–23, 2023*). This may be partly because access to mental health services is difficult. For example, 40,000 children waited more than two years for treatment. (*Children's mental health services. Children's commissioner report March 2024*). Young people may not seek help from professional services because of anxiety, from perceived social stigma of mental health problems and other reasons. (Radez, J., Reardon, T., Creswell, C., Lawrence, P. J., Evdoka-Burton, G., & Waite, P. (2021). Why do children and adolescents (not) seek and access professional help for their mental health problems? A systematic review of quantitative and qualitative studies. *European Child & Adolescent Psychiatry, 30*(2), 183–211.)

5 **Mental health needs of children and young people.** In 2023, 1 in 5 children and young people aged 8–25 years had a probable mental disorder. The total population in this age bracket is approximately 15 million. Increasing rates of mental health needs in children and young people occurred following the Covid pandemic but rates were more stable between 2022 and 2023. An overview of rates of disorder between 2017 and 2023 based on four national surveys in the UK showed increases in rates of probable disorders from 12.6% in 2017 to 20.8% in 2023 for 8–16-year-olds. (Newlove-Delgado, T., Marcheselli, F., Williams, T., Mandalia, D., Davis, J., McManus, S.,… & Ford, T. (2022). *Mental health of children and young people in England, 2022-Wave 3 follow up to the 2017 survey.)*

6 **Adverse childhood experiences (ACEs):** Adverse childhood experiences (ACEs) refer to stressful or traumatic events that occur during childhood, such as abuse, neglect, household dysfunction, or witnessing violence. These experiences can have long-lasting effects on physical, emotional and mental health throughout life. The first major study on ACEs reported that adults who had experienced multiple ACEs had multiple health risks later in life (Felitti, V. J., Anda, R. F., Nordenberg, D., Williamson, D. F., Spitz, A. M., Edwards, V., & Marks, J. S. (1998). Relationship of childhood abuse and household dysfunction to many of the leading causes of death in adults: The Adverse Childhood Experiences (ACE) Study. *American Journal of Preventive Medicine, 14*(4), 245–258.) Several other studies have confirmed these findings including the Dunedin longitudinal study and the Minnesota Longitudinal Study of Risk and Adaptation.

7 **Increase in rates of neurodevelopmental disorders.** The number of children and young people diagnosed with ADHD increased between 2000 and 2018. The increase was approximately double compared with rates in 2000. (McKechnie, D. G., O'Nions, E., Dunsmuir, S., & Petersen, I. (2023). Attention-deficit hyperactivity disorder diagnoses and prescriptions in UK primary care, 2000–2018: Population-based cohort study. *BJPsych Open, 9*(4), e121.). Even greater increases in the diagnosis of Autistic Spectrum Disorder (ASD) have been reported with *a sevenfold increase across the life span reported since 2000* (Russell, G., Stapley, S., Newlove-Delgado, T., Salmon, A., White, R., Warren, F.,… & Ford, T. (2022). Time trends in autism diagnosis over 20 years: A UK population-based cohort study. *Journal of Child Psychology and Psychiatry, 63*(6), 674–682.)

8 **Increasing referral rates to CAMHS.** Based on NHS data, the number of under 18s referred to Child and Adolescent Mental Health Services (CAMHS) rose by 53% between 2019 and 2022. A number of studies showed increased referral rates following the Covid pandemic but a longer-term increase in referrals, not just related to the pandemic, has also been observed. This data can be found on the Mental Health Services Monthly Statistics Dashboard, which is hosted at NHS England Digital—NHS England Mental Health Services Monthly Statistics.

9 **Effectiveness of mental health treatments for children and young people.** This research has been comprehensively summarised by Professor Peter Fonagy and colleagues (Fonagy, P., Cottrell, D., Phillips, J., Bevington, D., Glaser, D., & Allison, E. (2015). *What works for whom? A critical review of treatments for children and adolescents.* Guilford Press. ISBN 9781462525928.)

10 **Diversity of child mental health problems.** Child mental health problems are defined by a classification system called the International Classification of Diseases (ICD) overseen by the World Health Organization (World Health Organization (WHO). (2018). *International classification of diseases for mortality and morbidity statistics (ICD-11)).* This system has identified several hundred different psychiatric conditions that apply to children and young people. Not everyone agrees with all aspects of the classification system, but it clearly illustrates the way that mental health problems, like physical health problems can be experienced by children and young people in many different ways.

11 **Difference between evidence-based treatments and usual care.** A study carried out by John Weisz and colleagues showed that the difference between evidence-based practice and usual care was relatively modest. The effect size for this difference was 0.29 which is generally considered a small effect size. (Weisz, J. R., Kuppens, S., Eckshtain, D., Ugueto, A. M., Hawley, K. M., & Jensen-Doss, A. (2013). Performance of evidence-based youth psychotherapies compared with usual clinical care: A multilevel meta-analysis. *JAMA Psychiatry*, *70*(7), 750–761.)

12 **Improvement rates for child mental health treatments.** A series of outcome studies in the UK has been carried out by the Child Outcome Research Consortium (CORC). CORC has been at the heart of promoting outcome evaluation work and has grappled with the problems of using data derived from mainstream services. Findings tend to suggest that improvement rates of around 50% are what professional help tends to achieve. (Bear, H. A., Edbrooke-Childs, J., Norton, S., Krause, K. R., & Wolpert, M. (2020). Systematic review and meta-analysis: Outcomes of routine specialist mental health care for young people with depression and/or anxiety. *Journal of the American Academy of Child & Adolescent Psychiatry*, *59*(7), 810–841; Edbrooke-Childs, J., Wolpert, M., Zamperoni, V., Napoleone, E., & Bear, H. (2018). Evaluation of reliable improvement rates in depression and anxiety at the end of treatment in adolescents. *BJPsych Open*, *4*(4), 250–255; Ruphrect-Smith, H., Davies, S., Jacob, J., & Edbrooke-Childs, J. (2024). Ethnic differences in treatment outcome for children and young people accessing mental health support. *European Child & Adolescent Psychiatry*, *33*(4), 1121–1131; Lereya, S. T., Norton, S., Crease, M., Deighton, J., Labno, A., Ravaccia, G. G.,... & Edbrooke-Childs, J. (2024). Gender, marginalised groups, and young people's mental health: A longitudinal analysis of trajectories. *Child and Adolescent Psychiatry and Mental Health*, *18*(1), 29.)

13 **Evidence-based practice.** Evidence-based practice (EBP) refers to a systematic approach to decision-making in professional fields such as healthcare, education, social work and others. It involves integrating the best available research evidence with clinical expertise and patient preferences or individual needs. The goal is to make informed, effective decisions that lead to better outcomes. The original definition of EBP came from a paper by David Sackett and colleagues (Sackett, D. L., Rosenberg, W. M., Gray, J. M., Haynes, R. B., & Richardson, W. S. (1996). Evidence based medicine: what it is and what it isn't. *bmj*, *312*(7023), 71–72.).

14 **Young people like to be helped in different ways.** Evidence-based practice tends to result in a few preferred ways of being helpful. However, young people themselves may have a much wider range of ideas as to what they find helpful to their sense of wellbeing. One study explored the value of much more diverse forms of help such as physical exercise, light therapy, dietary supplements, massage therapy, online peer support and contact with a dog (Wolpert, M., Dalzell, K., Ullman, R., Garland, L., Cortina, M., Hayes, D.,... & Law, D. (2019). Strategies not accompanied by a mental health professional to address anxiety and depression in children and young people: a scoping review of range and a systematic review of effectiveness. *The Lancet Psychiatry*, *6*(1), 46–60.)

15 **Individualised help.** Individualised help overlaps with ideas such as personalised care which has become an increasingly important part of mainstream healthcare. In the UK this is described on the NHS website (https://www.england.nhs.uk/personalisedcare/what-is-personalised-care/). A similar framework is described as person-centred care (Liu, T. C., Bozic, K. J., & Teisberg, E. O. (2017). Value-based healthcare: Person-centered measurement: Focusing on the three C's. *Clinical Orthopaedics and Related Research®*, *475*(2), 315–317; Coulter, A., & Oldham, J. (2016). Person-centred care: What is it and how do we get there. *Future Hospital Journal*, *3*(2), 114–116.) These approaches emphasise the benefit of adapting help to accommodate to individual preferences and contexts. Examples of adapting

help to take account of cultural differences have been less developed (Healey, P., Stager, M. L., Woodmass, K., Dettlaff, A. J., Vergara, A., Janke, R., & Wells, S. J. (2017). Cultural adaptations to augment health and mental health services: a systematic review. *BMC Health Services Research*, *17*(1), 8.)

16 **Adapting help to different faith groups.** The adaptation of evidence-based practice for Muslim families is now being extensively studied so that the core mechanisms of change can integrate cultural beliefs into the type of help that is offered (alHarbi, H., Farrand, P., & Laidlaw, K. (2023). Understanding the beliefs and attitudes towards mental health problems held by Muslim communities and acceptability of Cognitive Behavioral Therapy as a treatment: Systematic review and thematic synthesis. *Discover Mental Health*, *3*(1), 26.)

17 **Adapting help to LGBT groups.** Some work is beginning to be developed as to how to adapt help to take account of the needs of those with a sexual minority identity (Pachankis, J. E., Soulliard, Z. A., Morris, F., & van Dyk, I. S. (2023). A model for adapting evidence-based interventions to be LGBQ-affirmative: Putting minority stress principles and case conceptualization into clinical research and practice. *Cognitive and Behavioral Practice*, *30*(1), 1–17).

18 **Multi-agency help.** The challenges of providing effective help to children and young people and their families when this requires the involvement of more than one team have not been as extensively studied as other aspects of mental health care. NHS England published guidance around this aspect of help for children, and this can be found through the following link. (https://www.gov.uk/government/publications/the-multi-agency-response-to-children-and-families-who-need-help/the-multi-agency-response-to-children-and-families-who-need-help).

19 **Integrated care.** Integrated care is a widely supported principle of health and social care. However, the evidence for its effectiveness in improving health outcomes is more mixed. A review of this evidence was carried out which reported evidence for improved quality of care, increased patient satisfaction and improved access to treatment. The studies involved in this review were all adult studies so that we have much more limited research evidence about the value of integrated care from the perspective of children and young people. (Baxter, S., Johnson, M., Chambers, D., Sutton, A., Goyder, E., & Booth, A. (2018). The effects of integrated care: A systematic review of UK and international evidence. *BMC Health Services Research*, *18*(1), 350.)

Chapter 3

Providing Help

The Problems for Families

Introduction

Following the previous chapter, we now turn to take a parallel look at the challenges faced by parents, carers, families and communities in supporting children and young people with mental health needs. Some of these are common problems that overlap with those encountered by professional services, such as identifying the core problem and determining the best way to help. However, families also face unique struggles. Although these issues are addressed in separate chapters, professional and family support are deeply interconnected. The gradual but significant expansion of child mental health services over the past 30 years, along with the vast amount of professional advice available through various media, has influenced how families understand and respond to their children's needs.[1] Despite—or perhaps because of—the sheer volume of this advice, parents may experience greater uncertainty about how best to help and support their child. This chapter explores how these uncertainties contribute to parenting challenges and, in turn, drive families to seek external support, particularly from specialist services.

Parental Anxiety

Anxiety about their children seems to be an inherent part of the core job description of being a parent. Few parents would deny that their child is a source of worry, often acknowledging this with humour and affection. This concern is likely adaptive and a way that nature keeps us on the job ensuring continued attention and care. But many parents experience anxiety far beyond this level.[2] Some estimates suggest that around a quarter of parents meet criteria for high levels of anxiety, characterised by persistent and uncontrollable worry, an inability to relax, feeling continuously tired, poor concentration, irritability, physical tension, sleep difficulties and episodes of intense fear or discomfort. This type of anxiety can be deeply distressing, dominating daily life and relationships. For parents, it may be difficult to distinguish anxiety

DOI: 10.4324/9781003145523-3

in general from anxiety about themselves as parents or about their child or children. But a high proportion report feeling ‘overwhelmed’ by their responsibilities which suggests that parenting itself contributes to these heightened levels of distress. Severe parental anxiety has been increasing for decades, a trend that predates the Covid pandemic. This increase is probably due to many factors ranging from financial insecurity, poverty, educational pressures, societal expectations of children and a growing awareness of mental health issues. There is also a complex interplay between parental anxiety and childhood mental health, with each reinforcing the other.

Parental anxiety played a significant role in the lives of three of the young people we are following, but in different ways. Simone’s parents were highly anxious, and their worry centred on Simone, amplifying her own anxieties in a cycle of mutual escalation. Brigitte exhibited many features of an anxiety disorder, experiencing persistent worry about Simone, particularly when separated from her. At times of separation, she would panic, as if experiencing Simone’s distress within herself. This made it unbearable for her to see her daughter struggle. Judith, Daniel’s mother, also suffered from anxiety, but hers was not solely focused on Daniel although it had a major impact on her relationship with him. Her financial insecurity and fear of losing her job weighed heavily on her, leaving her terrified of becoming homeless. She struggled in her work setting, hated the work itself but was constantly anxious that she was not performing well enough. Even vague criticism of any of her work would trigger strong reactions. She worked to support Daniel, but her frequent absences due to periods of depression only deepened her sense of helplessness. In her relationship with Daniel, she was responsible and supportive; he was the most meaningful part of her life. When she was well, Daniel felt better and clung to the hope that these good periods would last. But he was frightened of her fragility and kept his own emotional and social struggles to himself, not wanting to burden her further. Bernadette was not generally anxious, but she was deeply worried about Teresa, and with good reason. Teresa was volatile, unpredictable and prone to violent outbursts, some of which were directed at Bernadette. These episodes frightened her. She dreaded the confrontations and was left to deal with this on her own by Teresa’s father who would absent himself whenever tensions escalated. Anxious parents understandably may seek professional help for their worries about their children. Their fears do not invent their child’s difficulties; the problems are real, and they hope professionals will have ways to address some of the difficulties that they are carrying. For many, professional services represent a last hope. However, they may be unprepared for the reality that meaningful change nearly always requires their active involvement. Rather than professionals taking the problem away and ‘fixing’ their child for them, they may be disappointed to discover that effective help nearly always depends on collaboration with them.

Parental Uncertainty: Is This Normal?

Parents and carers lookout for their children, staying aware of how they are managing in life and, to varying degrees, taking action when they believe their child needs some extra help, love or protection. Their judgement is shaped by their understanding of the nature of their child's difficulties and how openly they can discuss concerns with them. A common dilemma for parents is feeling unsure whether the problems that they are concerned about are common to children in general or are signs of something more worrying. Uncertainty is everywhere. 'Is this how most young people react to the breakup of their first romantic relationship?' 'Should my daughter be this upset about not making the football team?' 'Is it normal for siblings to fight this much?' 'Why is he always so angry and irritable?' 'Is he really being treated differently by his teachers, or is this just his perception?' 'If she stays in her room all weekend, is this just a passing phase or something more worrying?' How does a parent know? Every day, they face what Donald Rumsfeld famously described: the known knowns, the known unknowns and a lot of unknown unknowns about their child's life.

Parental anxiety is closely tied to these uncertainties about what it means to be a parent and what should be done. This is especially true when it comes to mental health concerns. Is this normal, or is there something wrong? The boundary between what might be called the common miseries of childhood and the distress associated with mental health 'disorders', 'conditions' or 'additional needs' is never going to be tidy, and there are major differences of view about where such a boundary should be drawn. These differing views provide a context in which parental uncertainty makes sense. For some, there is concern that the common challenges of childhood such as making and losing friends or the anxiety of starting a new school—are increasingly being professionalised (medicalised) as mental health issues. Others argue that these struggles have been overlooked for too long and require more professional recognition and intervention. The same child might be described as 'shy' by one family and as having 'social anxiety' by another. The difference is significant: the latter suggests the possibility of treatment and change, whereas shyness may be accepted, even embraced, as part of a child's personality— 'His dad was just like that when he was young, and he turned out fine.'

Simone's experience highlights this uncertainty. Her struggle with separation when starting primary school was deeply distressing for both her and her parents. She experienced overwhelming fear at being apart from her family, and her parents found her distress unbearable. What made it worse was its persistence; the longer it continued, the more entrenched it became. Her parents felt stuck, unable to support her successfully and certain that professional help was needed. The problem was clearly affecting Simone's early education. Yet from another perspective, this was a familiar situation for reception class teachers, who are generally very experienced (and kind) in supporting children through the distress of starting school. They are not mental health specialists, but they have extensive experience in helping children navigate separation anxiety as part of normal development. Their expertise lies not in eliminating distress but in guiding children through it, helping them face short-term discomfort so that they can adjust. From their viewpoint, Simone's struggle was a common developmental challenge rather than a mental health condition. Sometimes, the right kind of support comes not from clinical intervention but from adults who are confident and familiar with helping children overcome specific fears in everyday situations.

The implication here is not that specialist mental health support was unnecessary or that, left to themselves, Simone's family and school would have resolved her difficulties. Her distress, and Brigitte's, was exceptional and severe. Brigitte's own childhood experiences shaped her response to Simone's struggles. She had been separated from her parents and placed in the care of her paternal aunt, whom she was frightened of. She had cried every night, and her aunt had been frustrated by the way she was so inconsolable. An important turning point in the helping process was recognising how much this past experience unconsciously influenced her response to Simone's distress. As in many cases, distinguishing between the common difficulties of childhood and more entrenched, severe problems was not straightforward. Some may view professional involvement as 'making a fuss' over a common issue, while others may see it as an example of where skilled therapeutic support was crucial to helping the child through her distress. Was Jacqui's grief an example of the everyday sadnesses of childhood, or did it require professional help? Both. Jacqui was deeply affected by the death of her grandmother, but she got stuck in the sadness of her grief. Moving house shortly afterwards severed her from her old life, and she missed an entire term of school—a major developmental setback. She could not share her feelings with her mother, burdened by guilt that she had always loved her grandmother most of all. She experienced grief in isolation, cutting her off from those who might comfort her. She was alone with it and a common grieving process became prolonged and disruptive. Her daily routines collapsed, and her absence from school triggered secondary problems. She argued with her parents, felt hopeless and withdrew further. This combination of emotional distress and external disruption to her life moved her across the threshold where professional help became valuable. Not everyone agreed. Her Head of Year believed her parents should have been firmer and insisted she attend school, doubting that young people could experience depression in the same way that adults do.

Teresa's difficulties were often minimised by her family as being 'just like all teenagers'. Yet, despite holding this view, they felt powerless in the face of her emotional storms and turned to professionals for help. Teresa's rages, often triggered by seemingly minor events, were overwhelming. A neutral text message could be read as rejection, a casual meet-up between friends as betrayal. Many young people experience similar emotional sensitivities, but Teresa's reactions were extreme, impulsive and persistent. Her distress disrupted daily life—she struggled to attend school, and she sought excitement and relationships which put herself at risk. It was not the nature of her difficulties but their severity that made professional help essential.

Parental Uncertainty: Is Everything a Trauma?

Let us take another example where it can be difficult to make sense of children's distress, namely the issue of trauma. There is now much encouragement in supporting schools, social care teams and other child services to adopt a 'trauma-informed' approach.[3] While this is valuable, it risks broadening the definition of trauma to include all distressing, sad, frightening or unexpected experiences of childhood. This is unhelpful. Trauma refers to experiences that the child or young person has been unable to process in a normal way. Instead of being assimilated into the mind as a past memory it becomes stuck in the present, repeatedly intruding on their mind as if it were happening now. This terrifying and repetitive experience results in highly distressing mental states, such as flashbacks, nightmares and hypervigilance, where the child is constantly scanning their environment for anticipated threats.

Some children endure repeated experiences of terror and cruelty, often described as relational trauma.[4] The impact of such experiences can be profound, leading to rage, deep distrust of others, an expectation of malevolence from others and a sense of being alone and repeatedly poorly understood. However, these experiences are distinct from the moments of fear, threat or distress that all children occasionally encounter—experiences they can process, and which are followed by subsequent recovery to safety. A fundamental aspect of early attachment involves learning that fear and sadness are temporary and can be overcome. Through repeated experiences of comfort and reassurance, children learn that the pain of an injection or the distress of being temporarily left with a babysitter will pass. Emotional regulation is not about avoiding strong emotions but about learning that they are transient. The nature of an event alone does not determine whether it is traumatic; a street mugging, for example, may or may not result in trauma, however distressing it is at the time. Equally, just because an experience is common does not mean it cannot be traumatic. One of the authors experienced trauma at 14 simply from going to the cinema. A scene depicting a man having his throat cut left him with unexplained neck pain for nearly two decades. He frequently wore thick scarves until he re-experienced the memory, after which the physical symptoms gradually faded.

For parents, this discussion about trauma raises difficult questions. Is loving parental care enough to help a child through an adverse experience, or do they need specialist treatment from an expert? Does not seeking professional help mean neglecting their child's needs? These uncertainties can feed into parental anxiety as we have already discussed. As described in the previous chapter, about half of children who experience so-called traumatic events do not develop traumatic symptoms, and most who do will not experience lasting distress. Only a small proportion develop enduring trauma responses. However, such rational data may not be reassuring when parental anxiety is high, like being told suicide is rare when you are terrified about your own child. Data alone is unlikely to ease parental fears.

Parental Uncertainty: What Helps My Child to Be Resilient?

For many parents, the current conversation around mental health feels like a confusing battleground of conflicting advice. Unsurprisingly, this fuels rising anxiety about how best to support their child. Helping a child build resilience in the face of adversity is a common goal for most parents, but the path to achieving this can feel like an impossible choice between offering empathy and support or encouraging the child to 'face their fears' and 'give it a try'. Several decades ago, these dilemmas would likely have been handled differently—not because parents were less concerned about their children's well-being, but because mental health was not as dominant a narrative as it is now. One of the authors attended school in the 1960s and was in the same class as a child who died by suicide at 15. The tragic event was not followed by a process of explicit reflections or emotional processing as might be expected today. Talking about it simply wasn't part of how resilience was fostered. In some ways, society has moved from one theory of resilience to another—one where open communication and verbal support play a much greater role. It is also likely that there was once a more shared cultural response to adversity, whereas today, views on how to respond to serious distress vary widely. The large presence of therapists and counsellors at Grenfell Tower in the days after the terrible fire reflects how our collective beliefs have shifted. Similarly, responses to public tragedies, from the death of famous figures in the UK like Princess Diana to the horrific violence in Gaza, now place far more emphasis on emotional expression than in previous decades. For parents, this shift may make decision-making more difficult. They often feel caught between encouraging self-reliance ('You'll be okay') and providing emotional validation and support. These are not entirely separate approaches, and parenting likely involves a combination of both. But in specific situations, parents can feel deeply uncertain about which stance to take. Should I encourage my child to go on her friend's sleepover when she tends to avoid any situation where she can't sleep at home? Few parents are free from these dilemmas, and even fewer can say they have never made a judgement that, in hindsight, turned out to be less helpful than they had hoped.

Parental Uncertainty: The Stigma of Mental Health

So parental anxiety and uncertainty often drive some parents to seek professional help for their child. For others, the fear of stigma and shame associated with mental health services may lead them to minimise difficulties or avoid seeking help altogether. Some parents worry that even contacting services will leave a lasting mark on their child's medical record, potentially affecting future life opportunities. Others fear that seeking professional help will invite criticism of their parenting or expose their family to professional judgement. Many parents experience an internal struggle—balancing their concern for their child's well-being with the anticipated shame of engaging with mental health services. In recent years, stigma around mental health has been challenged in the UK, with high-profile figures, including members of the royal family, advocating for greater openness. Mental health education has also become more embedded in school curriculums. While stigma remains a significant issue, its power has reduced in many communities, making it easier for more families to seek help than in previous decades.

Parental Uncertainty: What Is Professional Help Like?

For many parents, uncertainty extends beyond whether to seek professional help—it also surrounds what that help involves. Will it mean things I don't agree with, such as medication? Will they think I'm a bad parent and consider whether my child should go into care? Will my child have therapy, and how long will it last? Do services take full responsibility for my child's support, or will I be expected to play a role? Will professionals simply tell us what to do and then leave us to manage on our own? Will they blame me, saying my child's difficulties are because of my parenting? Before seeking help for their child, most parents do not have direct experience of children's mental health services and will often have many of these uncertainties before deciding to attend.

Specialist mental health professionals are trained in understanding mental health needs and providing psychological therapies, and in some cases, prescribing medication or arranging hospital care. They have expertise in recognising and helping with a wide range of mental health problems including neurodiverse conditions such as ASD or ADHD, as well as in difficulties related to self-harm, eating problems, anxiety, depression and oppositional behaviour. Their role involves assessing these difficulties and helping a child or young person and their family to understand what is happening and offering interventions or treatments that may help. Some children and young people may actively seek their support, while others may be much more reluctant to take part in such professional help. But this detached description does not capture the emotional sensitivities involved in this process. Mental health support often requires discussing deeply personal and painful matters—things children and parents are highly sensitive about and may never have spoken about before. Even acknowledging feelings of sadness, anxiety or self-harm can be hugely difficult and distressing. Many of these difficulties carry layers of shame and fear both for parents and for children. Professional expertise is not just about understanding mental health conditions but also about helping a child or family to navigate these conversations with sensitivity. While professionals bring knowledge about mental health, families hold another type of knowledge—equally valid and essential for effective help. The family knows the child in a way that professionals never can. Parents have been there from the moment of their birth, witnessing every stage of development, understanding their child's personality and recognising when difficulties first emerged. They know how they get on with their brothers and sisters and what they like and don't like. Their knowledge is shaped by lived experience and cultural values, which may strongly influence their views on how such problems should be addressed. For those from faith communities, beliefs about parenting and childcare may be deeply rooted in their religious framework, contrasting with the secular, research-based knowledge of professionals. So, parents bring unique knowledge, personal beliefs and also concerns that go beyond the child's immediate difficulties. They may be wrestling with questions about how the problem arose, whether they were responsible, whether others will blame them and whether seeking help will lead to judgement. Feelings of shame, guilt, anger or helplessness often accompany their efforts to find support. Seeking professional advice is not a neutral process; it involves personal stakes for parents as much as for the child. For the child, the experience of meeting a mental health professional can be equally uncertain. They know the problem from the inside and may feel relief, apprehension or confusion. They might not know what they are supposed to say, worry about being told off afterwards or feel pressured to talk when they don't want to. Their understanding of their difficulties is often fragmented—a blur of feelings towards others where they may feel angry, guilty or frightened in a context which is strange and unknown to them. More than adults may realise, they may be trying to work out what others think they have done wrong.

Bringing these perspectives together—so that professionals, parents and children develop a shared understanding of the child's difficulties—is often hard to achieve. But when progress is made with this, it can bring enormous relief. Parents and children alike may feel affirmed when their struggles are recognised and respected. Naming the problem in a way that enables the child and parents to both feel heard can be a significant step forward, leading to the question about what help is needed.

Many parents hope that professionals will have clear answers about this and how they will do it. But this is where, for some parents, expectations may meet disappointment, as much of the support a child needs will come not just from professionals but also from the family itself. Professionals can provide guidance, therapy and structured interventions, but day-to-day help that their child will need will often involve all sorts of requirements for the family and often by the child's school. Professional recommendations—whether for managing emotions, improving communication or changing behaviour patterns—often require significant effort from parents and teachers. Alongside professional interventions like individual therapy, family therapy or parent training, these daily interactions play a crucial role in how the child copes and recovers. Despite the importance of professional help, therapy sessions make up only a small fraction of a child's weekly life. What happens in the everyday moments matters just as much, if not more.

All six young people in this book had significant mental health needs that could be described using formal psychiatric language. Jacqui had depression, Martin had an attachment disorder, Abdul had autistic spectrum disorder, Daniel had body dysmorphia, Simone had separation anxiety and Teresa had an emerging personality disorder. Daniel did not accept or engage with the term 'body dysmorphia', and Teresa, while aware that others described her as having a personality disorder, rejected the label with contempt. Still, at times, she felt painfully different from others and experienced unbearable periods of emptiness, as if she disappeared even from herself. Treatments existed for all these conditions, aimed at alleviating distress and supporting improvements in their lives, which might be understood as a form of recovery.

For Jacqui, learning to manage her depression involved both professional help and a shift in how her parents responded to her. Over time, her mood and self-perception improved, but much of this was linked to changes at home. Her parents moved from seeing her as difficult and oppositional to recognising that she was struggling with an illness. Their new stance—supportive rather than critical—was crucial. They were the ones who put in the hours between therapy sessions, helping Jacqui practise what she learned, encouraging her when she lost heart and supporting her return to school. Therapy played a vital role, but one of its key functions was enabling her parents to regain confidence in their parenting, restoring the helping system around her that had been disrupted by depression.

It is hard to convey how difficult this can be for parent when faced with a highly distressed, angry or oppositional child. Yet, re-establishing a sufficiently confident helping system is often essential to effective support. The most obvious example is in eating disorders where professional guidance of what is needed is for the family to resume having family meals together. What may be discussed and agreed in sessions with the therapist are the rules that parents and the young person may be encouraged to comply with as part of this. Such rules may be about parents agreeing not to 'nag' about eating, or parents and the young person jointly planning meals. The task is to maintain as normal a routine as possible despite intense anxiety and disagreement. There is a collaboration with families to create a functioning support system, but it is the family who does the work each day.

The same principle applied to Martin's rages and an avoidant, oppositional stance towards things he disliked or resented. He frequently refused Sandra's requests—whether to go to bed, get ready for school or stop playing on his PlayStation. Most evidence-based interventions around negative behaviour include the need for consistent responses and a focus on reinforcing positive behaviours. However, the idea that consistency is a universal feature of 'good parenting' is misleading. Most families function well enough with all kinds of inconsistent parental responses to their children's behaviour. Children usually know that their parents are not equally strict about things, but they agree sufficiently for the family to muddle along happily enough from day to day. To help Martin cope with family and school life, and to support him when he felt angry or threatened by others, Sandra, her adult daughter Polly, Sandra's mother and Fatima (his teacher) had to maintain a level of consistency that most families do not achieve. They had to be super consistent. This was exhausting, requiring them to hold a shared approach to his non-compliant behaviour. Their plan was to focus on Martin's emotional state when he was upset, helping him name his feelings and supporting him to calm down, rather than engaging in negotiation when he was angry. They praised him when he regained control and reinforced his successes—whether managing in class or in a family situation and listening to him when he felt like talking about things that happened. This long-term approach depended on a strong working relationship between Sandra and Fatima, ensuring Martin received the same message across home and school. But super-consistency is not how most families operate. But for Martin, as with Jacqui, sustained effort from his family and school—alongside professional input—was essential in rebuilding the support system around him.

Collaboration of Parents and Professionals

Help for children with mental health needs nearly always requires collaboration between professionals, parents or carers and schools. This theme will recur throughout the book, but for now, we will briefly explore what this collaboration can look like. The role of parents in individual cases varies depending on family preferences and the treatment approach recommended by professionals. For example, Professor Cathy Creswell and colleagues have developed a highly effective approach for treating severe anxiety in children, placing parents at the centre of the therapeutic process. Parents are trained to help their child overcome their anxiety by following a carefully structured programme to help their child gradually face and manage previously avoided situations. Professionals train the parents, and the parents work directly with their child. Similarly, for behavioural difficulties in early childhood, the most effective approach is often the parent group approach where parents reflect on and adjust their responses to their child's oppositional behaviour. Rather than focusing primarily on managing negative behaviour, these interventions prioritise increasing positive interactions—encouraging play, connection and positive reinforcement. By sharing their frustrations and experiences with other parents, they develop a more balanced and hopeful approach to helping their relationship with their child to be a balance of play and containment, of listening and instructing. Once Simone had settled into school, Brigitte attended a 12-session parent group, which helped her understand her own feelings towards Simone and develop a clearer approach to supporting her daughter.

These are clear examples where parents are at the centre of the intervention, guided by mental health professionals to interact with their child in a structured, consistent way. Here, professionals act as trainers, and parents are the 'practitioners'. However, with other problems, the parent's role may be less direct. For depression, a young person may find it easier to speak with a therapist rather than their parents about their feelings. This was true for Jacqui, though later in treatment, therapy supported her in talking more with her parents. She first needed space to process her guilt and shame around her loss before she could open up to her family again. Similarly, for young people experiencing persistent post-traumatic symptoms, therapy is often central to helping them re-process distressing experiences in ways that may not be possible through parental support alone. Although the balance between professional and parental contributions varies, both play a crucial role in helping children navigate their difficulties. However, it is not always clear what this balance should look like, and there is often resentment and confusion for both professionals and for families about this. For families, in their exhausted and overwhelmed state, may feel that they have done more than their share already and hope that professionals will take over, only to find that much of the responsibility still rests with them. Professionals, on the other hand, may feel that families are handing over too much responsibility and need to remain more actively involved in their child's recovery. These tensions are real, deeply felt and not easily resolved. The aim of this book is to explore how a more balanced collaboration can be more regularly achieved, ensuring that both professionals and families are supported in their shared task of helping children and young people move forward.

Summary and Conclusions

This chapter has explored the vital role that parents and families play in supporting children with mental health needs, working alongside professional services. Just as professional services face challenges in providing effective support, families encounter significant difficulties in understanding, managing and responding to their child's needs. We have highlighted some of these challenges, including parental anxiety and the uncertainty many parents feel about how to make sense of mental health concerns in their child and how professionals may be able to help them. In our view, parental uncertainty has increased with the expansion of mental health services and the sheer volume of advice now available. This can have both positive and negative effects. On the one hand, it encourages parents to think differently about their child's experiences, question their assumptions and remain open to new ways of understanding and supporting them. On the other hand, it can erode parental confidence in their own instincts and actions, even when what they are already doing aligns closely with professional recommendations. We have also explored how parents vary in their level of collaboration with professionals—sometimes playing a central role, sometimes feeling more like observers. What is often needed is the restoration of parental confidence in their ability to help their child. As in many areas of life, confidence can be the crucial factor that makes a difference.

Both professional services and families bring their own challenges to this task. The interaction of these challenges has contributed to the rapid rise in identified mental health needs and the growing pressures on both services and families. Addressing these problems does not require a completely new approach to mental health service design or another large-scale reorganisation. Such changes have little evidence of improving outcomes for children and families and are often disruptive for professionals and services alike. Instead, we need to build on what already works, drawing on the expertise of the existing workforce and well-established methods for supporting children's mental health. However, a rebalancing is needed—one that better integrates the contributions of families and professionals to create more effective helping systems. In this book, we will use the widely adopted **Thrive** framework as a foundation for this rebalancing. Thrive provides a structure that allows us to focus not just on mental health services but also on broader helping systems that include families, schools and communities. The aim is not to build a system in which professional services are the sole providers of help but to create one that is cohabited—and perhaps even co-owned—by professionals, families, young people and children themselves. Before we explore what this means in practice, the next chapter will introduce the **Thrive** framework in more detail. This will serve as the floor plan for understanding how we can move beyond helping services to strengthening the helping systems that surround children and young people. Our focus is on our experiences in the UK, but we have been influenced by work in other countries and hope these ideas will have relevance to those working in those contexts too.

Key Practice Points

1 For most children and young people with mental health needs, parents and carers play a central role in helping their child with such needs.
2 Parents and carers may experience high levels of anxiety and uncertainty about how best to help their child. It is often unclear whether a child's difficulties require professional intervention.

3 Effective helping systems usually involve some level of collaboration between parents and professionals.
4 Professional methods must be adapted to consider the beliefs, experiences and context of the family—including both the parents and the child or young person.
5 A key goal of the helping system is to restore parents' confidence in their ability to support their child, particularly when they assume that responsibility rests primarily with professionals.

A Parent's Life: Maggie

Maggie, a 30-year-old single mother, sought help for managing the behaviour of her three-year-old son, Matt. When we met, she spoke openly about everything on her mind. She was warm, friendly and chaotic, and clear that she wanted help. She was angry with Matt, describing him as unreasonable and defiant, constantly demanding her attention and ignoring her instructions. At the same time, she felt guilty about her own exhaustion and hopelessness as a parent. Matt struggled to settle at night, and Maggie had to lie beside him until he fell asleep, often falling asleep herself. He frequently woke during the night and settling him again was difficult. At home, she felt he was uncontrollable, constantly needing her attention. She was exhausted, often depressed and felt criticised and unsupported by her own family. While the nursery staff were kind, she found their advice unhelpful. Everyone told her to set firm boundaries, but this only made her feel worse. Maggie knew one thing for certain—she did not want to parent like her own mother. She wanted something different for Matt, but she had no clear idea of what that looked like. It was a blank in her mind. She had never realised this before. What she remembered from her own childhood was being frightened—of her parents, of their shouting at her. She knew she didn't want Matt to be frightened of her, but the advice she received made her worry that he would end up hating her and she couldn't bear that. She would give him whatever he wanted because she couldn't bear the thought of him hating her. Yet, when she spoke about this, she realised she also didn't want him to be in charge. Over time, in our sessions, she began talking about her own childhood, her parents and the impact of her early experiences. Slowly, she started to form a clearer picture of how she wanted to parent Matt. She valued the help and, for the first time, felt able to seek more support. She joined a parenting course and, to her surprise, started trying out new approaches to managing Matt's behaviour in a calm way. Her relationship with Matt improved, and he began sleeping in his own bed. Maggie was finding her own way—different from how she had been raised but shaped by what she wanted for her son. She was filling in the blank in her mind about this.

Notes

1 **Impact of professional knowledge about children and parenting on parents.** The growing body of knowledge about children's mental health has had a profound impact on parenting over the past few decades including greater awareness of their children's emotional needs, more open and empathetic communication with their children (often called emotional intelligence), more focus on mental health as part of well-being, more awareness of the signs of mental health challenges in children. One example of this dissemination of professional knowledge is the influential book by Jonathan Haidt (Haidt, J. (2024). *The anxious generation: How the great rewiring of childhood is causing an epidemic of mental illness*. Penguin) which highlights the impact of increasing safety and the greater use of the internet on the emotional well-being of children. He highlights the need for more encouragement to teach children resilience and healthy coping strategies. In summary, the impact of mental health knowledge on parenting has led to considerable change in parental ways of raising children.

2 **Rates of anxiety disorders in parents.** There is a large literature on rates of anxiety and depression in parents. Studies during Covid described high rates of parental anxiety (e.g. McGoron, L., Wargo Aikins, J., Trentacosta, C. J., Gómez, J. M., & Beeghly, M. (2022). School support, chaos, routines, and parents' mental health during COVID-19 remote schooling. *School Psychology*, *37*(2), 173; Skripkauskaite, S., Creswell, C., Shum, A., Pearcey, S., Lawrence, P., Dodd, H., & Waite, P. (2023). Changes in UK parental mental health symptoms over 10 months of the COVID-19 pandemic. *JCPP Advances*, *3*(2), e12139). Some studies have suggested increased rates of parenting stress and burnout in more individualised cultures (e.g. Roskam, I., Aguiar, J., Akgun, E., Arikan, G., Artavia, M., Avalosse, H.,… & Mikolajczak, M. (2021). Parental burnout around the globe: A 42-country study. *Affective Science*, *2*(1), 58–79.) A more recent survey in the UK reported approximately 50% of parents having concerns about their mental health needs (UNICEF UK 0–4 Parents Survey by YouGov (10th May -2nd June 2024). Similar levels of concern in the United States have also been reported. (Murthy, V. (2024). *Parents under pressure: The US surgeon general's advisory on the mental health & well-being of parents*. US Department of Health and Human Services (US), PMID:39250580). The relationship between increased parental stress and reduced well-being was reported in a comprehensive review (Rusu, P. P., Candel, O. S., Bogdan, I., Ilciuc, C., Ursu, A., & Podina, I. R. (2025). Parental stress and well-being: A meta-analysis. *Clinical Child and Family Psychology Review*, *28*(2):255–274, doi:10.1007/s10567-025-00515-9).

3 **Trauma-informed services.** The UK NHS provides guidance on the definition of trauma-informed practice. https://www.gov.uk/government/publications/working-definition-of-trauma-informed-practice/working-definition-of-trauma-informed-practice a range of sites provide additional information on this approach. https://www.traumainformedservices.co.uk/; https://www.traumainformedcare.chcs.org/what-is-trauma-informed-care/

4 **Relational trauma.** The term relational trauma refers to the experience of trauma or abuse within close, intimate or family relationships. Bessel Van der Kolk has been particularly influential about this concept. (Van der Kolk, B. A. (2003). *Psychological trauma*. American Psychiatric Pub). Specific applications to different need groups have been done such as with respect to infancy (Baradon, T. (Ed.). (2009). *Relational trauma in infancy*. Taylor & Francis.)

Chapter 4

The Thrive Framework

Introduction

This chapter may feel a bit distant from the lives of the young people that we have introduced to you as it moves into how services are planned and delivered. We recognise that for some readers, this shift to more organisational language may be off putting but our aim is to bring together lived experience with the structure of helping systems and services. As much as possible, we will avoid jargon and use everyday language to connect these ideas to the experiences of young people.

What Is the Thrive Framework?

Thrive is a framework for designing and delivering child mental health services, widely adopted across parts of the UK.[1] It was developed in 2012 by a working group of mental health professionals from the Tavistock Centre and Anna Freud, led by Professor Miranda Wolpert. The group produced four guidance documents between 2014 and 2019.[2] Previously, services were organised into four tiers: Tier 1, primary care support; Tier 2, targeted services for more complex needs; Tier 3, specialist services; and Tier 4, highly specialised services. This expert-led system assumed that the right treatment for a young person was determined by a specialist based on the severity of their problem. While this structure encouraged the expansion of community-based services, it also became bogged down in debates about which problems should be treated at which tier. It struggled to support young people with multiple, unpredictable or changing needs. Thrive took a different approach, placing the child's needs—rather than the organisation of services—at the centre. Needs were defined as a combination of the difficulties the child or young person was experiencing and the type of help they wanted. Four broad 'need groups' were established: Advice and Signposting, Help, More Help and Risk Support. These categories, deliberately non-specialist in language, recognised that different children and

DOI: 10.4324/9781003145523-4

families needed to be helped in different ways. While evidence-based practice remained important, this was balanced with the views and preferences of young people and their families.

Each of the four need groups plays a distinct role. **Advice and Signposting** applies to young people and families who primarily want information—about their difficulties, typical experiences and the best ways to manage them. They are not necessarily seeking therapy or treatment but want guidance on self-management, peer support or relevant community initiatives which may be helpful to their needs. The advice includes information about the risks that the problem might present both now and in the future. Some families and young people prefer to navigate their challenges independently, without active involvement from mental health professionals. Daniel fits within this need group. He did not want professional treatment but actively sought out information to make sense of his experiences. He searched the web, listened to trusted sources and made his own decisions about what support, if any, he wanted to engage with.

The **Help** need group is for children, young people and families who want to engage in structured treatment with a specialist mental health practitioner using an evidence-based approach for a mutually agreed problem. For example, a child with anxiety might be offered cognitive behavioural therapy (CBT), while a young person with an eating disorder would be offered family-based community treatment. Help is what most families would recognise as counselling or therapy in its various forms. Jacqui fell into this category. With encouragement from her family, she attended individual CBT for her depression. Similarly, Simone and her parents received Help for her severe separation anxiety when starting primary school. Given her young age and stage of development, help was primarily delivered through her parents in collaboration with school staff. Abdul was also in this group, taking part in an adapted CBT programme designed for children with autistic spectrum disorder (ASD) to help manage anxiety.

The **More Help** category recognised that some children and families needed longer or more intensive help. This group included those whose difficulties had not improved with initial treatment and who required additional intervention—either more intensive community support or, in rarer cases, inpatient care, alternative living arrangements or specialist education. Teresa needed More Help following her suicide attempt. This was provided through a period of inpatient care, followed by intensive help from an outreach team after her discharge from hospital. But some children, young people and parents or carers do not wish to engage in **Help** or **More Help**. The reasons vary. Some have previously tried therapy without improvement and concluded it was not useful. Others dislike the nature of therapeutic work itself. Some of these families have long-term, ongoing needs likely to result in future re-referrals. This group falls under **Risk Support**, estimated to make up around 10% of all families accessing child mental health services. Risk

Support is not about treatment but ensuring an active, multi-agency approach to prevent deterioration and maintain a support system for times of increased difficulties. Martin was in this group. He had previously received Help when prescribed medication for ADHD, but after it was discontinued, he was not actively engaged in treatment. However, his ongoing needs were recognised, and it was anticipated that he might require professional support at key moments, such as during crises or major life transitions. Rather than closing the case, as would typically happen, the mental health team remained available to his social worker, Matt, and his foster carer, Sandra, ensuring that support could be accessed when needed.

A critical aspect of the Thrive approach was its focus on the helping process rather than simply the structure of services. It introduced key standards of practice that applied to all four need groups. Thrive aimed to encourage a shared language across the helping system, promote active participation of children and young people in their support, ensure that interventions were informed by measurable change, encouraged joint agency work based on outcomes and addressed stigma around mental health. Since 2012, gradual but significant changes have taken place, including the increased use of outcome monitoring[3] (especially in voluntary sector services), wider adoption of goals-based measures,[4] and the development of single points of access where health and social care teams work together to provide advice and signposting for families and young people. The national Thrive team have developed leadership and practitioner training to support implementation, focusing on key challenges that could arise. The framework was designed to be applied at three levels: the micro level, which referred to direct practitioner-family interactions; the meso level, which involved embedding Thrive within teams and services; and the macro level, which focused on shaping national policies, service planning, funding and evaluation. By 2024, the UK's health system had undergone another major reorganisation with the introduction of Integrated Care Boards (ICBs).[5] The Thrive framework had already been embedded in a large proportion of Local Implementation Plans, which preceded the creation of ICBs. The commitment to cross-agency working in these plans translated relatively smoothly into service planning within ICBs, reinforcing Thrive as a key part of how local services should be designed and delivered. The presence of Thrive in these plans became the responsibility of each ICB, reflecting a shift away from tiered models towards a more needs-led approach. This was a major step forward, largely due to the work of the Thrive Implementation Team, which provided expert guidance to local boards. In areas such as Greater Manchester, Thrive became a cornerstone of the integrated care model promoted by ICBs. At the strategic (macro) level, Thrive has been highly influential. However, at the level of teams and families, adoption of Thrive has been inconsistent. In some areas, it has been embraced more in name than in practice. The shift to a community-based, needs-led approach with shared decision-making at the heart of its approach has been difficult to implement, and progress at the micro and meso levels has been uneven. Meaningful change requires whole-system transformation, a highly ambitious task that demands both long-term commitment and the alignment of shared objectives across multiple organisations. These macro conditions have not been consistently present in the UK over the past decade. Limited investment in public services, coupled with separate large-scale restructuring across health, education and social care, has hindered integrated system development. The introduction of ICBs in health, alongside national reforms in children's social care,[6] has absorbed much of the capacity for change within these sectors. Although some progress has been made, separate organisational priorities have often acted as a barrier to building integrated helping systems across agencies. A second reason for Thrive's partial and inconsistent implementation may lie within the framework itself. While it has been highly successful at the planning level, making a strong case for a needs-led approach, it has been less clear at the team and practitioner level about how professionals should change their day-to-day practice. Those responsible for designing and funding services often see the logic of this approach, but for frontline teams working under significant pressure, Thrive can seem impractical or even burdensome. If a service's primary concern is reducing waiting times for first appointments, shifting to a needs-led approach may feel irrelevant or extremely unrealistic. There has been considerable local variation in how well this approach aligns with efforts to address immediate service challenges. But there have also been notable successes. The widespread adoption of integrated referral systems, linking health and social care, represents a significant step towards more joined-up practice that aligns with Thrive principles.

However, as explored in Chapters 2 and 3, profound difficulties remain for both services and families. The ambition of creating an integrated, needs-led, child-empowered, multi-agency approach is still far from fully realised. The remaining chapters of this book will explore how to move forward. Achieving this will require renewed collaboration between families, communities, health services, social care and education—far beyond what has been achieved so far. Such ambitions can easily seem like empty rhetoric. We recognise this, and the purpose of the rest of this book is to ensure that it is not. We will outline six principles of good practice that aim to rebalance the system by focusing on helping systems before helping services. First, we will describe the helping process—both help-seeking and help-giving—for professionals and, secondly, for families, highlighting its role in meeting children's needs as a vulnerable and dependent group. Third, we will consider how effective help needs to recognise the importance of safety for children and young people, particularly those in threatening environments or abusive contexts of care, and how we need to adjust help to such circumstances. Fourth, we will emphasise the importance of young people and families actively participating in their own support—what is often referred to as participation, but which we will call

Active Help. Fifth, we will argue that measuring help is essential to improving how needs are met, and lastly, we will stress the importance of a whole-system approach. Supporting children and young people with mental health needs cannot be the sole responsibility of specialist practitioners. We believe it takes a village to support a child—but we must rethink what that village looks like in modern urban settings and virtual social networks.

Summary and Conclusions

The Thrive framework provides an established structure for understanding how best to support children and young people with mental health needs. It emphasises that families and young people engage with help in different ways, seeking and receiving support through multiple routes. Thrive identifies four key need groups, ranging from those who wish to help themselves but require advice and signposting, to those seeking treatment for distress, as well as those who may not seek professional help despite experiencing difficulties. These categories serve as starting points, recognising that help can take many forms and that non-professional help—whether from families, peers, schools or communities—plays a critical role.

At the macro level, Thrive has influenced the planning and organisation of mental health services. However, implementation at the meso level (team structures) and the micro level (direct work with families) has been more challenging. Despite these difficulties, Thrive has provided a widely supported framework that highlights the multiple forms of effective help and reinforces the need for multi-agency collaboration in supporting children and young people. This book builds upon the Thrive framework, expanding on key principles of effective practice for teams, practitioners and families. The aim is to move beyond structural planning and explore how these ideas can be translated into meaningful, practical change in everyday interactions with children and young people.

Key Practice Points

1. Thrive provides a comprehensive framework for understanding the many components of a helping system around a child or young person with mental health needs.
2. Thrive establishes a common language between agencies and families, ensuring a coherent approach to understanding and addressing mental health needs. A shared narrative across all service levels is essential for effective support.
3. Thrive recognises that there are multiple ways to provide support and that young people's views and experiences must be central in shaping a helping system that is both effective and respectful of their preferences.

4 Thrive acknowledges that not all children, young people and families actively seek professional help for mental health needs. Some may distrust services, fear stigma or prefer alternative forms of support. This need group is as important as those who actively seek help.
5 Thrive advocates for coherence between strategic priorities, service organisation and direct work with families. If services are expected to provide individualised care, then teams must be supported and trained to deliver this in practice.

A Child's Life: Lawrence

Lawrence was eight years old with a diagnosis of learning difficulties and ASD. He was profoundly disabled, had almost no language and displayed unpredictable behaviour patterns. He attended a specialist school for children with severe learning disabilities and was cared for by his two devoted parents, who were determined to do their best for him. His parents sought help because Lawrence had begun smearing faeces on his bedroom wall each night for the past two months. They felt desperate and exhausted. Despite trying everything they could think of—using nappies, keeping him awake later, talking to him—nothing changed the behaviour. Not knowing what else to suggest, I offered to visit their home in the evening to observe what was happening. After being settled in bed and left alone in his room, Lawrence smeared faeces on the walls. His parents, checking on him frequently, discovered this and immediately began cleaning up. I offered to help and joined them in wiping down the walls. Once the room was cleaned, they settled Lawrence back into bed, and he went to sleep without difficulty. At the time, Lawrence's behaviour was incomprehensible to all of us. But my visit turned out to be more significant than I had anticipated. Later, his parents told me how much it had meant to them—not just that a psychologist had come to their home, but that I had helped them clean the walls. Their shame and distress over this deeply upsetting behaviour ran deep, and in that moment, I was simply another person sharing their struggle rather than an expert telling them what to do. My psychology skills were limited in the face of this severe difficulty, but I was able to come alongside in the way that the context allowed. The visit increased my feeling for their distress. We now shared the challenge in a way that we hadn't before. Despite having no immediate answers, they attended every subsequent appointment. I provided support, curiosity and encouragement as they tried different approaches. Over the next few months, Lawrence's smearing behaviour gradually declined and eventually stopped altogether. It was not technical expertise or a behavioural strategy that resolved it, but rather the parents' ability to persist despite feeling helpless or ashamed. My role was to help them sustain a helping system around their son, ensuring that they did not collapse under the weight of the problem or lose hope. For me, I admired them profoundly—not for finding a quick fix, but for their endurance, patience and love. I believe this, more than anything else, helped them through.

Notes

1 **The Thrive model.** The main source of information on the Thrive model can be found on the website for the national I-Thrive Implementation Team: i-THRIVE | Implementing the THRIVE Framework. This site provides information on the Thrive model, guidance on how to implement Thrive in a service and examples of successful implementations.

2 **Key references for the Thrive model.** These can all be found at THRIVE Framework for system change | i-THRIVE

a Wolpert, M., Harris, R., Jones, M., Hodges, S., Fuggle, P., James, R., Wiener, A., McKenna, C., Law, D., & Fonagy, P. (2014). *Thrive. The AFC-Tavistock model for CAMHS.* CAMHS Press.

b Wolpert, M., Harris, R., Jones, M., Hodges, S., Fuggle, P., James, R., Wiener, A., York, A., McKenna, C., Law, D., & Fonagy, P. (2015). *Thrive elaborated.* CAMHS Press.

c Wolpert, M., Harris, R., Jones, M., Hodges, S., Fuggle, P., James, R., Wiener, A., York, A., McKenna, C., Law, D., Fonagy, P., Fleming, I., & Munk, S. (2016). *Thrive elaborated second edition.* CAMHS Press.

d Wolpert, M., Harris, R., Jones, M., Hodges, S., Fuggle, P., James, R., Wiener, A., York, A., McKenna, C., Law, D., Fonagy, P., Fleming, I., & Munk, S. (2019). *The thrive framework for system change.* CAMHS Press.

3 **Outcome monitoring.** Outcome monitoring has been supported by the Child Outcomes Research Consortium (CORC) which was set up in 2002 by a group of mental health professionals determined to understand the impact of their work. The network now includes mental health providers, education services, community groups, professional bodies and research institutions. Their website https://www.corc.uk.net/ provides a wealth of information and references about how to support outcome monitoring in services, the challenges that this poses and examples of how these challenges have been met.

4 **Goals based measures.** Information about the use of goal-based measures can be found on the CORC website (https://www.corc.uk.net/). Comprehensive guidance on the use of goal-based measures is provided by Duncan Law and Jenna Jacob (Law, D., & Jacob, J. (2015). *Goals and goal based outcomes (GBOs) some useful information.* CAMHS Press). Research on the goals set by children has been reported (Jacob, J., Edbrooke-Childs, J., Holley, S., Law, D., & Wolpert, M. (2016). Horses for courses? A qualitative exploration of goals formulated in mental health settings by young people, parents, and clinicians. *Clinical Child Psychology and Psychiatry, 21*(2), 208–223).

5 **Integrated Care Boards.** Integrated Care Boards (ICBs) were introduced in England as part of the Health and Care Act 2022. The aim is to create more coordinated, patient-centred care by integrating services across primary, secondary and tertiary health sectors and with social care. ICBs are responsible for overseeing local delivery of health care across a geographical area. Explanations about integrated care systems can be found at the Kings Fund. https://www.kingsfund.org.uk/insight-and-analysis/long-reads/integrated-care-systems-explained in 2024 the impact of the introduction of ICBs was reviewed in a report by the Integrated Care Systems Network (Bliss, A., Williamson, S., & Alayo, L. (2024). *The state of integrated care systems 2023/24: Tackling today while building for tomorrow.* Integrated Care Systems Network. NHS Confederation).

6 **National review of children's social care.** The independent review of children's social care in England led by Josh MacAllister took place in 2021–2022. (MacAlister, J. (2022). The independent review of children's social care: Final report. May 2022. Gov UK.) The report emphasised the need for early intervention

to avoid issues escalating into crisis and reducing the need for children to enter the care system in the first place. The report also encouraged regional collaborations and a new focus on workforce development and support. A series of proposals was published in 2023 by the Department of Education as statutory guidance which is periodically revised. This document is titled Children's Social Care: national framework and provides more detailed information about the implementation of the proposals in the review and the standards of practice for social care that this requires.

Chapter 5

The Helping Process

The Role of Families

Parents/carers have a key role in helping children to overcome their mental health needs, usually working collaboratively with child professionals.

Introduction

The next six chapters will each explore a key principle. We will briefly explain the reasoning behind each principle, followed by outlining core processes that demonstrate how the principle operates in practice. A principle is not a protocol or procedure; there are multiple ways these principles can be applied in practice. Each principle will be linked to the lives of the six children and young people who form the thread of this book.

Jacqui disliked others knowing how she truly felt. She didn't know why she felt this way and assumed everyone thought as she did. She fondly remembered her grandmother, who would talk with her after primary school about all sorts of things including all the things that upset her at school. When her grandmother became seriously ill, Jacqui enjoyed bringing her the things she needed. She had always felt closer to her grandmother than to her mum, Chisomo. In secondary school, she didn't share her worries with Chisomo or her dad, Kande. She felt unable to ask for help, expecting that she would somehow feel told off. However, life became overwhelming, leading to daily arguments with Chisomo and a refusal to attend her new school. Then Kande, in a rare conversation, shared how unhappy he had been at her age. This made Jacqui feel they were trying to help. She began talking more with Chisomo and eventually agreed, albeit reluctantly, to see a mental health professional.

The helping process is the foundation upon which everything else rests. Due to its significance, it will span two chapters: one focusing on the helping process between children and families and the other on the relationship between children and professionals. Seeking help for mental health needs has many similarities to help-seeking in general. A shared understanding of this process is essential for the rest of the book to be meaningful. In exploring the helping process, we aim to reflect common experiences that may resonate with you as a child, a parent, or both.

DOI: 10.4324/9781003145523-5

Key Aspects of Family Help

Help as a Core Process of Childhood

Throughout the journey from infancy to adulthood, all children need help.[1] In early life they need help with all their fundamental needs—eating, dressing, using the toilet and learning the right words for things. But they also need help with things that frighten or excite them, managing intense feelings of excitement, threat or confusion. This help involves addressing both the situation itself and the intense emotions that may arise, whether excitement or fear.

As children grow older, help shifts towards navigating the social world—understanding others' behaviour and expectations. They need guidance in acquiring new skills such as reading, playing football and making friends. Additionally, they must begin to make sense of their family's cultural values and the social norms of the complex societies they belong to.

In adolescence, help becomes more focused on supporting young people to discover who they are: understanding where they fit in, who likes or dislikes them and managing the complexities of attraction, relationships and sexual intimacy. At this stage, parents may become less influential compared to peers and wider social influences including the internet. They may often seek help in indirect ways due to heightened awareness of social shame and the humiliation of not knowing what others appear to know. In their relationships, they begin to imagine the kind of adult they wish to become while discovering both opportunities and limitations in their world. They realise that the world is not equally fair for everyone. And, unlike in a book, all this rarely goes smoothly. They will learn that they have to choose who they trust, and who are cruel and exploit their vulnerability. They will encounter situations where they feel unfairly treated or rightly held accountable for their actions. The helping process must be carefully managed to avoid worsening feelings of guilt, inadequacy or anxiety. During this process, parents' direct influence on daily behaviour may diminish but their long-term significance remains unique. Other adults—grandparents, teachers, sports coaches, dance instructors, career advisors—may provide valuable and sometimes life-changing help but this is usually relatively short-term compared with the parents. Parents are there for the long haul.

All families develop patterns of who they can seek help from about what. This book aims to locate how we respond to the specific mental health needs of children and young people within this universal process of giving and receiving help, a core aspect of childhood. Countless small, caring acts—like preparing breakfast—occur daily between children and their caregivers. These moments often seem routine and insignificant, merely practical tasks to ensure children are fed and watered and have some sort of idea about how the day will be spent safely and perhaps enjoyably. Yet, within this web of interactions, children learn profound lessons about themselves, their relationships and the world they are in. These discoveries may not be explicit or named but are the building blocks of how they grow to be the adult they become. Alongside this, children learn about the delicate process of giving and receiving help. Humans are inherently social beings, dependent on others to navigate complex social environments while also discovering the joys and frustrations of helping and being helped. During childhood, learning how to give and receive help shapes personal growth and future relationships.

For example, Jack is three years old and staying with his grandparents along with his six-year-old sister, Alice. While getting ready for bed, Jack realises his soft toy panda, Paney, is missing from his bag. He always sleeps with Paney and becomes upset. He tells his grandma during bedtime stories, and she reassures him that he will be alright. Jack doesn't know what else to say. After his grandma leaves, he grows more upset and begins to cry. Unable to sleep, he gets up to find his grandma but instead encounters his grandad, who notices Jack has been crying. His grandad gives him a cuddle, and Jack tells him that he is missing Paney. Grandad asks him all about Paney and says that he can see why he misses him. They ring home to check that Paney is alright at home and then find an old soft toy cat, Catty, and that Catty would enjoy some company. Jack agrees to let Catty sleep in his bed. Though it's not the same as having Paney, with his grandad telling him a story, Jack settles and falls asleep.

Jack is learning about help, even if he doesn't recognise it as such. He discovers that both grandparents are kind but help him in different ways. His grandma offers reassurance, while his grandad shares a personal story about feeling unhappy when away from home. Jack feels better. This small moment of asking for and receiving help is one of countless experiences shaping his journey through childhood. Jack's grandparents may not see themselves as part of the children's mental health workforce, but they are.

Good Enough Family Environments

Jack's story is about a child in an environment where adults love and care for him as best they can. They may forget things or misunderstand him at times, but they are doing their best.[2] While many children grow up in families where they feel loved and cared for amid everyday family challenges, not all do. Some children face environments filled with threat, aggression, fear, blame and criticism. In focusing on the helping process, we must not overlook children whose needs are met with dismissal and harshness, or worse. We will turn to the needs of these children in Chapter 7. This was Martin's experience. In early life, he faced unpredictable and neglectful care from his birth mother, Maisie, who struggled with alcohol and substance misuse. Sometimes Maisie was caring and responsive, but other times she was harsh and punitive. Martin never knew which version of his mother he would encounter. From a young age, he learned to avoid trouble and managed his world rather than feeling supported by it.

At this point, we focus on the majority of children in environments of good enough care, where children are loved and helped as best as parents and carers are able to do.

We do not mean every interaction is sensitive, thoughtful or kind, nor that the child is always happy. Childhood involves ups and downs—sadness, conflict, misunderstandings, disappointments and hurts. It carries its own share of suffering. However, in general, children and carers adapt and find a way through. Through this process, children come to recognise both kindness and unkindness, patience and impatience, availability and unavailability. This learning is crucial in preparing them for adulthood. It's this mixed experience that helps a child to discriminate, to learn who and when to trust others and when not to. This process has been most thoroughly described through attachment theory, and due to its central importance, we will provide a brief overview.

The first system of help a child experiences is best described as the attachment process.[3] Many view this as a form of love—a connection formed between a baby and their parent or carer, involving feelings of obligation, care, love, affection and warmth. Some may feel that the term 'attachment' lacks emotional depth or fails to capture the mysteries of this bond. However, psychologists are not poets and use this language to explain the process of connection. Attachment forms the foundation of a child's emotional development, fostering survival by creating strong emotional bonds with primary caregivers. These early attachments shape how a child engages in future help-seeking relationships. A baby's or young infant's attachment behaviour is how they seek closeness, comfort or safety from a familiar caregiver when they feel frightened or threatened. When hungry, uncomfortable or wary of strangers, the infant seeks proximity and help—this is the first helping relationship. Not all children engage in this process in the same way. The majority (about two-thirds) are described as securely attached. These children are comforted when reunited with their caregiver and learn that this part of the world is safe. While attachment is not the only factor influencing future helping relationships, it plays a significant role. Jacqui, for example, was securely attached to her grandmother, who cared for and responded to her in ways that made Jacqui feel supported and accepted. This trust in others allowed Jacqui to consider new ideas and try things, even when it wasn't her preference. This adaptability proved important when her mother encouraged her to seek professional mental health support, despite Jacqui's reluctance. Similarly, Daniel had a secure bond with his mother, Judith. However, as he grew older, he became aware of Judith's fragility, which made him anxious about her well-being and inhibited his willingness to seek help from her.

Around one-third of children are described as 'insecurely attached'. These children may display more anxiety or avoidance towards their caregiver during comfort and repair, making the process of seeking and receiving help more challenging. Insecure attachment is sometimes misunderstood as resembling a disorder, but this is inaccurate. Most insecurely attached children develop as well as their peers. However, for some, it can mark the start of a pattern where seeking help feels more fragile and uncertain. Simone exemplified this pattern. Her parents were deeply devoted and attentive, believing it was essential to spend significant time with her in the years before she went to school. However, Simone struggled with brief separations during routine care. When left with her dad while her mum was out, she was overly concerned about when her mum would return. Her parents viewed this as simply part of Simone's personality and adapted their care accordingly. Yet, starting school was particularly difficult for Simone and her parents, requiring additional support to navigate this transition.

There is a third attachment group of children described as having disorganised attachment patterns. This group represents a small proportion of all children and are particularly challenging for caregivers to form a consistent pattern of care with. They may intensely seek closeness but then abruptly become rejecting. Typically, they struggle significantly to seek and accept help. Martin and Teresa's life stories illustrate this pattern. Teresa's difficulties extended beyond managing her intense emotions; her relationships with adults and peers were marked by a cycle of seeking closeness followed by feelings of hurt, disappointment and rejection. She oscillated between intimacy and distance, often accompanied by overwhelming emotions of rage and abandonment.

Much attention is given to the formation of attachment in early life, but attachment continues to evolve throughout the lifespan. For instance, adults experiencing distress, such as during a divorce, may temporarily return to their parents for comfort and support. Similarly, adolescents may seek proximity to caregivers in subtle or indirect ways while striving for independence and autonomy. Strong attachment provides children with a sense of safety. In early life, children need to understand that they could be eaten by tigers if they wander off. Their natural wariness of strangers makes sense and is protective. They need reassurance from familiar caregivers that new adults will be kind to them. Through these interactions, children learn about the helping process—seeking comfort when frightened and regaining a sense of safety through connection. They learn that others can help them feel better.

As children grow, their ways of seeking and receiving help become more diverse, involving language, varied communication and more nuanced interactions.[4] This development aligns with their growing cognitive, emotional and social competencies and experience. They need help with learning about the world (largely through education), navigating social relationships and making sense of their emerging identities. They encounter confusing or unfair situations, feel misunderstood and gradually develop the complex skills of knowing when and how to seek help when they don't know what to do or how to do it, or when they are unsure, upset or hurt by events or other people. These early experiences of help shape the patterns of help-seeking that children and young people carry into adulthood. All children are not the same in this regard, and the creation of effective helping systems must adapt to these variations in how children and their caregivers are comfortable receiving support. How we help must be influenced both by the nature of the problems they face and by these individual ways of being in the world. For many children, young people and families, the first step in the helping process is trying to work out the nature of the problem—and this is where we will begin when exploring family help processes.

Key Processes of Family Help

Working Out What Is the Problem

Help-seeking and help-receiving is a precarious process for everyone, involving the risk of further hurt or upset.[5] This is true for adults and even more so for children in relation to adults. For children, naming the problem can be difficult. They may struggle to find the words to express how they feel or question whether it is acceptable to have the problem at all. This is especially true for mental health concerns, which often come in all sorts of disguises, creating much confusion and self-blame. "Is it my fault that I feel so scared to go to school?" or "Does this make me a bad person or just weak?" are common. Children may wonder if they caused their parents' arguments after wetting the bed or if their struggles reflect something fundamentally wrong with them. They navigate these uncertainties partly on their own and partly through interactions with others, often with their parents or carers in early childhood. Children frequently need help working out what the problem is before they can consider what help they need. For example, being bullied can be very unclear and confusing whether certain experiences qualify as bullying or not. Jacqui felt rejected by her new peer group at secondary school, and her identity as a black young person led her to accept this rejection as something to be expected. Abdul dealt with targeted behaviour from a small group of children but didn't label it as bullying. He often felt stressed by this but didn't know how to make sense of it. Like many children, it was not clear to him when the usual ups and downs of peer conflicts crossed the line into bullying. He wondered, "Is it my fault that other children are mean to me? Will my parents understand or just tell me to toughen up? Should I be able to make them stop?"

Often, it takes the perspective of a family member or a friend to help work this out.[6] Dialogue with others can help a child recognise a problem like bullying. Ideally, this understanding is co-constructed, with parents and peers bringing their own experiences and anxieties into the conversation. Some parents may respond with anxiety or anger, while others may dismiss it as a normal, if unpleasant, part of childhood. Parents frequently help their children make sense of experiences, often without even realising it. Help-seeking for a child often begins with a parent helping to identify the problem. A parent might ask, "Are all children this scared to go to school?" or wonder, "Haven't most children stopped wetting the bed by now?" Adolescents also often struggle to name their problems. Young people experiencing low mood or depression rarely begin by calling it that. They may feel like they don't want to talk to people, that they feel useless, unattractive, have no energy and other people irritate them a lot. The experience is a blur, a muddle of life circumstances and internal emotions, often accompanied by a sense of self-blame. Recognising and naming the problem is often the first and most challenging step in seeking help.

If a child doesn't understand what the problem is, seeking help becomes extremely difficult. For example, young people often need support to recognise that what they are experiencing is something adults call depression and that they could benefit from help for this. They may have worked this out from online information, conversations with peers or discussions with parents, identifying their feelings as being 'stressed'. This process of working this out can be filled with uncertainties and fears. Will their parents respond with sympathy or dismiss their feelings by telling them to 'pull themselves together'? Parents, too, bring their own anxieties and emotions into these situations. A parent might recognise similar struggles from their own childhood—such as disliking school or feeling isolated—or might feel disappointment if their child faces challenges that they hoped to prevent. Understandably, it can be difficult for parents to simply mirror a child's emotions when they are powerfully involved and managing their own stresses too.

For the child, the first challenge in seeking help is understanding what they are experiencing and anticipating how others will react. Even in loving and supportive environments, from the child's perspective, adults' responses to their distress can feel unpredictable. Sometimes a child may receive kindness and sympathy; other times, they may feel criticised or dismissed. Responses may also differ between parents or carers, leading young people to seek help selectively or indirectly. They often wait for moments when they feel safer to open up. This might occur when a younger child is being read a bedtime story, walking home from football with a parent, sensing a parent is in a good mood or combining their problem with something they think will please their parent. Helping children make sense of their lives, build coping strategies and develop resilience is not a simple exchange. It's a complex process where problems may be unclear, disguised or feared before they can be identified and addressed.

Daniel had a strong relationship with his mother, Judith. He felt comfortable discussing school events, friendships and music—a shared passion that led them to attend concerts together. He was acutely aware of Judith's emotional struggles—her work-related stress and the distress caused by her marital separation. Daniel felt responsible for supporting her and, at times, took on a caregiving role. He feared burdening her with his own problems, believing it would add to her stress. As a result, he kept his personal struggles hidden from his mother. Despite Judith's attempts to engage with issues she suspected, Daniel avoided and deflected these conversations.

Family Work: Helping with the Problem

It is impossible to capture the countless ways families support children with their mental health needs.[7] This help ranges from practical assistance to emotional care, deeply intertwined within family relationships. This book acknowledges, for better or worse, that most of the help children receive in managing their emotions, developing their identities comes from relationships outside formal mental health services. This support occurs within family and peer relationships, often without being explicitly labelled as 'help'. It can be indirect, informal and often disguised. At other times, it is more explicit, particularly when a child or adult recognises the need to address an issue together. This help is often facilitated by setting the right conditions for communication—ensuring privacy or being clear about who will be involved and who will know the outcome. Although common, providing this help is neither easy, uniform or routine. Quite the opposite.

Kande and Chisomo were deeply distressed by Jacqui's withdrawal, depression and the constant arguments they had with her. They struggled to understand what Jacqui was experiencing and what had caused it. In their attempts to help, they oscillated between kindness and the firmness they believed she needed. At times, they felt passive and helpless; at others, they wanted to take full control. Two key events improved the situation. First, after speaking with their GP, Chisomo began to view Jacqui not so much as a defiant teenager but as a young person who was unwell. Although the concept of depression in a young person was difficult for her to accept, she started responding differently, avoiding battles with Jacqui. Second, Kande, prompted by advice from a work colleague, shared his own struggles as a young man with Jacqui. She had always been somewhat afraid of him, but his vulnerability resonated with her. In that moment, he stopped instructing her and connected with her emotionally. These two shifts marked the beginning of a supportive system that blended family understanding with professional guidance.

Sandra was dedicated to caring for Martin. Although she found him hard work, she recognised his anger and restlessness as stemming from his early life experiences. Having fostered several children, Sandra had developed a practical warmth in her caregiving. She often felt anger and frustration towards Matt, Martin's social worker, due to indecision over Martin's long-term care plans. Sandra believed Martin needed clear consequences if he behaved badly, and that sometimes she felt that she wasn't allowed to deal with things her own way. She felt she understood Martin best, and it made her feel good that Martin was gradually settling at school and forming a strong bond with her older daughter, Polly. Sandra's understanding and consistent care were instrumental in helping Martin feel more secure.

For Aisha and Ali, Abdul's diagnosis of ASD was a significant event in their family life. It brought relief by explaining why Abdul struggled with certain aspects of life, but it also carried feelings of shame, making it difficult to discuss within their extended family. As practising Muslims, the views of their mosque community were deeply important to them. Initially, the diagnosis seemed to isolate them from the community. However, after Ali spoke with the Imam about Abdul, he felt accepted and supported. To Aisha's surprise, some women at the mosque began offering help to Abdul, even volunteering to care for him when she needed to focus on her other children. For Patrick and Brigitte with Simone, they were overwhelmed by the feelings that Simone's difficulties evoked in them. It dominated their family life creating high levels of anxiety in her parents, making her seem all-powerful. Changing this pattern was extremely difficult and required extensive support from both the school and health services to help Simone settle into school. A turning point came when Simone's maternal grandmother visited from France. She was uniquely able to contain her daughter's anxieties and help her see beyond the immediate challenges, providing much-needed perspective and support.

These four families responded to their children's needs in a variety of ways—through wider family involvement, community support, shifts in parent-child relationship or simply recognising the distress behind their child's behaviour. While these responses did not solve all difficulties—and in some cases, like Teresa's, family responses worsened the situation—they marked the starting point for building a broader helping system that could in different ways include professional support. This will be the focus of the next chapter.

Conclusions

Families have natural ways of supporting, protecting, loving and helping one another. These processes begin at birth (or even earlier) and involve countless human interactions that help a child learn about themselves, others and about the world at large. In this learning are sophisticated ways of recognising distress and offering comfort. These systems are not perfect, and misunderstandings often occur, but for most families, they are sufficient to navigate the challenges of childhood. However, mental health problems in children and young people often put a serious strain on these natural helping processes. Identifying the nature of the problem can be difficult, and both children and parents may struggle to articulate and discuss these challenges. Even when the problem is recognised, determining what will be helpful is rarely straightforward and may involve conflicting views on the best course of action.

To address this, we propose in the next chapter that children's mental health needs are best supported through collaboration between families and professionals. This partnership must consider the existing helping processes already surrounding the child. Standardised approaches to care should be adapted to fit the helping styles and the helping system that already exists around the child. Uniform methods of help are unlikely to be effective for all families. Professional support should not replace family help but instead work alongside and strengthen both family and community support to best help the child or young person.

Key Implications for Good Practice

1. The dependency and vulnerability of children mean that all children require help and support from their family and community throughout their journey to adulthood.
2. The vast majority of support for children's mental health needs—often complex and stressful—is provided by the family.
3. Mental health needs are often confusing, hidden and disguised and can be very difficult for families to discuss openly.
4. Professional help must place at the centre of their work how they complement and strengthen family methods of help when determining how best to help a child or young person with their mental health needs.

A Parent's Life: Maggie

Maggie was a 30-year-old single parent with a three-year-old son, Matt. She was referred for help in managing Matt's behaviour. During our meeting, Maggie spoke openly about her thoughts and feelings. She was warm, friendly and chaotic, but clear that she wanted support. She expressed anger and frustration with Matt, describing him as unreasonable and unwilling to follow her instructions. However, she also felt guilty about her own sense of hopelessness in caring for him. Matt struggled to settle in the evening, requiring Maggie to lie in bed with him until he fell asleep—often causing her to fall asleep as well. He frequently woke during the night, making it difficult to soothe him back to sleep. Maggie felt he was uncontrollable at home, constantly demanding her attention and care. She felt criticised and unsupported by her own family and was chronically exhausted, often feeling depressed and demoralised about her life. Although the nursery staff were supportive, Maggie found their advice unhelpful. Everyone encouraged her to set firm boundaries with Matt, but this advice only made her feel worse. Maggie was certain of one thing: she did not want to parent Matt the way her own mother had parented her. She wanted to care for Matt differently, but she had no clear idea of what that looked like. Reflecting on her childhood, she remembered being frightened of her parents, particularly their shouting. She didn't want Matt to be frightened of her, but she worried that following others' advice would make him hate her. To avoid this, she gave in to his every demand, allowing him to take control. Maggie had never spoken about these feelings before. Gradually, through several sessions, she opened up about her parents and began to work out how she wanted to parent Matt. Out of this process, she decided to attend a parenting course and successfully implemented behavioural strategies to manage Matt's behaviour in a calm manner. Over time, her relationship with Matt improved, and he began sleeping in his own bed. Maggie was discovering her own parenting style—one that differed from her parents—and was filling in the blank space she once had in her mind about how to parent.

Notes

1 **The helping process.** Help is a fundamental aspect of human relationships. A useful general introduction to the helping process is provided by Edgar Schein (Schein, E. H. (2010). *Helping: How to offer, give, and receive help.* Berrett Koehler Publishers, Oakland, USA). Michael Rutter's classic overview of child mental health problems in 1975 set the context for emphasising that helping children took place in a social context (Rutter, M. (1975). *Helping troubled children.* Plenum). There are multiple psychological texts providing a broad overview of the role of helping in the social/emotional development in childhood and adolescence (Leggett, E. S., Roaten, G. K., & Ybañez-Llorente, K. (2016). Early childhood: Emotional and social development. In D. Capuzzi & M. D. Stauffer (Eds.), *Human growth and development across the lifespan: Applications for counselors* (pp. 217–248). John Wiley & Sons, Inc). The helping process is also central to how children learn in school, and the evidence for the key components of this was reviewed by John Hattie who concluded that the key aspect of effective helping (or learning) was to be able to see the problem from the perspective of the child or learner. (Hattie, J. (2012). *Visible learning for teachers: Maximizing impact on learning.* Routledge).

2 **Good enough family environments.** The term 'good enough' care was first proposed by Donald Winnicott (Winnicott, D. W. (1973). *The child, the family, and the outside world.* Penguin) and has been used extensively to recognise that children learn to manage caring relationships which are not ideal, but which provide sufficient love and safety for a child to thrive.

3 **Attachment.** Attachment theory originated in the work of John Bowlby. (Bowlby, J. (1988). *A secure base: Parent-child attachment and healthy human development.* Basic Books. Bretherton, I). There are many reviews on current thinking about attachment processes (Fearon, R. P., & Roisman, G. I. (2017). Attachment theory: Progress and future directions. *Current Opinion in Psychology, 15*, 131–136; Barlow, J., Schrader-McMillan, A., Axford, N., Wrigley, Z., Sonthalia, S., Wilkinson, T.,... & Coad, J. (2016). Attachment and attachment-related outcomes in preschool children–a review of recent evidence. *Child and Adolescent Mental Health, 21*(1), 11–20; Gregory, M., Kannis-Dymand, L., & Sharman, R. (2020). A review of attachment-based parenting interventions: Recent advances and future considerations. *Australian Journal of Psychology, 72*(2), 109–122.)

4 **Help-seeking.** Help-seeking behaviour is the act of actively seeking assistance from others when experiencing stress or difficulty. It can involve asking for guidance, treatment or support from a healthcare professional or a trusted person. Theories of what influences help-seeking were first proposed in the 1980s (Gross, A. E., & McMullen, P. A. (1982). The help-seeking process. In V. J. Derlega & J. Grzelak (Eds.), *Cooperation and helping behavior* (pp. 305–326). Academic Press. Recent more detailed cognitive behavioural models of help-seeking have been proposed (Hammer, J. H., Vogel, D. L., Grzanka, P. R., Kim, N., Keum, B. T., Adams, C., & Wilson, S. A. (2024). The integrated behavioral model of mental health help seeking (IBM-HS): A health services utilization theory of planned behavior for

accessing care. *Journal of Counseling Psychology, 71*(5), 315–327. Theories of help-seeking suggest that the recognition of the problem is an important determinant of help-seeking behaviour.

5 **Reluctance of help-seeking behaviour.** A number of studies have shown that help-seeking for mental health problems lags behind the level of need (Oliver, M. I., Pearson, N., Coe, N., & Gunnell, D. (2005). Help-seeking behaviour in men and women with common mental health problems: cross-sectional study. *British Journal of Psychiatry, 186*(4), 297–301; Doll, C. M., Michel, C., Rosen, M., Osman, N., Schimmelmann, B. G., & Schultze-Lutter, F. (2021). Predictors of help-seeking behaviour in people with mental health problems: A 3-year prospective community study. *BMC Psychiatry, 21*, 432; O'Neill, A., Stapley, E., Rehman, I., & Humphrey, N. (2023). Adolescent help-seeking: An exploration of associations with perceived cause of emotional distress. *Frontiers in Public Health, 11*, 1183092).

6 **The role of the family in helping children with mental health needs.** The important role of families in supporting children's mental health is widely supported by both research and literature about professional practice. For example, Hoagwood and colleagues completed a large-scale review of the role of family support which supported the value of family support (Hoagwood, K. E., Cavaleri, M. A., Serene Olin, S., Burns, B. J., Slaton, E., Gruttadaro, D., & Hughes, R. (2010). Family support in children's mental health: A review and synthesis. *Clinical Child and Family Psychology Review, 13*(1), 1–45). Professional bodies, the NHS and the Children's Commissioner provide position statements about the importance of families in addressing these needs. (https://www.childrenscommissioner.gov.uk/blog/mental-health-and-family/).

7 **Parents support children in different ways.** Studies have shown that parents have different ways of supporting their offspring. Stapley and colleagues followed a group of families where a young person was being treated for depression and showed that parents may have different approaches to providing support. (Stapley, E., Target, M., & Midgley, N. (2017). The journey through and beyond mental health services in the United Kingdom: A typology of parents' ways of managing the crisis of their teenage child's depression. *Journal of Clinical Psychology, 73*(10), 1429–1441.)

Chapter 6

The Helping Process

The Role of Professionals

Mental health professionals need to adapt well-tested methods to take account of how parents/carers and children wish to be helped.

Introduction

Alongside family help, professional help is provided by doctors, therapists, social workers, psychologists, teachers, counsellors and others dedicated to assisting children, young people and their families. For professionals, obviously enough, helping is a job and the help they provide is very different from informal family help, where individuals choose when and from whom to seek support. In contrast, professional help usually begins with a meeting at an agreed time in an unfamiliar place. Beforehand, the child may know relatively little about what is going to take place, who they are seeing and what such people do. The therapist or 'talking doctor' is a stranger and, combined with the unfamiliarity of the situation for both the child and carer, this does not create ideal conditions for beginning a helping process. It is entirely different from the type of helping process which we have described in the previous chapter in which help takes place within existing relationships and familiar settings. This contrast with family help means that professionals need to develop sensitive and thoughtful ways of enabling a child to feel comfortable in these initial interactions.

Professionals become involved when parents/carers or young people feel the problem exceeds their ability to cope, goes beyond typical parental management or raises concerns that the child may have a disorder or is experiencing distress beyond the normal ups and downs of childhood. The decision to seek professional help can be collaborative, involving both child and parent, as with Jacqui. Alternatively, it may be driven primarily by the parent/carer, even when the child is reluctant or disagrees that a problem exists, as seen with Martin and Abdul. Less commonly, a young person may independently seek help without involving their parents when they recognise a problem but choose not to involve them. Children who seek or are brought for professional help are always receiving some level of family support. When any sort of

DOI: 10.4324/9781003145523-6

support is entirely absent this may indicate abuse or neglect, which will be explored in the next chapter. At the point of seeking professional help, the family support system may be highly anxious or nearing collapse where the family don't know what to do or how to help their child. This was evident with Jacqui's parents, who were in despair over her prolonged absence from school, and with Martin's foster carer, who feared his placement was at risk of breaking down.

This shift towards professional help is well illustrated by Sam's experience. Sam, a parent, contacted a mental health service for her 15-year-old daughter, Margot. Sam had supported Margot through various childhood challenges and viewed her emotional ups and downs as a normal part of growing up. Although sometimes exasperated, she enjoyed parenting and helping her daughter. However, when Margot recently confided that she sometimes wanted to die and had suicidal thoughts, Sam was terrified and unsure how to respond. For her, suicidality went beyond the job description for a parent. It terrified her and crossed a line between family help and the need for professional intervention. Understandably, she wanted Margot to see a mental health professional. Despite Sam's concerns, Margot was deeply unhappy about coming to see a professional whom she did not know. She was upset that Sam had shared her feelings with others and felt ashamed and hostile towards attending any sort of appointment. Margot complied with attending the session but did so more out of obligation than a personal desire for help. Her main motivation was to avoid further involvement with the service. However, at the meeting itself, she was reassured about the approach that the doctor took, particularly that part of the meeting took place without Sam being present.

Key Aspects of Professional Help

Professionals Joining the Helping System

Seeking professional help for children and young people is a complex and delicate process, often marked by differing views between parents and children about the problem itself. Such disagreement is a common feature and can often be a major part of the problem itself. Typically, initial sessions will involve working out what the problem is (an assessment) and then developing a therapeutic plan, in which the family usually plays a crucial role. Rarely does a plan exclude parental involvement. For all of the six young people discussed in this book, parents/carers were part of the helping process although in very different ways. Daniel was different as he did not involve professionals in his needs, but his mum actively cared for and supported him although his mental health needs were not explicitly recognised. The other five families involved a delicate process of integrating professional guidance with family perspectives. This usually involved developing an active parental role in the helping process so that with Teresa, because of her volatile relationship with her parents, the professional input tried to play an active role in reducing the frequency of the repetitive conflicts between them.

Professional help often involves the child or family attending a planned series of sessions targeting a specific issue identified during the assessment. The assessment clarifies the problem, which may range from family relationship difficulties or parenting challenges to more child-focused concerns like anxiety, depression, anger, eating disorders or self-harm.

Professional help generally aims to help the child and family develop a shared understanding of the issue, improve communication and explore ways to change relationships or behaviours to alleviate the problem. Therapists offer expert knowledge and an outsider perspective, which can be valuable in strained family relationships caused by mental health struggles. While showing empathy for the distress, frustration or guilt present in the family, professionals are less embroiled in these feelings in the way that the family are likely to be. Commonly, the treatment may involve helping a family to talk with each other, and the sessions may provide a neutral space for families to communicate more effectively. Therapy sessions alone rarely constitute the entire treatment. Most treatments will involve the invitation by the practitioner for children, and parents to try things out between sessions. These activities often involve communicating more with each other, to face a situation that they had previously avoided or adopting new safety measures discussed in therapy. While these actions require conscious effort, other positive changes—such as better relationships, feeling understood or reduced stress—may occur implicitly. Conversely, sessions may also surface long-standing conflicts, temporarily increasing tension. Applying therapeutic changes in daily life is one of the biggest challenges in child mental health care. Changes in behaviour or emotional shifts achieved during sessions can be difficult to maintain in familiar home or school environments, where ingrained habits quickly resurface. Although a vast range of therapies and treatments exist for children with mental health needs and their families, nearly all rely on collaboration between professionals, children and parents.[1] Certain aspects of this collaboration are essential for building effective helping systems around a child, which we will now explore.

Creating Trust between Professionals and with Parents/Carers and Families

In collaboration between a young person, their parents and a mental health professional, it is unlikely that all three will share identical views on the nature of the problem and how to address it. For example, some parents may believe their child simply needs to "get on with it", reflecting expectations from their own upbringing. This difference isn't necessarily problematic if it is openly discussed. While such differences cannot be eliminated, establishing a degree of trust between professionals and parents about the overall approach is essential. This is a core responsibility of the professional, perhaps even the most crucial.[2] Trust develops when parents and the child feel the professional has some understanding of what it is like to be them, not perfectly but sufficient for trust to emerge. This may involve recognising aspects of a family that aren't openly acknowledged, such as tensions between parents or siblings. For families facing oppressive environments—racism, bullying or discrimination related to sexual identity—it is especially important that these experiences are acknowledged. Similarly for families in practising faith communities, recognising differences in belief systems can help families from faith communities feel understood. Professionals foster trust by explicitly sharing their understanding with the family and inviting correction when they misunderstand. For example, as a white older male, recognising that a white male psychologist may not grasp the lived experience of a 15-year-old black girl can build trust more effectively than offering superficial empathy. Acknowledging these differences shows genuine understanding rather than relying solely on general knowledge of mental health issues.

Supporting Change: Different Roles for Professionals and Parents/Carers

Beyond trust, collaboration between parents, children and professionals requires all the things that are involved in any collaborative relationship—reliability, honouring agreements, problem-solving and genuine interest in each other's experiences. While the general components of collaboration are well-documented, our focus here is on the specific challenges that occur between professionals, parents/carers and children in addressing mental health needs.

Children are not miniature adults. They differ from adults in the way they think and feel, in their life experience and in their capacity to make decisions about their own lives. In this collaborative process, they are equal in value but not in power. Typically, others define their problems and decide on the help that they should receive. But, in their involvement in education, children and young people are also actively engaged in learning about the world, a process that mirrors collaboration between adults and children. This process of collaborative learning may provide useful insights as to how parents, children and professionals can work together to support a child's mental health. Effective teachers understand what needs to be learned from the child's perspective—a skill like that required by parents and mental health professionals. Beyond understanding, education designs ways for children to practise and reinforce what they've learned. Supporting children to learn and practise new ways of doing things in the world is vital in creating an effective helping system for mental health. We have a lot to learn from education about how parents, professionals and children collaborate together in helping children learn and, to explore this, we will take a specific example around how children learn to read but it will be easy for the reader to see parallels with how children learn about many other things, both of the world and themselves.

How Children Learn to Read

It may seem unusual in a book about helping children with mental health needs to discuss how children learn to read.[3] However, this example offers valuable insights into effective ways to help children, as many principles of effective help are reflected in the learning process. This comparison can make it easier to understand the components of the helping process than the often complex nature of mental health needs. Notably, it highlights the distinct but complementary roles of professionals (teachers) and parents in providing help. Almost all children receive help from adults in learning to read. While a few may teach themselves, this is rare. Learning to read involves adults teaching the necessary skills, the letters of the alphabet, the way words are made up of letters and how words are separated by spaces. They are shown how letters and groups of letters sound, enabling them to read words aloud—a process known as phonics. These foundational mechanics are taught gradually, with early reading books designed to reinforce these concepts. Initially, children observe adults reading books to them and are gradually encouraged to participate by reading letters and words themselves. Yet, mastering the mechanics is only part of learning to read. The other part involves fun, discovery, humour, happy and sad endings making reading engaging and meaningful. Through stories, children explore imagined worlds: caterpillars become hungry, children journey down rabbit holes and tigers talk and come to tea. This imaginative aspect develops alongside the technical skills needed for reading. Once reading is mastered, it's easy to forget how complex the process is. For those familiar with the English alphabet, looking at Japanese or Chinese scripts can remind us of the astonishing achievement reading is and highlights how remarkable it is that such texts can be deciphered. So learning to read requires practice; lots of it.

To learn to read, children receive help in two ways. First, they need to be taught the basics by professionals—teachers who understand the principles of reading and have developed effective teaching methods. These methods have been refined over time so that teachers know how to introduce phonics, select suitable books for beginners and recognise the stages of reading development. They are skilled in encouraging children to persist through challenges, understanding that tasks must be appropriately difficult to sustain interest. A guiding principle is the "zone of proximal development", where children should be able to read most words in a book, struggling with only a few. If a book is too easy, they don't learn; if it's too hard, they become discouraged and disengaged from the story. Importantly, children don't learn to read by being told they have got a word wrong. Mistakes are best met with curiosity and playfulness, not criticism. This approach encourages learning and resilience, fostering a supportive environment where children feel safe to make mistakes and keep trying.

To learn to read, a child needs to be shown and taught the fundamentals of reading, but they also need ample opportunities to practise. They need teachers to instruct them, but they also need 'practicers'—an informal team of parents, older siblings, grandparents and others who sit with children helping them to practice. Practicers are not coaches or experts; their life experience is sufficient. They need patience, dedication and most importantly, a shared sense of enjoyment in the learning process. This involves having fun, being amused and being able to imagine what it's like for a child to be learning to read as if for the first time. Practicers need to understand that children may want to read the same story rather too many times and find gentle ways to introduce new books. They help build both meaning and skill, and parents and family members are not strangers to the child. It can be deeply satisfying for a child to show their parents what they've learned, and they enjoy sharing their achievements with them. Most parents instinctively know how to support their child with this, often recalling how they themselves learned to read. They don't need expertise in phonics or detailed knowledge of reading schemes; they can leave this to the teachers. Eventually, active assistance with learning to read naturally comes to an end. This occurs when a child can independently read texts and begin deciphering unfamiliar words for themselves. They become self-learners, no longer relying on others to expand their vocabulary or engage with more complex stories. They are truly launched into the world of words and books, easily forgetting that reading was once a skill they had to learn—much like walking. The helping system has fulfilled its purpose, and active help is no longer needed. Most children reach this stage without too much trouble. For some, reading becomes a lifelong source of enjoyment, while for others, it serves as a practical tool for navigating daily life—buying train tickets, using the internet or reviewing a restaurant bill. Literacy transcends generations, becoming a shared human experience.

However, for some children, learning to read is more challenging, requiring additional help to grasp the mechanics or discover the joy of reading.[4] For these children, the helping system needs to show its colours. More help will be required of both the teachers and the practicers and for these children the parallels with helping children with mental health needs should again be apparent. There are many approaches to helping children who find reading hard. Some focus on fostering pleasure and enjoyment, while others prioritise mastering the mechanics of reading. However, all effective approaches recognise the need to balance both aspects. One structured approach is Reading Recovery, which provides intensive, systematic teaching and practice for children who find reading particularly difficult. This method acts as extra scaffolding during the critical phase of helping children reach a point where they can read more independently. Importantly, children still need both a professional teacher and a 'practicer'. Specialist teaching alone is not enough; consistent practice with non-professionals is also essential.

Reading Recovery recommends that a six-year-old child struggling with reading should receive daily 30-minute sessions with a specialist teacher for 12–20 weeks. This expert support is vital but does not replace the need for regular practice with family members or others. But helping children who face significant challenges is different from supporting those who progress more easily. Practicers can unintentionally fall into unhelpful patterns, such as offering too much assistance, by providing word solutions too quickly or overestimating the child's reading ability. This tendency often stems from the practicer's anxiety and desire for the child to succeed. As a result, practicing reading may become tense and frustrating, shifting focus from learning to performance. The child may begin managing the adult, trying to meet their expectations rather than focusing on learning, leading to frustration and avoidance for both. Teachers can help address these pitfalls by guiding practicers on how best to support the child without falling into these patterns. This differs from practicers working with children who learn to read with ease, as they typically need little direction. For children facing greater challenges, more collaboration between professionals and practicers is essential, and practicers do best if they can set aside their own beliefs about how to help the child. For reading, this is hard but for mental health problems this can be very difficult. It requires significant trust in the professional, a trust that may take time to develop. Learning to read highlights that childhood is a period where learning about the world is a central part of daily life, facilitated by various adults who provide different types of help. We will now apply these key principles to common mental health needs, illustrating how professionals and parents, and children can collaborate to help children manage and overcome their mental health challenges—just as additional support helps children who struggle with reading.

Key Processes of Professional Help

Professionals, Practicers and Cheerleaders

Learning to read demonstrates that effective help involves a blend of professional expertise and supported practice. Those facilitating practice do not need to possess the professional's level of expertise. In reading, teachers provide the expertise, whereas in mental health, psychologists, therapists, social workers and doctors fulfil this role. Applying this to mental health, consider a child's growing ability to regulate their emotions—a progression from the intense emotional outbursts of feeling (both excitements and more negative feelings) when they were infants to managing strong feelings in a more contained and controlled way. This is a journey that all children make and for some children the route to self-control is much more difficult than for others.[5] Developing some understanding of what has led to these difficulties can be helpful, but, as with those who struggle with reading, a significant part of the help that the child needs may be about supporting the child to practise self-control in daily life.

For many children, the core ‘practice’ involves learning to calm down and the ways to support this may be like those used with any child, although children with greater difficulties will need much more of it. Helping a child calm down requires the adult to remain calm themselves. When these situations occur frequently, this is tough work, and it is difficult for carers to maintain consistency. Children struggling with managing their feelings may have outbursts in various settings—at home, school, when they are staying with friends or when they are being cared for by their grandma. What can be most helpful is for all adults in the child's life to adopt a consistent approach to helping them calm down. The most effective help for the child is likely a combination of family and professional help and that family help is harnessed as fully as possible. Again, as with reading difficulties, relying solely on professional support, such as weekly sessions with a mental health specialist, is unlikely to be sufficient. The challenge lies in integrating family and professional efforts to address the child's needs, with a significant emphasis on family support. The challenges for practicers in helping a child manage his feelings are similar to those in supporting reading development. These include focusing on success rather than failure, the need to go at the right pace, recognising the frustration that can come with the role and fostering trust and collaboration between the professional expert and the practicer.

This collaborative approach between parents and professionals should not be limited to behaviour alone. Parents can provide encouragement, understanding and support across a wide range of mental health challenges. For instance, encouraging a child with depression to maintain friendships, supporting a child with anxiety to face their fears or helping a child navigate family meals despite overwhelming emotions are all vital roles parents often take on. For many, this is simply parental love in action. Yet, reassurance that their efforts align with professional guidance is crucial for families to sustain their support, especially when challenges become severe. When a child refuses to eat or turns to self-harm for relief, the helping system can easily lose confidence, overwhelmed by the anxiety these situations provoke. Some parents may feel this level of responsibility exceeds what they signed up for as parents, leading to feelings of resentment if they perceive the burden of care being shifted back onto them. Professionals must acknowledge and validate these feelings of frustration and exhaustion when fostering a collaborative family-professional support system. Parents might believe that more comprehensive and effective professional services should be available for common mental health issues and that professionals should carry more responsibility. While more resources are indeed necessary to meet the mental health needs of children and young people, relying solely on professional support can be less effective. Leveraging existing family relationships as part of the child's support network is often more impactful than positioning help solely within professional services.

To conclude this section, let's revisit the real-life example of Sam and her daughter Margot, who was experiencing suicidal thoughts. Sam sought professional help for Margot, hoping a professional could provide the support her daughter needed. However, as discussed earlier, it is easy for a young person to be brought to an appointment without much consideration as to what sort of help the young person may feel they would like. The young person may be placed in a position of passive compliance rather than active help-seeking. Margot regretted confiding in her mother because it led to an unwanted appointment. During a conversation with Sam, the mental health practitioner suggested asking Margot who she might feel comfortable talking to and exploring her concerns about seeing a professional. The goal was to support Margot's sense of agency—one of the core principles discussed in Chapter 8—regarding the help she wanted to receive. They also discussed whether talking about suicidal thoughts increases the risk of acting on them (it does not) and outlined what steps to take if Sam believed Margot was in immediate danger (developing a safety plan). Sam agreed to talk with Margot. After several conversations and follow-up calls, Sam and Margot attended an appointment together. Despite the high anxiety surrounding the situation, the intention of this initial process was to convey that effective help was likely to involve a combination of family and professional help, and professional help did not replace family help but came alongside to support it. There was recognition that there was already a helping system in place that needed strengthening through professional input. However, how this collaboration unfolds will differ for each young person, and there are cases where family involvement may be entirely rejected by the young person at that time.

Let us now apply these ideas to Jacqui, Martin, Abdul, Simone, Daniel and Teresa. For Simone, her parents were central to the entire approach, which involved gradually increasing her separation from them at the start of the school day. This began with one parent staying with Simone for a period of time in school and gradually withdrawing support. Professional input helped the school and parents collaborate on a clear plan and manage the parents' anxiety when Simone showed distress. Similarly, Martin's foster carer, Sandra, played a key role in managing his aggressive outbursts. Close collaboration between Sandra and his class teacher, Fatima, proved helpful. Together, they developed consistent, calm responses to Martin's behaviour, avoiding unpredictable consequences and explicitly recognising instances when Martin demonstrated self-control and restraint. Their approach also considered Sandra's beliefs about boundaries and the importance of setting limits at home. The warmth of the relationship between Sandra and Fatima was crucial to the success of this strategy. For Abdul, his mother Aisha supported him by reinforcing the stress-reduction techniques he had practised with his therapist. Her role was to highlight situations where these skills helped him. Essentially the approach was to allow Abdul a degree of withdrawal from stressful situations, followed by a return, aiming to prevent this strategy from becoming avoidance rather than a tool for self-regulation. Chisomo, Jacqui's mother, was instrumental in supporting Jacqui's help-seeking behaviour, becoming more involved towards the end of therapy. Her role was to continue supporting Jacqui after treatment, learning ways to provide effective support without being intrusive or causing shame. This involved practising with Monica, Jacqui's therapist, on how to discuss feelings of low mood in a supportive and non-threatening manner. Daniel's situation was different. He preferred to manage his challenges independently. However, significant progress occurred when he discovered that his emotional state improved through participation in an exercise group. He particularly enjoyed intense physical exertion, which helped shift his focus away from his preoccupation with his physical appearance.

Finally, there is one other key aspect of effective helping systems within the collaboration between professionals and parents: the role of cheerleading.[6] This involves explicitly recognising the efforts made by the child or family to create positive change. Some mental health approaches emphasise building a supportive 'backup team'[7] around the young person —a concept similar to the helping system—which may include professionals, family members, community members, friends and peers. The backup team's role is to ensure that the child's efforts and small positive changes are noticed and celebrated. This is crucial because progress in addressing mental health needs is often gradual, particularly in the early stages. Without recognition, children and young people may become discouraged if early achievements go unnoticed. Cheerleading is a skill in itself. General, non-specific praise such as a casual "well done" that lacks connection to the child's real-life experiences is far less effective. The backup team must recognise and celebrate specific actions, such as when a child confronts their fear of attending PE on Wednesday afternoons with a stand-in teacher who makes them anxious. Recognising such efforts shows genuine understanding of the child's daily challenges. For example, Jacqui always felt that her head of year was unsupportive. She was surprised when, after her first week back at school, he told her he was pleased she had returned. What stood out to Jacqui was that he mentioned a teacher had praised how she honestly answered classmates' questions about her absence and her grandmother—something she had practised with her therapist, Monica. This was meaningful cheerleading because it demonstrated that her effort was genuinely noticed. Similarly, Sandra and Polly developed a routine with Martin after he came home from the farm. Instead of offering vague praise about his good behaviour, Polly highlighted specific moments when Martin showed kindness to animals, such as caring for a donkey or a sheep. Cheerleading is not about excessive, empty praise but about reflecting back to the child meaningful, positive behaviours they may not recognise in themselves.

Conclusions

Mental health problems in young people often place significant strain on the family and community helping systems. We propose that these needs are best supported by creating a collaboration between family and professional support, recognising and building upon the existing helping systems around the child. This approach suggests that standard interventions or evidence-based practices should be adapted to complement the family's natural helping styles and systems. Uniform methods are unlikely to be effective for every child and family.

In cases of abuse, neglect or harm, professional intervention must take a more central role. However, in most situations, professional help should not replace family help but work alongside it, strengthening both family and community networks to better support the child or young person. By framing child mental health problems within the context of these universal helping processes, we aim to encourage the integration of preventative initiatives with effective professional interventions—viewing them as interconnected rather than separate approaches.

Implications for Good Practice

1 Effective help is likely to be a combination of family, community and professional help that is organised around the views and wishes of the child or young person.
2 Professional help for mental health needs should complement and not replace family help.
3 Combining professional and family help is a complex process that must balance evidence-based approaches with family and community beliefs about what help is likely to be effective. Integrating these two sources of knowledge is often the greatest challenge in providing effective help for children.
4 Parents and family members play a vital role in helping children overcome mental health challenges by creating environments where they can practise key changes in how they relate to others and behave in the world.
5 Working alongside and strengthening family support must be adapted if there is a risk of harm in doing so.

A Young Person's Life: Monica

Monica was 13 years old when she came home from school to find her father hanging in the hallway. She was the first to discover him. Monica was referred to the local mental health team and attended with her social worker. She presented as cheerful, mischievous and dismissive of adult concerns. She openly said she disliked her father, who had been violent when he drank, and insisted she didn't need help. I agreed with her but invited her to come back to see me with her ten-year-old sister. Monica's mother refused any contact with our service. With the support of her social worker, we established a pattern. Monica came at lunchtime with her sister and a classroom assistant. We had picnic lunches on the floor of my office and created a large picture book of things she and her sister enjoyed. This went on for several months without any involvement with her mother. Monica was wonderfully caring towards her sister, but neither wanted to speak much about what had happened. They drew pictures of positive things that they remembered about their father, and they talked about feeling safe with their maternal grandfather. The goal was to support positive narratives about themselves and their future and affirm that they were not responsible for their father's actions. Monica expressed that she liked coming. Although her mother was invited, she never joined the picnics. Sadly, years later, I learned that Monica had run away from home and was reportedly homeless in London. Her behaviour made sense to me, but I was saddened that the helping system had not been able to support her more effectively.

Notes

1 **The involvement of parents in children's treatment of their mental health needs.** There is a high degree of professional consensus from professionals, from government policy and national that parental involvement in providing help for children with mental health needs is important and beneficial agencies (Advice for parents—NHS; Royal College of Psychiatry—Worries and anxieties information for parents; NSPCC—Positive parenting | NSPCC Learning). Several reviews have highlighted that parental involvement in their child's treatment is likely to improve effectiveness. For example, Haine-Schlagel and Walsh showed that parent involvement enhanced attendance for treatment (Haine-Schlagel, R., & Walsh, N. E. (2015). A review of parent participation engagement in child and family mental health treatment. *Clinical Child and Family Psychology Review*, *18*(2), 133–150). Some studies show little difference in outcomes depending on parent involvement. For example, parent involvement and child-only treatments for childhood anxiety indicated that there was not a substantial difference in these two approaches and that child-only interventions did slightly better (Thulin, U., Svirsky, L., Serlachius, E., Andersson, G., & Öst, L. G. (2014). The effect of parent involvement in the treatment of anxiety disorders in children: A meta-analysis. *Cognitive Behaviour Therapy*, *43*(3), 185–200). Lawrence and colleagues highlighted the multiple ways that parents provide support for their children and that these different ways of offering support may explain why studies do not demonstrate improved effectiveness as they may not be measuring key aspects of support (Lawrence, P. J., Parkinson, M., Jasper, B., Creswell, C., & Halligan, S. L. (2021). Supporting the parents of children and young people with anxiety and depressive disorders is an opportunity not to be missed: A scoping review. *The Lancet Psychiatry*, *8*(10), 909–918).

2 **Trust between mental health professionals and parents.** There is a strong professional consensus that trust between parents and professionals is a key aspect of providing effective help to children and young people with mental health needs (Department of Education—Help for early years providers: Working in partnership with parents and carers; Parents as partners—Birth To 5 Matters). In addition, this has been shown in several specific studies. (Boelsma, F., Bektas, G., Wesdorp, C. L.,

Seidell, J. C., & Dijkstra, S. C. (2021). The perspectives of parents and healthcare professionals towards parental needs and support from healthcare professionals during the first two years of children's lives. *International Journal of Qualitative studies on Health and Well-being, 16*(1), 1966874; Gómez-Zúñiga, B., Pulido Moyano, R., Pousada Fernández, M., García Oliva, A., & Armayones Ruiz, M. (2019). The experience of parents of children with rare diseases when communicating with healthcare professionals: Towards an integrative theory of trust. *Orphanet Journal of Rare Diseases, 14*(1), 159); Dewan, T., Whiteley, A., MacKay, L. J., Martens, R., Noel, M., Barnard, C.,… & Thorne, S. (2024). Trust of inpatient physicians among parents of children with medical complexity: a qualitative study. *Frontiers in Pediatrics, 12*, 1443869).

3 **How children learn to read.** There has been significant progress in recent years to develop a consensus about how children learn to read which includes the key role of instruction of phonics as a key part of the process. (Castles, A., Rastle, K., & Nation, K. (2018). Ending the reading wars: Reading acquisition from novice to expert. *Psychological Science in the Public Interest, 19*(1), 5–51.). This review also emphasised the role of practice in how children move from novice readers to fluent consumers of complex text and that families have a key role in supporting such practice.

4 **Supporting children who find reading hard.** Apart from universal teaching of reading, there are programmes which offer additional specialist help for children who find the acquisition of reading skills much more challenging. We have drawn from the approach called Reading Recovery, a programme that has been well described and evaluated. https://www.ucl.ac.uk/reading-recovery-europe/about-reading-recovery. The approach has been evaluated as showing long-term effectiveness (Hurry, J., Fridkin, L., & Holliman, A. J. (2022). Reading intervention at age 6: Long-term effects of Reading Recovery in the UK on qualifications and support at age 16. *British Educational Research Journal, 48*(1), 5–21).

5 **Emotional self-regulation.** This is a process in which children develop their ability to regulate their emotions which arise in relationships with others. It is often described as a process of co-regulation in which both child and adult together find ways to manage the present feelings. Advice on self-regulation can be found on many sites e.g. Self-regulation—Birth to 5 Matters; NL-Emotion-regulation-e-leaflet-02.21.pdf). Research on emotional regulation has been reviewed (Alarcón-Espinoza, M., Sanduvete-Chaves, S., Anguera, M. T., Samper Garcia, P., & Chacón-Moscoso, S. (2022). Emotional self-regulation in everyday life: A systematic review. *Frontiers in Psychology, 13*, 884756) which acknowledges the relational aspects of how self-regulation develops in children. Some research has suggested that self-regulation in childhood can predict achievement, interpersonal behaviors, mental health and healthy living in later life (Robson, D. A., Allen, M. S., & Howard, S. J. (2020). Self-regulation in childhood as a predictor of future outcomes: A meta-analytic review. *Psychological Bulletin, 146*(4), 324).

6 **Cheerleading.** Cheerleading is simply a process of recognising the efforts made by children and young people to make positive changes to their lives whether this be trying to create friendships, or to reduce cannabis use or to not argue with their parents at bedtime. This overlaps with the concept of 'praise' although the assumptions about the value of praise have been questioned (Robins, G. (2012). *Praise, motivation and the child.* Routledge) as some praise by adults may not be much believed by children. A more mentalizing approach to positive feedback is suggested which aims to include an understanding of the state of mind of the child and not just their behaviour (Chelouche-Dwek, G., & Fonagy, P. (2024). Mentalization-based interventions in schools for enhancing socio-emotional competencies and positive behaviour: A systematic review. *European Child & Adolescent Psychiatry, 34*(4),

1295–1315, doi:10.1007/s00787-024-02578-5). We have used the term 'cheerleading' as it is more playful and because it places the positive emotion in the adult or parent who is experiencing the efforts of the child or young person.

7 **Interpersonal Psychotherapy (IPT) and the backup team.** We are grateful to Roslyn Law, our colleague at Anna Freud who has generously shared so many of her insights in using IPT to support children and young people (Law, R. (2016). *Defeating teenage depression: Getting there together*. Hachette UK; Law, R., Ravitz, P., Pain, C., & Fonagy, P. (2022). Interpersonal psychotherapy and mentalizing—synergies in clinical practice. *American Journal of Psychotherapy*, *75*(1), 44–50). The explicit idea of a backup team was taken directly from this approach.

Chapter 7

Supporting Safety

Families and professionals' support for children's safety is a key part of helping them with their mental health needs.

Introduction

In the previous two chapters, we described key aspects of how families and professionals help children and young people with their mental health needs. This approach assumed that the child's family relationships and social environments were safe and non-harmful. Sadly, this is not the reality for all children. Indeed, the assumption that children are not vulnerable to abuse by adults around them contradicts both historical and current understandings of childhood. Inadequate, hostile and abusive relationships and environments remain part of what an important minority of children endure. In England, in 2024, 49,900 children were protected through child protection plans coordinated by social care—a rate of approximately 40 children in every 10,000.[1] But if we broaden our perspective on what makes children feel unsafe, estimates suggest that 95% of young black children have experienced racist abuse at school or college.[2] Similarly, 40% of pupils report being bullied within the past year, with 6% experiencing bullying daily.[3] These experiences profoundly affect how children perceive the world, their sense of safety and their ability to trust others.

A comprehensive approach to mental health provision for children and young people must prioritise supporting safety and reducing the impact of continuous threats. This is a crucial aspect of mental health care as the absence of safety and exposure to abuse are inherently harmful. Additionally, chronic threats can erode trust in the world and weaken a child's capacity to seek help from others. A sense of safety is essential for children to engage openly about their needs. However, this does not imply that children should be shielded from the negative aspects of human relationships, such as aggression, anger and conflict, which are a familiar part of relationships both between children and adults and among peers. Children need to find their way through the complexities of negative feelings both in themselves and others. This is a normal

DOI: 10.4324/9781003145523-7

part of childhood. Nevertheless, professional services have a duty to protect children from relationships characterised by systematic threat, cruelty or a lack of love and respect for them.

When children and young people are asked about the stresses of their life bullying is often the most frequently cited problem that they face. Peer bullying is a significant adversity that undermines their sense of safety. It can dominate their experience, and even in warm, supportive parent-child relationships, children may not tell their parents about the bullying that they experience. It is not uncommon—and this includes the authors of this book—for parents to only learn of their children's bullying experiences when they are adults. Like racism, bullying can be minimised or dismissed as being just part of growing up, but this is not so. Bullying involves ongoing, systematic intimidation of a child by a more dominant group, leading to feelings of hopelessness and diminished self-worth. It increases vulnerability to anxiety, low mood and self-harm.[4] This is what children and young people report, and any comprehensive mental health strategy must acknowledge the seriousness of this harmful environment many young people endure.

Jacqui had to change secondary school in Year 8. Following this move, she had found it hard to establish a new set of friends. As a black young person in a predominantly white peer group, she became increasingly aware of racial differences in her peer allegiances. The racism she encountered was often subtle and ambiguous but sometimes overt. She experienced peer rejection, which she believed was racially motivated, and faced explicit hostility from older pupils during her journeys to and from school, where she endured racist comments and abuse. Without an established friendship group for support, Jacqui felt isolated and unsure how to approach teachers about her experiences. Despite the school's stated zero-tolerance policy on racism, she did not feel safe confiding in staff. Attempts to discuss this with her parents were met with sympathy but they downplayed her distress by comparing it to their own experiences which they felt were worse. Racism, like other forms of abuse, is often minimised and tolerated when it should not be. For Jacqui, these experiences exacerbated her vulnerability to social withdrawal and feelings of personal rejection. Over time, however, developing peer friendships helped mitigate the impact of the racism she faced.

Abdul's school experience was generally positive, except during breaks and lunchtimes. During these periods, he was subjected to ongoing teasing and verbal hostility from a small group of classmates. Abdul disliked this and eventually shared his experiences during sessions with Rachel, who supported him in communicating what was happening at school. Rachel relayed this information to his teacher, Fenulla, who addressed the issue by speaking directly to the pupils involved and encouraging Abdul to engage in preferred solitary play activities during the lunch breaks. This approach was partly effective, but it also reinforced Abdul's pattern of withdrawing in response to hostility by others. The school, his family and the mental health team worked together to support Abdul's safety and well-being.

Most abusive, hostile and intimidating environments are partially hidden. While the severe impact of abuse on children must be recognised, the disguises and uncertainties surrounding specific situations often make the recognition of such abuse far from easy. Martin's situation illustrates this. For the first three years of his life, he lived with his mother, Maisie. Her substance misuse made her care unpredictable—sometimes responsive and playful, but at other times neglectful, leaving Martin hungry and ignored. He would experience uncontained fear and rage which would be either dismissed or mirrored with anger and intimidation. He became increasingly prone to uncontrollable tantrums, abated only by exhaustion. He learned to use emotion as a weapon, finding satisfaction in hurting others. Martin experienced emotional, verbal and physical abuse and neglect in the context of relational trauma. His safety was only achievable through alternative care. However, when placed with foster carers, he brought what he had learnt from his early years into his new relationships. He was described as being emotionally dysregulated, distant and distrustful traits that were adaptive for survival in his birth family. Identifying Martin's behavioural and emotional challenges was straightforward but addressing them was more difficult due to his negative and frightening early experiences of care.

Key Aspects of Supporting Safety

Abuse Increases a General Vulnerability to Developing Mental Health Needs

Abusive family care (parental abuse), hostile environments (racism), intimidation and fear (bullying) and early trauma (witnessing violence, intimidation and terror) have a profound negative impact on children and young people.[5] These factors heighten the risk of mental health difficulties, though their effects are not uniform. Abuse and adverse environments do not result in specific mental health problems but increase vulnerability to various difficulties, such as anxiety, low mood, self-harm, behaviour problems, substance misuse and relationship problems. It is as if such experiences create a general susceptibility rather than directly causing particular disorders. For those offering support, it is crucial to avoid assumptions about how abuse may affect each child or young person.

Abuse Negatively Impacts on the Capacity to Seek Help

Children and young people who experience the world—especially caregiving adults—as unkind, abusive or cruel naturally distrust those offering help.[6] This distrust is not a disorder to be treated but a survival strategy born from living in unpredictable, harmful environments. Seeking and receiving help involves vulnerability, exposing children to feelings of shame, humiliation and helplessness. These feelings are common even in safe environments as children are vulnerable by their own dependency and absence of power. These feelings are intensified when children have been repeatedly told they are stupid, unkind, disobedient and bad. So inviting a child into a helping relationship with a practitioner who they do not know in order to speak about themselves is unlikely to be easy to navigate. Many children feel that they are not being referred for help with a problem, they feel that **they are the problem** because that is a narrative that they have heard repeatedly. Help must be approached differently for these children.

Rather than assuming they are open to trying to make their life better, we need to assume that they are wiser than that and that they know that the promises that adults make cannot be trusted. It is essential to recognise their distrust of adult promises. Practitioners should focus on exploring ways of discovering what they imagine might be helpful to them. Rather than start with the problem, we need to start with curiosity about when or who or what they have experienced as helpful to them in the past, to learn about their experience of kindness and support. It is clearly an oversimplification to categorise children as either help-seeking or help-avoiding. Most children navigate a continuum of trust and mistrust, and what is important is to include curiosity about the process of help itself as a legitimate aspect of how to provide effective help. If we simply focus on the nature of their problems, there is a risk that we inadvertently position children as being the problem which repeats their experience of abuse and harm.

Negative environments have a 'double whammy' effect—first causing harm and then impairing the ability to seek help. It is like being cast adrift at sea in a small boat, only to find the boat lacks both a sail and rudder to find one's way back to land. Jacqui experienced racism but she was left without guidance to navigate these experiences. Abdul faced bullying but struggled to recognise and articulate it, complicating his ability to seek help. Martin's early trauma made him reluctant to reconnect, finding more comfort in isolation and the company of animals than in human relationships. Supporting safety for children like Jacqui, Abdul and Martin requires acknowledging both the primary harm and the secondary barriers to seeking help.[7]

Poverty

Poverty is not an adverse environment in the same way as direct abuse or intimidation, but it imposes significant constraints.[8] Most families experiencing poverty are deeply committed to providing supportive and nurturing environments for their children. However, financial hardship creates barriers. For example, a parent working multiple low-paying jobs may be unable to support their child with school routines or listen to their worries due to simply being unable to be present at home. This lack of availability is not a relationship issue but a consequence of financial pressures. If childhood is like a game of snakes and ladders—with opportunities for advancement and setbacks to be overcome, then poverty reduces the number of ladders on the board. An absence of ladder might be a parent unable to take time off from work by their employer in order to attend a mental health appointment with their child due to inflexible work conditions. Such a parent is not unmotivated but fearful of job loss.

Poverty often receives limited attention in strategic planning for children's mental health needs. It should play a more prominent role. While addressing poverty is beyond the direct scope of mental health programmes, there are lessons to learn from other countries. Some nations protect employees' rights to leave work in time to collect their children from school, aligning work and school routines. Implementing such policies could support working parents, especially those unable to afford alternative childcare, enabling stronger relationships to develop between parents and their children.

Key Processes of Supporting Safety

Taking Action

The first task in supporting safety is ensuring that concerns about a child or young person's safety are shared and acted upon. Unlike other aspects of child mental health practice, addressing safety concerns is governed by joint agency protocols and a professional duty of care to protect children at risk of harm or neglect.[9] This often involves sharing information with social care. While families may sometimes agree to this, it is not unusual that professional relationships with families may be severely and negatively affected by this process of information sharing. Parents and families may feel misunderstood, betrayed, heavily criticised or threatened by information being passed to social care. There is a common fear among families that social care aims to remove children from their homes.

For children facing bullying or racism, the initial step may involve working with them to share their experiences with parents, family and school. Children may be very wary about this fearing that adults may do things to make things worse with their peer group. A common anxiety is that the bullying would get worse if those involved in the bullying learn that their behaviour has been 'reported' to others. Although these are sometimes valid, involving key adults usually leads to reduced bullying and increased safety. Prioritising a child's safety may not always align with their immediate wishes, but fostering communication between children and parents is often crucial.

In Abdul's case, collaboration between Rachel, Aisha and Fenulla significantly reduced bullying at school. For Jacqui, involving Chisomo in therapy sessions enabled discussions about her experiences of racism and the support she needed. With Jacqui's consent, Chisomo spoke to her head of year, creating a supportive network between Jacqui's family, school and therapist to enhance her sense of safety.

Working with Distrust

Recognising distrust: the narratives of our six children. Consider the experiences of the six children and young people introduced earlier in this book. Jacqui did not want to attend a mental health service and went because her mother asked and persuaded her to do so. Chisomo had a degree of trust in her GP and accepted his advice about Jacqui attending a mental health service, and Jacqui had sufficient trust in her Mum to be willing to try something that she didn't know about. There was a thread of trust, not strong but sufficient. Her relationship with her mother was not especially close, but it was strong enough to encourage her to explore unfamiliar support. Once Jacqui began sessions at the clinic, she formed her own opinion about the help offered. She liked Monica, her therapist, and engaged with her suggestions, which led to her feeling better.

Martin, however, disliked the support he received at both school and the mental health team. Despite reassurances, he felt that he was being told off but in a kind way. He didn't like any talk about himself. He didn't want to talk about Maisie (his mother) and was always worried that he would be asked questions about her. He felt trapped, and his main motivation was to escape as best he could. Because he was hard to help and was often silent or passive with his carers, in school and with his psychiatrist, Martin was at risk of being referred to more specialist teams. While greater expertise can be beneficial, an alternative approach might involve focusing less on Martin's problems and more on fostering trust. Exploring what strengthens his relationship with his foster carer and his enjoyment of the urban farm could prove more effective than specialist intervention.

Abdul depended heavily on his mother, despite frequent arguments. She encouraged him to explore more than he was comfortable with. Abdul equated trust with feeling safe, a feeling he had with his mother, who understood how to help him learn. He was happy to attend sessions with Rachel, his psychologist, as he liked learning new things which he practised with Aisha and he enjoyed it when he did it with her. So, the help he received at the mental health service was closely aligned with his home experiences. While the process may not have been driven by trust, it was familiar and effective for him.

Simone's journey towards independence was facilitated through her parents. Their ability to trust the advice of the early help team, supported by the psychologist, was crucial. Both parents were highly anxious, fearing they were harming Simone when she became distressed during separations. Her father feared Simone would hate him forever, though he rationally knew this wasn't true. However, in moments of Simone's distress, rational thinking was difficult. Trust in the early help team developed because the parents felt their fears and experiences were acknowledged and respected. Feeling understood allowed them to trust in the helping process that was established.

Daniel deeply hated himself and his appearance, believing his unattractiveness was a fact, not perception. When he hinted at these feelings, reassurances from his mother and others left him feeling profoundly misunderstood. His severe distress led to self-harming, which briefly alleviated his pain and validated his suffering. Responses from others often minimised his struggles, leaving him feeling humiliated. Daniel longed for surgery to change his face but knew he'd have to wait until adulthood. His suffering was private, inward and consuming. Yet, he shared a warm, affectionate relationship with his mother, Judith, discussing many topics except his appearance. He had a couple of close friends at school but felt socially anxious in larger groups. He was unsettled when a girl in his class showed interest in him, unable to comprehend why. Daniel ruminated over his looks and sought help through information online rather than through those he knew.

Teresa frequently changed her mind about others, viewing adults and peers as either marvellous (e.g. nobody understands me like you do) or hopeless (e.g. you haven't a clue about young people). Her work with Molly, her outreach nurse, Molly aimed to avoid triggering Teresa's volatile attachment patterns. Molly remained reliable, factual and interested, guiding Teresa to recognise the fluctuations in her feelings towards others. When Teresa began idealising Molly, she gently reminded Teresa of previous negative feelings to help her understand her shifting mindset. This approach gradually reduced ruptures in their relationship.

Jacqui, Abdul, Martin, Simone, Daniel and Teresa each had distinct relationships with help and varying experiences of trust and distrust. Young people often hesitate to seek help from strangers about personal feelings or life circumstances. However, each child faced additional vulnerabilities that intensified these challenges. This process is typically mediated by parents or carers. In these six examples, parents and carers played crucial roles in fostering trust—either by providing direct support, as with Simone, or by facilitating engagement with professionals, as with Jacqui and Abdul. For Martin, building a supportive process remained difficult, while Daniel sought help through information rather than relationships.

Summary and Conclusions

Many children suffer abuse or endure adverse social environments where they do not feel safe or able to be themselves. Attitudinal and behavioural change around racism, bullying and gender and sexual identity is essential to improving safety for children and young people.

Supporting safety involves expanding access to a wider system of help—not just professional support but fostering trust in others within a child's world. This chapter highlighted how distrust increases the risk of harm and exposure to negative experiences, such as bullying, racism and discrimination. While entirely eliminating negative environments is unlikely in the near future, recognising that distrust in well-intentioned helpers can hinder safety is key. For children experiencing abuse, distrust may be what has enabled them to survive, to get them through.

We cannot assume children will trust those offering help or that helpers always know the best approach. Building trust is crucial and is more likely when parents and children feel understood—not only in their problems of living but also in their concerns about the help being offered. For some children, help is the last thing they want, and they spend their energy managing adults who try to assist them. In these cases, attention to the helping process is as important as addressing the problem itself. This curiosity can lead to more diverse and effective ways of providing support—a theme explored further in later chapters in this book.

Implications for Good Practice

1 Supporting safety must be integral to comprehensive approaches in children's mental health. Reducing racism, bullying, homophobia and discrimination should be prioritised in mental health work.
2 Unsafe relationships and environments hinder the helping process. Children with such experiences may distrust adult or professional help.
3 Young people who have experienced abuse or harm are more vulnerable to a wide range of mental health needs.
4 A broader range of support strategies is necessary for children who distrust help compared to those more inclined to trust helpful adults.

A Parent Life: Rosanne

Rosanne was 45 years old and came to see me with Paul who was 12 years of age. She was quietly spoken, thoughtful, respectful but deeply anxious about her son who she thought was being bullied at school. She thought that he was only safe when he was with her at home. Paul was shy and deferred to Rosanne before saying anything. Rosanne came to see me for about four years. Over that time, she gradually shared the key aspects of her life, much of which she had never spoken about before. As a child, Rosanne had been brought up on a farm in a remote country area. Her family was very poor and, as a young teenager, she had been traded for sex with the neighbouring farmer in return for food for the family. At about 18 years, she told someone outside her family what had happened to her, and she was disowned by her family and ejected from the family home. She came to London and never returned to her family even for her parents' funerals as the family would not allow her to come. Paul attended psychotherapy with a colleague and attended school some of the time, but his attendance was always intermittent. He changed schools three times in this period. Efforts to encourage her to seek therapeutic help for herself were unsuccessful. After about three years, she decided she wanted to die, contacting me to tell me and to thank me for the support I had given her. Then she hung up. I was in the middle of a senior leadership meeting. I asked one of my colleagues to help me and we found her in the park with a large bottle of whisky and a half-empty bottle of tablets. An ambulance took her to hospital and she recovered. She continued to refuse treatment for herself but had intermittent support from myself and from the family social worker. The social worker did a great job in encouraging Paul to sign up for a course in college which he attended quite regularly. Over time, she gradually told the story of her life dominated by a profound sense of shame about herself that silenced and paralysed her. Despite what happened to her, she always wanted to go back to her home and sometimes she would talk about making plans for a visit with Paul. As far as we know she never did and perhaps that would have been the outcome that she would have wanted most of all.

Notes

1 **Child protection plans**. Social care provides support to families through child protection plans (CPP). The number of children on CPPs was reported by the Department of Education in the UK. (Government Report on Child in Need. (October 31, 2024). *Department of education. Children in need, reporting year 2024 – Explore education statistics – GOV UK*).

2 **The impact of racism on children**. Many reports have highlighted the high prevalence of experienced racism for young people in the UK. A report by the NSPCC (NSPCC. (2021). *Not making the grade*. NSPCC) includes a summary of the experiences of racism in the UK for children and young people. Similarly, a report by the YMCA (YMCA. (2020). *Young and Black: the young black experience of institutional racism in the UK*. YMCA) reported that 95% of young black people hear racist language or witness racism at school. A research roundup by the UK Trauma Council highlighted the relationship between racism and increased vulnerability to mental health needs (UK Trauma Council. (2022). *Racism, mental health and trauma*. UK Trauma Council).

3 **Bullying in the UK**. The Mental health survey of children and young people in 2023 reported that children aged 11–16 years with a probable mental disorder were five times more likely than those unlikely to have a mental disorder to have been bullied in person (36.9% compared with 7.6%) (Newlove-Delgado, T., Marcheselli, F., Williams, T., Mandalia, D., Dennes, M., McManus, S., Savic, M., Treloar, W., Croft, K., & Ford, T. (2023). *Mental health of children and young people in England, 2023*. NHS England, Leeds). A summary of these reports about bullying can be found at the website of the Anti-Bullying Alliance (National Children's Bureau (2024). *Bullying, school experiences and wellbeing: a picture of pupil experience in England*). This report highlighted that 40% of young people experienced bullying in the last 12 months and 6% faced bullying daily. A review by Richard Armitage provided a global perspective on the serious impact of bullying on children's mental health (Armitage, R. (2021). Bullying in children: impact on child health. *BMJ Paediatrics Open*, *5*(1), e000939).

4 **The long-term effects of bullying.** The effects of bullying are not short-term and have been shown to have substantial long-term effects on children and young people (Wolke, D., & Lereya, S. T. (2015). Long-term effects of bullying. *Archives of Disease in Childhood*, *100*(9), 879–885).

5 **Abuse increases general vulnerability to mental health needs.** The negative impact of child maltreatment and abuse on increasing mental health needs is very widely recognised (Lippard, E. T., & Nemeroff, C. B. (2023). The devastating clinical consequences of child abuse and neglect: Increased disease vulnerability and poor treatment response in mood disorders. *American Journal of Psychiatry, 180*(8), 548–564). The degree of impact has been shown to be influenced by ways of coping and social support (Su, Y., Meng, X., Yang, G., & D'Arcy, C. (2022). The relationship between childhood maltreatment and mental health problems: coping strategies and social support act as mediators. *BMC Psychiatry, 22*(1), 359).

6 **Abuse negatively impacts on capacity to seek help.** Low levels of help-seeking are reported for children who have experienced abuse (Pereira, A., Peterman, A., Neijhoft, A. N., Buluma, R., Daban, R. A., Islam, A.,... & Palermo, T. (2020). Disclosure, reporting and help seeking among child survivors of violence: A cross-country analysis. *BMC Public Health, 20*(1), 1051). The reluctance to seek help has been powerfully demonstrated in the results of the Independent Inquiry into Child Sexual Abuse (The Report of the Independent Inquiry into Child Sexual Abuse IICSA: Report of the Independent Inquiry into Child Sexual Abuse (2022). The scale of sexual abuse is indicated from the report of the Office for National Statistics (March 2020) which estimated that 3.1 million adults in England and Wales had experienced sexual abuse before the age of 16.

7 **Barriers to help-seeking.** Many factors which affect help-seeking in young people have been reported such as the role of stigma, poor mental health recognition and a preference for self-reliance (Gulliver, A., Griffiths, K. M., & Christensen, H. (2010). Perceived barriers and facilitators to mental health help-seeking in young people: A systematic review. *BMC Psychiatry, 10*(1), 113). Some studies have shown that distrust reduces help-seeking in young people (Corry, D. A. S., & Leavey, G. (2017). Adolescent trust and primary care: Help-seeking for emotional and psychological difficulties. *Journal of Adolescence, 54*, 1–8).

8 **Poverty and increased vulnerability to mental health needs.** The mental health survey of children and young people in 2023 reported that 15.3% of children with a probable mental disorder lived in a household that could not afford to buy food or had to use a food bank, compared with 3.5% of those unlikely to have a mental disorder. It also reported that young people aged 17–24 years with a probable mental disorder were about four times as likely to report falling behind with bills, rent or mortgage (20.6%) than those unlikely to have a mental disorder (5.4%) (Newlove-Delgado, T., Marcheselli, F., Williams, T., Mandalia, D., Dennes, M., McManus, S., Savic, M., Treloar, W., Croft, K., & Ford, T. (2023). *Mental health of children and young people in England, 2023*. NHS England, Leeds). Other studies have shown that poverty increases risks of mental health problems (Knifton, L., & Inglis, G. (2020). Poverty and mental health: Policy, practice and research implications. *BJPsych Bulletin, 44*(5), 193–196).

9 **Information sharing about child abuse concerns.** Professional codes of conduct for health care staff, social workers, police and teachers require professionals working with children to report concerns of abuse to social care. Failure to report child abuse may result in disciplinary action. It is not considered that a professional has discretion about whether to report information about a child but is required to do so. This is not the same as a legal requirement. A professional has not broken the law if they do not report. This is currently being considered as part of a response to the Independent Inquiry into child sexual abuse (2022) referred to previously.

Chapter 8

Taking an Active Part in Help

To create effective help for their mental health needs, children and young people need to take an active part in designing, understanding and participating in the help they need.

Introduction

Helping processes can easily become muddled regarding who is driving the process—the helper or the person being helped. The primary motivation for change or recovery may unintentionally shift to the helper rather than the individual whose life is affected. This is often unconscious for both parties and is particularly pronounced when working with children and young people due to their dependent position in society. Children are accustomed to having decisions made for them: parents often choose their school, determine where they live and teachers decide what they learn. Many children adapt well to adult decision-making, but in certain matters, it is preferable—or even essential—that they have more say. For mental health support to be effective, children and young people must have a meaningful say in the type of help they receive. This involvement is not just beneficial; it is crucial. We argue in this chapter that effective support requires children and young people to actively engage in designing, understanding and participating in the help that they need. Without this involvement, they may comply with interventions they neither believe in nor find helpful. Many children are very good at that.

Parents and carers may see this differently, often feeling that their children have quite sufficient say in things, and they are constantly struggling to accommodate to their child's wishes and preferences. For children, decision-making can seem inconsistent—sometimes they have a choice, sometimes they don't and the reasons are not always clear to them why. However, as children mature, they gradually develop greater capacity to decide for themselves about both minor and major issues. We refer to this growing ability to express and act on personal preferences as 'agency'.[1] Effective help should nurture this agency

DOI: 10.4324/9781003145523-8

in ways that align with a child's developmental stage and the cultural norms of the family. But this is often hard to do. This chapter will explore how to support children and young people's agency in mental health care.

No one perfectly balances when a child should decide for themselves versus when an adult should decide for them.[2] From the time that a toddler wants to choose which chair she sits at for a family meal to a 17-year-old wanting to borrow money to buy a car, there will be pushes and pulls between the two. Agency about things is rarely entirely fixed and to a child it may seem to depend on random things like a parent's mood or even the day of the week. There is also a gap between how we would like things to be and real-world practice. One author attended a full-day workshop on children's participation in treatment and strongly supported child choice. Yet, upon returning home, his 13-year-old son declared that he did not want to attend his dental appointment the next day. The author's immediate response—insisting his son would definitely attend—contradicted the very principles he had advocated earlier in the day!

At first, Jacqui did not want to visit the mental health clinic. Her parents felt that Jacqui's views were important, but she should not decide this on her own. They believed they had a responsibility to follow their GP's advice. However, it was a balance. Jacqui and Chisomo agreed that she should give it a try, with the understanding that if she disliked it, she could choose not to continue. This was like the way other things were decided in her family. Her parents did not discount what she said but expected her to consider their views too. Martin felt he had no choice about seeing his psychiatrist. It was simply something adults required children to do. His desire was to be left alone by such adults, although his relationship with Sandra, his current foster carer, was slowly becoming a space where he could express his preferences and disagreements. So, supporting agency in children is not a simple process and often requires compromises and imperfect solutions. It exists within broader societal and cultural contexts where expectations about a child's agency are shaped and developed. These cultural norms can be deeply ingrained and vary significantly, such as differing attitudes towards young people's dating preferences. This chapter will focus on three specific ways children's agency in mental health is currently being shaped: the development of children's legal rights, the involvement of young people in designing mental health services and the recognition that personal agency is fundamental to healthy functioning and well-being.

Key Aspects of Taking an Active Part

Children's Rights and the Role of Participation

Historically, children were the property of their parents who could decide what happened to them. Parent rights about their children were unchallenged. But in the twentieth century this has gradually changed through the development of children's rights, of which the United Nations Convention of the Rights of the Child (1989) with its 54 articles has been perhaps the most influential.[3] 196 countries (including the UK) have signed up to support the rights articulated in this convention. These rights include the right to safety, to be cared for in a family home (or equivalent) and to access to education. Three of these rights are particularly related to supporting a child's agency, namely Article 12 which states that 'every child has the right to express their views, feelings and wishes in all matters affecting them, and to have their views considered and taken seriously'. Article 13 supports their freedom of expression so that 'every child must be free to express their thoughts and opinions and to access all kinds of information, as long as it is within the law'. Article 14 asserts their freedom of thought so that 'every child has the right to think and believe what they choose'. This powerful statement of the rights of children has placed an obligation on signatories to the Convention to create the conditions by which these rights can be met. In the UK, for those concerned with the development and design of mental health services for children and young people, it is their obligation to ensure that the services are consistent with these rights.

These principles may appear to be somewhat remote from the realities of children's lives and the design of services to help them. How does this make any difference in practice? Don't we already ask children what they think? Perhaps not as much as we might imagine and in real world situations it may be less clear cut than we would like. Somewhat impulsively Teresa took a large quantity of paracetamol, then panicked and told her mum who at first ignored her as Teresa had done this before and it had turned out to be untrue. Her dad called for an ambulance, and she was taken to A and E and stayed in hospital overnight. When seeing the nurse from the psychiatry team, she presented as flat, depressed, despairing and suicidal. She wanted to go home but her parents would not agree. The team felt she was highly vulnerable and felt that she needed to be admitted to hospital but there was no bed available that day. She would need to stay in the paediatric ward for one more night before being transferred to a young people's psychiatric unit. At first, she refused to agree to this plan and became angry and threatened to run away from the ward. The effort of the hospital team was to make decisions in a collaborative way with Teresa. But in such situations, it would be misleading to imagine that the young person is given a range of options that she can independently decide upon. In such situations of high risk (and high emotion) the range of options may be very limited. What would happen if Teresa refused the admission? Further discussion would have taken place with her family as to who could look after Teresa and/or if she came home, what support could be provided for them. Alternatively, usually in the last resort (and relatively rarely in practice), Teresa may have been admitted to hospital using mental health legislation which placed her safety above her right to choose. This is commonly referred to as 'sectioning' and applies if the risks to her life were considered sufficiently severe. Eventually, after further discussion with the hospital team, she agreed to the admission the following day. In this example, Teresa's views were invited and listened to and considered in the decision-making. But, from Teresa's perspective, it was clear that some of her views were more acceptable than others and she was very aware of the power of the adults around her in this process.

In the UK, the application of Article 12 to the provision of services for children has been taken forward by the work of Laura Lundy.[4] This framework aims to extend participation beyond young people having some voice in their own care to provide a conceptual framework for young people's participation. This has four components: Space (the opportunity to express a view), Voice (support in expressing their view), Influence (these views must be listened to) and Audience (they must be acted on or explained why not acted on). Many efforts to involve young people may create space but often are less clear as to how their views are supported, listened to and acted on. This framework is a statement of values, of beliefs about how children should be treated, what position they should hold in their relationships with their peers and with adults. It is an ethical component of help itself which strongly promotes agency for children and young people.

The Lundy approach promotes the influence of children and young people in how services are run and delivered. These are not a required component of services and may be both temporary and somewhat piecemeal, often dependent on the commitment of local service leaders. However, there are many specific examples of how young people's participation has impacted on core service processes in the UK. For example, young people have been trained to be part of selection panels for appointments of staff in child mental health services, in which their view could be decisive in final selections of staff. Young people have also been trained to co-chair national mental health strategy meetings and have contributed to training of mental health staff. Some services have had participation workers to facilitate the inclusion of children's views in monitoring the quality of work. For example, a Court Assessment Service at Anna Freud had a service consultation group where reports submitted to court were periodically reviewed by professionals and by those with lived experience such as a young adult who had been in care and a foster carer.

In social care, young people's participation has been more developed through the required consultation of service providers with young people in care.[5] Improvements in participation remain mixed but there are individual projects which demonstrate its potential to improve the practice of services. For example, the Children's Active Involvement Service provided systematic feedback about young people's care experience and was routinely involved in recruitment of staff to the looked-after children's service.[6] At a national level, young people were consulted about the reform of children's social care in the UK about what was important to them about the services that they would be offered. Their contribution was succinct; they wanted social workers who were 'kind, who listened to them and who stayed around'. Applying the

Lundy model to this process, young people had Space and a Voice, but it was not clear how much these views influenced the key recommendations of the subsequent proposals that emerged from the review. For example, workforce recommendations proposed greater training, specialisation and expertise of social work staff, clearly important but it was not clear how much the reforms would increase the likelihood of young people receiving this sort of help that they asked for. Overall, in the UK, young people's contribution to service delivery and design remains piecemeal and is not yet a required aspect of how services address the mental health needs of their peer group.

For examples of this, we need to look elsewhere, namely to Denmark. In 2023, Denmark passed new legislation about children's rights, called the Child Law (or Children First) which represents a paradigm shift in the legal position of children in society.[7] This law affirms that the views of the child are primary and need to be considered in all aspects of their care. This is a momentous change in cultural, legal and societal expectations about the position of children in society. The legislation is detailed and complex as it recognises and articulates the rights of parents as well. Parental rights are important but, at the heart of this legislation, is the principle that the child's views are primary in consideration of their needs and their life. The law states that 'the child's or young person's position and views must be obtained and considered on an ongoing basis through interviews and other direct contact, before decisions are made. Involvement and interviews can take place ***without the consent of the holder of parental authority*** and without their presence, when consideration for the best interests of the child or young person warrants this'. The law requires that children who are unable to communicate with language must be given the opportunity to communicate their wishes in nonverbal ways before any decisions are made. The law requires that every meeting about a child needs to begin with a statement about the child's views about the matter being considered. The practical implications for different children's services are substantial, and implementation is only in its early stages. This is being supported by the creation of a national knowledge centre, a three-way collaboration between local municipalities represented by a national board, a telephone and online support service for children and young people and a research unit. This centre will provide training and support to the staff in the municipalities to support the change of practice required by the legal framework. Social services, schools and health providers are required to work to this legal framework and all aspects of their practice now need to be reconsidered in the light of this change.

The consideration of changes in the legal framework for children in Denmark may seem a long way from the realities of Jacqui, Martin, Abdul, Simone, Daniel and Teresa. In some ways it is, but in other ways, as we have described earlier, it places 'help' at the centre of its framework. Chapter 4 of the Child Law has a title of 'help and support' which recognises the multiple ways of providing help including advice, counselling, alternative types of support and care and even the provision to pay children through gift vouchers. Help is dependent on placing children's views at the heart of the process. This legal framework is very different from that currently in place in the UK but the work in Denmark suggests that a legal framework for children's rights is essential if children's views are to go beyond the first two components of the Lundy framework of providing Space and Voice and really begin to provide substantive Influence and a required Audience.

Participation and Power

Children's sense of agency is nurtured by involving them in decision-making about their lives. But children do not hold power; they do not vote and, as discussed above, in the UK, parents/carers hold legal powers and responsibilities around their needs and lives. Inviting children and young people to have an active role in their lives and decision-making—i.e. participation—must make explicit connections with processes of power. If processes of power are ignored, then participation projects will eventually lead to disappointment and demise.

In 2020, a major research initiative (called the Kailo Project)[8] was funded to explore how young people could contribute to a radical redesign of how support and help for children with mental health needs could be provided. Many creatively facilitated engagement and consultation meetings with young people took place to generate their ideas about what they believed would be helpful to them and their peers. The intention was to recognise the social determinants of mental health difficulties and to include consideration of these rather than simply to focus on a narrow perspective of mental health problems as identifiable disorders. For example, if young people felt that their community did not provide them with a viable future as young adults, then this would be likely to exacerbate feelings of low worth and value for the young people themselves. Improving job and vocational opportunities could be a major contribution to improving young people's mental health. Such views were richly elicited in the participation work of the project. How this connected to wider community concerns about economic viability and job creation was unclear. It was not that there was not equal concern about this but the forums where these issues were being considered were entirely disconnected from consulting with young people about their mental health needs. This is not an isolated example but highlights the way that the expression of young people's views is not enough in itself and requires an analysis of processes of power so that these processes can be connected to them. This is why the Danish example is so important. The Child Law in Denmark connects child and young people's participation to processes of power, namely what is lawful. Adults and professionals can be held accountable in law for ensuring that decisions include the views of young people. It is not an optional extra, a way of improving the quality of services, an afterthought that can only be supported when services have funds available for this type of activity. In the UK it has been a common experience that participation projects would often be the first projects to be cut when service budgets were pressed or overspent. Having this legal framework does not solve the inevitable dilemmas that will continue to arise but the law represents power and is a vehicle by which power is exercised.

Who Is the Active Agent? Parent or Child Help

Concerns about a child or young person's mental health often begins with a parent or carer.

Chisomo, Jacqui's Mum, is worried that Jacqui was seriously unwell. Sandra, Martin's foster carer felt she couldn't cope with Martin's anger and distance: Aisha, Abdul's Mum, wanted to do everything she could to compensate for Abdul's neurodiversity: Simone's parents wanted her to take the next step in her young life; Daniel's Mum was highly anxious about Daniel's periods of isolation and withdrawal and Bernadette and Eamon both felt that Teresa had to take more responsibility for her behaviour and there needed to be negative consequences to her actions. They were all offering help already but felt that it was not enough. Their shared concern was that their child gets help and feels better. They were seeking help for another. But for children and young people it is not obvious whether their suffering is just an expected part of being a young person (like having to go to school), or is due to lifelong aspects of being human (like having one's heartbroken) or that is due to an aspect of health and mental health, i.e. an indication that things are not as they should be and one should seek help for. So, for a child they are often in a triangle in which they are doing things both for themselves and also for their parents.

In her sessions with her therapist, Jacqui had gradually moved from attending because Chisomo wanted her to. She started to find ways of dealing with her depressed feelings in a more adaptive way. She appreciated Chisomo's support, but this was no longer why she went. She became the agent of her own help and recovery. In some ways she was most like Daniel who rejected his Mum's efforts to encourage him to seek help but decided on his own approach to his distress. He liked being part of a chat room in which he communicated with his peers about his body shame and his self-harm. He did not think of it as help, but he was the agent of his own private and solitary way of trying to work something out. He had an agreement with Judith that if he was in any 'real danger' he would tell her although what this actually meant was left unclear. On her part, she monitored his school attendance as a way of gauging how to handle her worries. For Simone, the sense of agency around help was with her parents and similarly for Abdul. For Martin, he had a vague worry, guilt and loss about Maisie, his birth Mum although he never spoke of this and he had no thought to express this worry to others. In that sense, with respect to his Mum, he had no voice, no agency.

So promoting the ability for each child to be active in relation to their life challenges takes many different forms for each of our six young people. It cannot be tidily separated from the way that parents/carers also have a degree of agency in the process, a duty to care and protect their child. So, the process is always a matter of balance rather than a dichotomy where either the child's or parents' wishes would completely prevail. How this balance is achieved is often in the small steps, in the details of the helping process rather than the banner headlines. It is in the conversation that Kande had with Jacqui about going for therapy where he didn't tell her what to do (as was his general style) but he told her about his unhappiness when he first came to England living with his aunt. By sharing his experience, rather than telling her how to behave, he promoted the conditions that Jacqui could make up her own mind. He didn't usually do this.

Children and parents/carers are often asked extensively about the nature of the child's problems or needs. This process, typically referred to as an assessment, aims to ensure that the most suitable type of help is provided by aligning support with a precise understanding of the problem. For instance, distinguishing between social anxiety and obsessive-compulsive disorder is crucial, as the most effective interventions for these issues differ significantly. This process holds clear value. However, it is equally important to show the same level of curiosity about what the child and/or parent believes would be helpful to them.[9] This approach is neither straightforward nor resolved through a single question. Asking children directly what would help with their worries, fear of eating or low mood rarely yields productive answers. Often, they simply do not know, and the question may seem too difficult or irrelevant, reinforcing the notion that adults ask questions that are too hard or pointless to answer.

Exploring what might be helpful for a child or young person usually requires a more indirect and exploratory approach. Useful questions might include: "Can you think of a time when an adult was helpful to you?" or "If you were worried about something, who would you tell—or would you prefer to keep it to yourself?" Another question could be, "Can you remember a time when you helped someone else? What was that like?" These conversations often require persistence but can reveal valuable insights. Children may indicate they prefer talking to people who do not criticise them, tell them off, or who enjoy doing fun activities with them. The goal is to build a picture of what effective help might look like for the child and incorporate these insights into the support offered. For example, if a child says, "I like it when my parents don't just tell me what to do", it suggests that directive support may not be effective. Supporting a child or young person's sense of agency involves being curious about their perceptions of helpful support so they can actively shape the helping process. They are not simply receiving help—they are shaping it.

Martin was not easy to engage. He rarely spoke to Matt, his social worker, offering brief, predictable answers to Matt's enquiries and was similarly reserved in his interactions with the specialist mental health service. He seemed intent on keeping people at a distance. However, Martin communicated his preferences through his actions. As previously described, Martin enjoyed caring for animals and being around people who didn't ask personal questions. He preferred being shown how to do things, and he liked feeling that he knew what to do when asked to do something. He enjoyed Brian's weekly jokes about the posh people who visited the farm on weekends. He felt part of something. He liked it that Brian wasn't interested that he was in care and found this comforting to him. Fenulla, Martin's class teacher, learned from Sandra about Martin's positive experiences at the farm. She adapted some of his schoolwork to draw on his interests, leading him to complete a project on sheep, focusing on their care and lambing. Martin engaged with this work far more than with typical school tasks. His enthusiasm even inspired another student to visit the farm, where Martin showed him around. He moved from being helped to becoming a helper.

However, inviting children and young people to express what they find helpful is far from straightforward. For many of the young people discussed in this book, this approach presents dilemmas and challenges. Take Jacqui, for example. When she first began withdrawing from school and family life, feeling increasingly depressed, she wanted to be left alone and not be a bother to other people. Simply following Jacqui's wishes would not have provided effective support. Her mother's concern after a GP visit led Jacqui to agree to an initial appointment with a mental health practitioner. Over time, Jacqui's perspective changed, and she recognised that therapy sessions not only improved her mood but also encouraged her to reconnect with school and relationships. A warm welcome back at school and reassurance from her parents, especially her father, that she was not being judged, were pivotal. When therapy ended, Jacqui wished it could continue and worried about how she would cope without it. A plan to avoid her relapsing was developed, with Jacqui actively contributing to decisions about what support she found helpful.

Martin constantly worried about saying something that would get him into more trouble. He felt that decisions in his life were driven by others' beliefs about what was best for him, leaving him confused and powerless. When asked what helped him, he couldn't articulate it, but he sensed that some people felt safer than others. Gradually, he began feeling safe with Sandra, his foster carer, enjoying games with her and the way she made food that he liked watching films with Polly and talking about her interest in animals and how she was training to be a veterinary nurse. As previously mentioned, Martin eagerly anticipated his visits to the urban farm—the highlight of his week.

Similarly, Abdul struggled to express what helped him. His school experience had improved although other children were still unkind to him at times. What truly helped was how his family and school adapted to better meet his needs. For Simone, effective support focused on her highly anxious parents, who struggled with her distress during separations. Building their trust in professionals was essential—particularly when this trust was shared with Simone's maternal grandmother, who had a close bond with Simone's mother. Daniel believed in self-help, in working things out himself. He found others dismissive of his body image concerns, which left him feeling unsupported. However, in other areas of his life, he was influenced by school expectations and his sense of responsibility towards his mother. Daniel could engage in supportive relationships and was helpful to school friends, fostering a sense of resourcefulness despite his struggles.

These examples deliberately highlight that focusing on what children and young people believe would improve their lives is not straightforward or a simple formula easily turned into practice. However, avoiding such inquiry is unhelpful. Even when answers are unclear or absent, asking the question invites agency and signals that the child or young person's ideas and motivations matter in helping them feel better about things. But it often does more than this and provides crucial insights that help build a more trusting relationship between the child and their supporters. Yet, this approach can challenge professional systems of help, which often rely on standardised procedures.

Key Processes of Taking an Active Part

Shared Decision-Making

Shared decision-making (SDM)[10] is a key component of the Thrive model, encouraging children and their families to actively participate in decisions about the child's mental health care.[11] This approach balances the child and family's perspectives with professional expertise. Professionals are responsible for providing clear, understandable information about the problem, different options on how to help and the risks and benefits of these choices. This enables the child and family to make well-informed decisions. Their values, beliefs and preferences should be central to this process. This might involve considering cultural or personal factors that shape their views on mental health care. SDM empowers children by giving them a voice and fostering a sense of control and active participation. Age-appropriate communication is vital—for younger children, decisions may be guided by parents, but including the child's input supports their involvement. It personalises care leading to improved treatment adherence and better therapeutic outcomes.

Teresa spent four weeks in hospital. During this time, she calmed down and could actively discuss her support plan for when she left hospital. There were different options around this and her key worker in the unit carefully explained different options, ensuring Teresa understood them. At 17, she had choices about where to live. In joint sessions with her parents, she agreed to return home on the condition that she would avoid cannabis and other substances. She also needed to accept ongoing support from the Outreach Team. Teresa met Molly, the outreach nurse before she left hospital. She liked Molly. She had some sort of idea that Molly understood her as they were both of Irish background.

Supporting Simone's return to school took longer than expected. Her parents, Brigitte and Patrick, believed Simone was often unwell and needed to stay at home in order to get better. So progress was slow and often reversed. Over time, Sarah (early help worker) and David (clinical psychologist) felt that the parents' anxiety about school exceeded Simone's own. Their intervention had become a struggle between professionals and the family. They decided to meet with the family to review progress and explore different options for how to help the anxiety in the family, not just in Simone. Brigitte brought her mother, Isobelle, to the meeting. When David and Sarah presented various options, Isobelle suggested she could help by taking Simone to school in the mornings. Both parents agreed, and a new shared approach was formed. Implementing SDM in this challenging situation transformed what had felt stuck and hopeless into a collaborative path forward.

Creating an Empowerment Culture

Discussions about child mental health services often focus on increasing professional provision, but this must be balanced with the need to enable parents, families and community groups to make a larger contribution to the way that help is offered to children and young people. In the UK the degree of support for such forms of help is inconsistent and not a core component of service provision.[12] For example, in some areas, there are support groups for parents/carers of young people with eating difficulties to enable them to support each other, to share experiences and to offer ideas to each other in caring for their young people. Similarly, there may be voluntary organisations supporting the needs of families with a child with ASD such as Abdul. One of these was available in the area where Abdul lived and Aisha attended a local parent group supporting families with children with ASD. This group not only provided a space to share challenges but also campaigned for better services, including advocating for educational support plans to ensure full participation in mainstream education.

For Aisha, the group was transformative. It increased her confidence in working with schools and mental health teams, helping her secure a support plan for Abdul. This included additional in-school assistance and specialist psychological help for managing his anxiety in school. Perhaps most important was that Aisha did not feel alone with her worries about Abdul and made particular connections with other Muslim parents. These connections brought her solidarity and comfort, enabling her to better support Abdul while feeling part of a community.

Summary and Conclusions

Children and young people often face situations where they have limited power to influence decisions, ranging from where the family decides to go on holiday to which school they attend to which sibling they share a bedroom with. But healthy development, however, requires that their voices are heard and increasingly influence decisions about matters affecting them. While cultural norms vary, good practice in child mental health services should promote agency where culturally appropriate. The child's voice must be supported by adults, listened to by those involved and acted on by those who have authority to do so, either parents or professionals. This does not imply that a child's views should always prevail, but they must be considered. For the influence of children and young people to really take root, it is essential that their views are supported by a clear relationship to power and well-established methods for translating experience into actionable proposals for improving help. In the UK the Lundy approach provides a framework for this, but the country lags behind others in establishing a legal basis to support such approaches. A sense of agency—the belief in one's ability to influence events—is a vital component of well-being. Mental health challenges like anxiety and low mood often erode this sense of agency. It could be argued that a major harm of such conditions is their capacity to undermine agency. Shifting the narrative from children passively receiving help to actively shaping and understanding their coping and recovery is essential.

Children's perspectives differ from those of adults. Although adults have experienced childhood, it is often the case that they forget what matters most to children and think that their own views about their needs are the same as the child's. This is often not so, and children's collective views on many matters which affect them needs to be heard. One of the authors was responsible for managing an in-patient unit and each month there was a management meeting in which the young people attended part of the meeting. The issues raised by the young people were invariably different from the issues that were priorities for the staff. They were often proximal and immediate such as the lack of internet access, familiarity with weekend staff and feeling safe with night staff—differed markedly from those of the staff. Addressing these immediate concerns was crucial for creating a supportive environment and ensuring their perspectives shaped the service effectively.

Implications for Good Practice

Effective help involves supporting active participation by children and young people in making sense of their lives and enhancing their adaptability to their circumstances.

1 For younger children, it is often necessary for parents or carers to act on their behalf.

2 However, maintaining the child's active participation in such cases requires careful attention to prevent passivity within the helping system.
3 All professional services should integrate advice from children and young people into their work.
4 To be meaningful, this participation must reach those in positions of power who can enact change.

A Young Person's Life: Sarah

Sarah was fifteen and the oldest of three children. She came on her own to see me. She was engaging, confident in talking with me, expressive of her feelings and quite challenging of why she needed to see me. She told me that both her parents had died of cancer in the last two years and during these distressing events Sarah had become the primary carer for her younger siblings. After enduring this shared tragedy, Sarah and her siblings formed a deep bond. They were later placed with kinship carers. Although Sarah knew they were good people, she hated them; she hated their relationship with her brother and sister. She felt it was an intrusion. She felt ignored and disrespected. She had loved and cared for her siblings like their parent. She knew she wasn't their parent, but her feelings were all muddled. But, on moving to her new carers, her life went into a sort of meltdown. She didn't go to school, frequently ran away and experienced emotional turmoil. She cried unexpectedly and felt guilty, ashamed, angry and confused. Despite resenting the idea of therapy, she fully engaged in our sessions. Through these discussions, she began to understand her anger towards the carers. With her agreement, we held two joint sessions with the carers to share some of this with them. It ended with hugs and reconciliation. Sarah returned to school and encouraged by a friend, joined a local theatre group. She did not know why she did this, but she discovered that her feelings poured out of her on a stage. Her rage at the world had its say.

Notes

1 **Agency.** Early work on agency was done by Albert Bandura who developed cognitive behavioural theory around agency and self-efficacy (Bandura, A. (1982). Self-efficacy mechanism in human agency. *American Psychologist, 37*(2), 122–147; Bandura, A. (2001). Social cognitive theory: An agentic perspective. *Annual Review of Psychology, 52*(1), 1–26.)
2 **Children's decision-making.** Children's decision-making about their own health care was reviewed (Mårtenson, E. K., & Fägerskiöld, A. M. (2008). A review of children's decision-making competence in health care. *Journal of Clinical Nursing, 17*(23), 3131–3141). They concluded that children's decision-making competence was dependent on age-appropriate information and an invitation to participate in the decision itself. A review of children's decision-making in social care reported that children's voices were often not taken seriously, that participation was dependent on adult relationships and that the context played an important role (McCafferty, P., & Mercado Garcia, E. (2024). Children's participation in child welfare: A systematic review of systematic reviews. *The British Journal of Social Work, 54*(3), 1092–1108).

3 **United Nations Convention on the Rights of the Child (1989).** This is an international human rights treaty which has been signed by 196 countries relating to human beings under the age of majority (usually 18 years). Detailed information about the 54 articles can be found at the UN Convention on Rights of a Child (UNCRC) —UNICEF UK.

4 **Lundy model of children's participation.** This is the approach advocated by Laura Lundy (Lundy, L. (2007). 'Voice' is not enough: Conceptualising Article 12 of the United Nations Convention on the Rights of the Child. *British Educational Research Journal, 33*(6), 927–942; Kennan, D., Brady, B., & Forkan, C. (2019). Space, voice, audience and influence: The Lundy model of participation (2007) in child welfare practice. *Practice, 31*(3), 205–218).

5 **Children's participation in the care system.** A review of children's decision-making in social care reported that often children's voices were not taken seriously, that participation was dependent on adult relationships and that the context played an important role (McCafferty, P., & Mercado Garcia, E. (2024). Children's participation in child welfare: A systematic review of systematic reviews. *The British Journal of Social Work, 54*(3), 1092–1108).

6 **Children's Active Involvement Service (CAIS).** Details of this can be found on Islington Social Care website (Find Your Islington | Children's Active Involvement Service, CAIS (Children's Social Care).

7 **Denmark's The Children Act.** Further information about the Children Act can be found on the Ministry of Social Affairs and Housing website: The Children's Act—Ministry of Social Affairs and Housing.

8 **Kailo Project.** The Kailo Project is led by Dartington Service Design Lab and University College London (UCL) https://kailo.community/ Their approach has been to position children and young people at the heart of service design in response to young people's mental health needs (Hobbs, T., De Lima, E. S., Bevington, D., Preece, C., Allen, K., Barna, P., … & Fonagy, P. (2023). Kailo: A systemic approach to addressing the social determinants of young people's mental health and wellbeing at the local level. *Wellcome Open Research, 8*, 524). Its community focus is also described (Santana de Lima, E., Preece, C., Potter, K., Goddard, E., Edbrooke-Childs, J., Hobbs, T., … & Fonagy, P. (2023). A community-based approach to identifying and prioritising young people's mental health needs in their local communities. *Research Involvement and Engagement, 9*(1), 104).

9 **Children's views on what might be helpful.** There have been many studies reported on children's views of what they find helpful. Children often highlight general qualities rather than professional skills when considering what makes adults helpful (Farnfield, S., & Kaszap, M. (1998). What makes a helpful grown up? Children's views of professionals in the mental health services. *Health Informatics Journal, 4*(1), 3–14.); Young people want services to be accessible, for them to be heard and to be useful (Persson, S., Hagquist, C., Michelson, D. (2017). Young voices in mental health care: Exploring children's and adolescents' service experiences and preferences. *Clinical Child Psychology and Psychiatry, 22*(1), 140–151. doi:10.1177/1359104516656722). Similar themes were reported by Crispin Day and colleagues who reported that young people's satisfaction with services related to the quality of the relationship, a sense of privacy and engaging session activity (Day, C., Michelson, D., & Hassan, I. (2011). Child and adolescent service experience (ChASE): Measuring service quality and therapeutic process. *British Journal of Clinical Psychology, 50*, 452–464. doi:10.1111/j.2044-8260.2011.02008.x). Helen Freake and colleagues carried out a review which reported similar key themes (Freake, H., Barley, V., & Kent, G. (2007) Adolescents' views of helping professionals: A review of the literature. *Journal of Adolescence, 30*(4), 639–653, ISSN 0140–1971, doi:10.1016/j.adolescence.2006.06.001)

10 **Shared decision-making.** There is extensive literature on shared decision-making in healthcare (Edwards, A., & Elwyn, G. (Eds.). (2009). *Shared decision-making in health care: Achieving evidence-based patient choice.* Oxford University Press). However, there is little evidence to show that efforts to promote shared decision-making are effective (Légaré, F., Adekpedjou, R., Stacey, D., Turcotte, S., Kryworuchko, J., Graham, I. D.,... & Donner-Banzhoff, N. (2018). Interventions for increasing the use of shared decision making by healthcare professionals. *Cochrane Database of Systematic Reviews, 7*(7), CD006732, doi:10.1002/14651858.CD006732.pub4).

11 **Shared decision-making in child mental health.** Shared decision-making has been actively supported by the IThrive team who provide training on how to apply this method in services. Evaluation of shared decision-making has been carried out by Professor Edbrooke-Childs and colleagues based at Anna Freud highlighting factors influencing implementation (with improved treatment outcomes (Hayes, D., Edbrooke-Childs, J., Town, R., Wolpert, M., & Midgley, N. (2019). Barriers and facilitators to shared decision making in child and youth mental health: Clinician perspectives using the Theoretical Domains Framework. *European Child & Adolescent Psychiatry, 28*(5), 655–666; Edbrooke-Childs, J., Jacob, J., Argent, R., Patalay, P., Deighton, J., & Wolpert, M. (2016). The relationship between child- and parent-reported shared decision making and child-, parent- and clinician-reported treatment outcome in routinely collected child mental health services data. *Clinical Child Psychology and Psychiatry, 21*(2), 324–338) and different ways that shared decision making took place in practice (Cheng, H., Hayes, D., Edbrooke-Childs, J., Martin, K., Chapman, L., & Wolpert, M. (2017). What approaches for promoting shared decision-making are used in child mental health? A scoping review. *Clinical Psychology & Psychotherapy, 24*, O1495–O1511).

12 **The role of support groups in supporting family carers.** There is some evidence that psychoeducation and support groups both contribute to reducing carer stress when caring for adult relatives with mental illness. (Yesufu-Udechuku, A., Harrison, B., Mayo-Wilson, E., Young, N., Woodhams, P., Shiers, D., ... & Kendall, T. (2015). Interventions to improve the experience of caring for people with severe mental illness: Systematic review and meta-analysis. *British Journal of Psychiatry, 206*(4), 268–274. doi:10.1192/bjp.bp.114.147561). There are fewer studies of relatives of children but there is some evidence of their benefit (Gísladóttir, M., & Svavarsdóttir, E. K. (2011). Educational and support intervention to help families assist in the recovery of relatives with eating disorders. *Journal of Psychiatric and Mental Health Nursing, 18*(2), 122–130). There is some evidence for the value of parent support groups for children with ASD (Luther, E. H., Canham, D. L., & Cureton, V. Y. (2005). Coping and social support for parents of children with autism. *The Journal of School Nursing, 21*(1), 40–47).

Chapter 9

Measuring Help

Measuring help is essential to learn what leads to improvement or recovery.

Introduction

Because of its significance to human life, people have theorised about rain for thousands of years.[1] Why does it rain? How long will it last? What forms clouds? The Greeks pondered why clouds don't fall to the ground, and Aristotle, in 600 BC, made substantial progress in understanding rain. However, during the Christian era, explanations of natural phenomena were stifled by the belief that all events were dictated by divine will. With the rise of science, the mysteries of rain began to unravel and in the eighteenth century, the key breakthrough came with the accurate measurement of air pressure. Today's weather forecasts still rely on areas of high and low pressure to predict rain. The breakthrough in rain prediction was not only understanding the mechanisms of rain but also measuring the right things. In child mental health, we lack an equivalent to air pressure measurement, but this chapter argues that progress in measurement is crucial. Accurate measurement can improve short-term decisions (what is best for this child in this situation?) and long-term predictions (are children experiencing more stress and anxiety over time?). The analogy of rain science remains apt; while the mechanisms of rain are well understood, day-to-day forecasts are still imperfect, albeit improved.

Some readers may find it surprising that measurement is one of the six key principles of effective help, and this reaction is understandable. For many practitioners, tools like questionnaires or other measures may seem far removed from the sensitive and nuanced process of helping children, young people and their families. Because this principle can feel counterintuitive to those engaged in this work, the chapter begins by making the case for measurement and then illustrates how it can be used effectively. In essence, measurement is necessary because practitioners' beliefs about what works may not always be as reliable as they hope.[2] Measurement is vital because both the helper and the young person have only a partial understanding of what

DOI: 10.4324/9781003145523-9

might bring improvement. Just as predicting rain remains imprecise even with a sophisticated understanding of weather systems, predicting what will help a child or young person with mental health needs can also be prone to error. While we may have reasonable ideas about what might be helpful, these must be adapted to the beliefs and experiences of the child, young person or parent/carer, as well as the unique context of the identified problem. This inherent uncertainty increases the need for curiosity about whether the help provided is actually improving the young person's life or not.

But can't we simply ask the child or young person if they feel better? Yes, and measurement is often just a systematic way of doing this. However, it can also reveal things that might otherwise be missed. Measurement offers a way to check whether our beliefs about what will help are accurate. This matters because humans tend to seek confirmation of their own beliefs, even in the face of contradictory evidence. Daniel Kahneman,[3] whose work on cognitive biases earned him a Nobel prize, demonstrated this universal tendency. He showed, for example, that even elite financial professionals were no better than their peers at predicting future market opportunities over time. Yet, when Kahneman presented this evidence to prestigious financial firms, many dismissed it because it conflicted with their existing beliefs about the exceptional abilities of their top performers. This insight may feel comfortably removed from child mental health, but similar challenges apply. For instance, it is commonly assumed that smaller class sizes improve educational outcomes. However, large-scale studies suggest class size has relatively little impact.[4] If smaller classes are considered a key part of a child's support plan, it makes sense to measure educational outcomes for that individual child to see if the assumption holds true in this particular case.

Errors about assumptions as to what may be related to a particular outcome can have significant consequences, as a simple example demonstrates. A nursery faced a growing problem of parents collecting their children after closing time, requiring staff to stay late. Management decided to address this by introducing a fee for late collection. Unexpectedly, this led to an increase in late pickups. When asked, parents explained that the fee made them feel it was acceptable to be late since they were now paying for it. What was intended as a deterrent became a justification. This example highlights how beliefs about what creates change can be misleading. Here, the error was easy to measure because late collection was readily observable. However, much of the help provided to children and young people is not as straightforward to evaluate, and measurement may enable such unexpected consequences to become more visible.

Measurement is also critical because even recommended approaches do not always work as intended. Evidence-based practice, a cornerstone of healthcare, emphasises using methods supported by reasonable evidence of effectiveness. This principle has driven significant advances in many areas of health care. In child and adolescent mental health, key findings have emerged from evidence gathered over time that no treatment works for everyone. As mentioned previously, evidence-based interventions achieve significant improvement for 50–60% of those who receive them—better than less evidence-based methods, but the difference is not dramatic. Furthermore, while different approaches may exist for a specific problem, the differences in their effectiveness are often small. Many interventions yield comparable outcomes in terms of effectiveness and recovery rates.

This might suggest that the choice of intervention does not matter, but this is incorrect. Some problems clearly benefit more from specific approaches—for example, Cognitive Behavioural Therapy for children with obsessive compulsive disorder. Conversely, some interventions are demonstrably ineffective, such as in-patient care for young people with eating disorders.[5] Refining what works best for specific disorders remains an essential task because a substantial proportion of young people's mental health difficulties do not improve despite receiving evidence-based help. This does not mean these interventions lack value; children, young people and their families often report that respectful and sensitive practitioner relationships are meaningful and appreciated. However, the presenting problem—whether an eating disorder or social anxiety or not going to school—may remain unchanged. This creates several challenges for families and practitioners. There is curiosity about why change has not occurred, with families and practitioners often holding differing perspectives. In some cases, small changes may have occurred but gone unnoticed during the intervention. Practitioners are not always good at predicting which families will benefit from their intervention or recognising whether a session has been helpful. These uncertainties highlight the potential value of measures. While measures will not resolve all difficulties, they can provide a clearer understanding of the issues and challenges within the helping process.

During her first sessions with her therapist, Jacqui completed a questionnaire (the R-CADS) about her low mood and anxiety. She found it a bit strange to do this in the room with Monica, her therapist, but she went along with it. She had never been asked such questions before and wondered if her answers would be shared with her mum. When she asked Monica if it was private, she was reassured it was. She felt startled when asked about suicidal thoughts. After returning the questionnaire, Monica suggested they review her answers together. She highlighted areas that were not a problem for Jacqui and started by discussing these. Jacqui felt relieved by this approach. Monica explained that the questionnaire helped her understand how Jacqui was feeling and asked if it would be okay to repeat it in the future to track changes over time.

Martin hated being asked questions on paper, as it reminded him of schoolwork. His social worker encouraged him to rate aspects of his life on a scale from 0 to 10, with higher scores being positive: How much did he like school? How was his weekend? How angry did he feel? Martin often tried to guess what the adults wanted him to say, seeing the process as a sort of test. Similarly, during his psychiatrist appointments for his methylphenidate review, Martin's answers were often motivated by wanting to avoid trouble or further questions. A shift occurred when his foster carer asked him to rate which of the animals he liked best. Martin was okay with this, so they first put all the animals in order of preference, then assigned each a score. Martin liked the donkey best because he enjoyed stroking it and rated the ducks lowest because they were boring. Later, his foster carer used this system to help him describe his experiences, asking whether something was a 'donkey' or a 'duck' Martin knew this was silly, but it made him laugh. Working with the school, he described most days as ducks but occasionally had a donkey day. Over time, he began to have more 'donkeys' in a week, and Sandra would celebrate this in a playful way.

Abdul enjoyed filling things in, especially using colours. At the end of each session, he was asked what he liked about the session and what he did not like. He then coloured in an outline of a person to represent how he felt. Red meant feeling hot, and blue meant calm. Sometimes he was half red and half blue; other times, he was entirely one colour. Occasionally, he coloured in two figures—one for how he felt now and one for how he remembered feeling at school the previous day. While it was unclear how accurately Abdul recalled his feelings, his ratings were supplemented by weekly feedback from his class teacher.

These examples illustrate how helpers (therapists, parents, social workers or foster carers) could track change over time from the child's perspective. For Jacqui, the measure helped her make sense of her feelings and understand whether they were changing. For Martin and Abdul, the measures were more external, providing simplified and approximate insights into their daily experiences. Importantly, these measures did not tell the full story of giving and receiving help. As Professor Miranda Wolpert[6] often said, "All measures are wrong", meaning they cannot fully capture the richness, sensitivity or skill involved in providing effective help. This is not their purpose. Measures are not an absolute truth but, at their best, offer utility in supporting the helping process.

What Are the Benefits of Measuring Outcomes?

Noticing Small Changes

Helping children and young people with mental health needs is often a slow process, where progress can be gradual and easily overlooked. Early changes in the helping process may go unnoticed when relying solely on memory, which tends to emphasise negative events. When asked how the previous week has been, memories often focus on difficulties—Jacqui feeling particularly low or

Martin having an explosive outburst at school. Positive moments, when things went well, are less likely to stand out. Measures help counteract this bias and the unreliability of memory.

For example, Jacqui completed a mood questionnaire at each therapy session and kept a daily diary about how she felt. Her diary included a general rating of her mood, the best thing that had happened that day, and the worst. Initially, Jacqui needed encouragement to stick with this, but after three weeks, she found it helpful. The diary allowed her to recognise what upset her and what made her feel better. At times, she began sessions by saying everything felt the same as when she first started therapy, reinforcing her feelings of low self-worth and hopelessness. However, with her therapist's support, she noticed that her mood varied day to day and that some parts of some days felt better. Over time, she realised these better moments were becoming more frequent and often linked to avoiding situations that worsened her mood, such as spending too much time on social media, neglecting enjoyable activities or skipping exercise.

For Martin, who struggled with severe rages, his foster carer and class teacher kept a shared record of when these occurred. Alongside tracking his donkey and duck days, they noticed his rages were gradually becoming shorter. This record helped his foster carer and teacher respond to him more calmly and consistently during these episodes, fostering a reflective stance. Additionally, the process of documenting Martin's progress gave them a sense of encouragement and helped maintain their optimism. Sharing this progress with Martin reinforced his sense of improvement and supported his motivation.

Noticing When Help Is Not Making Any Difference

Measurement can also highlight when a helping process is not addressing the problem. Michael Lambert, an American psychologist,[7] developed a system where, after a set period of treatment, if there was no improvement—or if things worsened—this prompted a conversation between therapist and client about whether a different approach was needed. Therapies vary in how long they should be tried before considering a change, but it is helpful to have a set period as it is easy for therapists to persist in relationship building in the unreliable belief that this will eventually produce change. This was the case for Simone and her parents. The early help team supported her parents in gradually reducing comforting behaviours when taking Simone to school. Simone became very distressed near the school, and this distress was mirrored by whichever parent accompanied her. The parents recorded how long it took for Simone to settle in school each day and how much time she spent there, as she was attending for reduced hours to ease her adjustment. Although some days were better than others, the measurements showed little overall improvement in her distress after six weeks. Measurement helped the team and parents recognise this, despite the optimism of the early help team. Together, they decided to seek advice from the specialist under-fives mental health service. A new approach reduced parental involvement in escorting Simone to school, and the same measurement system showed a rapid reduction in the frequency and intensity of Simone's distress.

Helping Services Learn What Problems They Address Best

Measurement also allows services to learn which types of problems they address most effectively. For example, Islington CAMHS service[8] measured outcomes for over 80% of children seen over several years, collecting data on approximately 1,500 children and young people. The findings revealed that significant improvement was more likely when working with younger children compared to adolescents, and that young people referred by social care showed much poorer engagement with the service. This led to discussions within the service and with social care about how to improve outcomes for these referrals. As a result, there was more awareness in the referral process of the importance of ensuring that families were consulted more closely before being referred to mental health teams.

Encouraging Participation through Measurement

Measurement often encourages active participation in the helping process, particularly when children and young people are invited to provide feedback on their progress. Goal-based outcomes are especially effective for this.[9] Children, young people and/or their parents/carers identify goals they hope to achieve, typically expressed in everyday language rather than clinical terms. Goals may be vague, such as 'get on better with my mum' or 'not get into trouble at school', or more specific, like 'stay in class when I get anxious'. These goals are rated on a scale of 0–10, with initial scores often between 1 and 5. Over time, scores might rise by 2–3 points, reaching 6–8 by the end of the helping process. Crucially, improvement is judged by the child's ratings, placing their perspective at the centre of the process. While adults may perceive progress differently, it is the child's view that takes precedence. In practice, the most reliable indication of whether help is effective comes from combining the child's ratings with those of adults, providing a more comprehensive picture of change.

There are many comprehensive texts on measuring change and identifying the best measures for different types of difficulties.[10] This chapter focuses on the process of measuring as a key aspect of effective help. This applies not only to professional support in therapy but is something that can be used by young people and their parents or carers too. Daniel provides an example of this. At 15, Daniel was deeply private about his problems. He hated his physical appearance and believed that he needed surgery to address this with plans to one day undergo surgery to improve it. He spent hours online exploring websites and stories of others with similar feelings, a condition professionals referred to as a form of body dysphoria. He found comfort in learning he was not alone and sometimes engaged in chats with others who felt like him. Through these interactions, he discovered that young people with body dysphoria were often depressed. When his preoccupation with his appearance became overwhelming, he coped by self-harming in ways that were hidden, but he did not want to die. Daniel encountered online questionnaires about depression and suicide, which he used to explore his feelings. He began to identify factors that might worsen his depression and made small behavioural changes as a result. He also started checking himself against risk measures to take small steps towards keeping safe. For Daniel, measures became a tool for self-reflection and self-management, as he preferred not to involve others in his struggles.

More commonly, however, help is relational, and measures are used by professionals like teachers and therapists to collaborate with young people and their families in developing effective systems of support. Here, the key is to select measures that align with the purpose of the intervention, rather than attempting to encapsulate the complexity of the process itself. Effective measurement should be as simple as possible while meeting the needs of the situation. For example, if change is expected to be gradual, the measure should be sensitive to small improvements. If the young person's difficulties involve multiple intersecting issues, it may be more useful to track a key functional measure, such as attending school or college, staying at home or limiting alcohol consumption, rather than trying to measure all problems simultaneously. The central question for the helping system and for the young person is whether things are getting better or not.

Once a simple measure has been agreed upon, its use should be as straightforward and with as less burden as possible. Ideally, completing the measure should take only a few minutes and can be done on a phone. Tools such as the *POD* (Person Owned Data) app,[11] developed by the Anna Freud Centre, allow young people to log in securely, access a brief agreed-upon measure and complete it quickly—often in under three minutes. The system generates a graph showing trends over time, making it easy to track improvement or to see that things remain unchanged. As technology evolves, there will be an increasing variety of ways to incorporate online tools into the process of measurement. These tools can simplify the tracking of outcomes while supporting young people and their helpers in their shared efforts towards positive change.

These basic aspects of setting up effective measurement are only useful if the helper or therapist remains curious about what the measures reveal about the young person's experience. This is absolutely crucial. Meaning does not reside in the use of the measure itself but in the willingness of the helping system to engage with what it communicates about the young person's life. However, it is not uncommon for therapists to dismiss or distance themselves from the value of the measures, persuading themselves that their help is beneficial despite routine outcome monitoring showing that little or no change is occurring. A more constructive approach is to jointly consider what the ratings over time indicate, engaging both the young person and the therapist in understanding what is happening.

This was the case with Jacqui. For the first five weeks, her scores on the depression measure showed no change. While she liked her therapist, her low mood remained the same. Her therapist was curious about this and invited Jacqui to think about how she felt about the sessions and whether anything might need to change. Jacqui revealed that she was struggling with constant questioning from her mum, Chisomo, about her therapy, which she found depressing. She wanted more space at home to make progress. Together, they arranged a joint session with Chisomo to discuss this and adjust the home environment. Following this change, Jacqui's mood ratings began to improve, demonstrating how measurement supported a shift in direction to take place.

For Martin, medication was discontinued as teacher monitoring showed no evidence that it improved his attention or behaviour. A shared behavioural approach between his foster carer and class teacher was given greater emphasis although no immediate positive changes were expected. However, Martin's donkey-and-duck ratings of his school days showed a small but consistent improvement. This allowed his teacher and Sandra his foster carer to provide specific praise and encouragement, recognising progress that might otherwise have been overlooked.

In Abdul's case, his therapy sessions were enjoyable, but his experience of school showed little change. Without adult prompting, Abdul struggled to apply strategies learned in the clinic to school situations. However, the intervention was not without value. Abdul's mother, who had also learned strategies during the sessions, was able to prompt and support him effectively at home. This led to a more stable and contained environment, demonstrating a beneficial transfer of skills within the helping system around Abdul. These examples highlight the value of undefensive curiosity from practitioners in interpreting what routine outcome monitoring reveals. To maximise the benefits of measurement, teams can also develop a culture of curiosity about their collective outcomes. However, this is challenging. Recognising that a proportion of young people may not show significant improvement often evokes defensiveness and shame. Lack of progress may be seen as a personal failure by the therapist, fostering beliefs that more skilled practitioners would have achieved different results. Exploring shared data across a team can help reduce defensiveness. Such data typically reveals that all therapists have cases where they have not been able to achieve significant change. This recognition helps to normalise these outcomes and fosters an open discussion about what types of young people and circumstances lead to better results within the service. For example, as noted earlier, exploring differences in outcomes across the team enabled changes in service practices based on these insights.

Summary and Conclusions

Providing effective help for children and young people is an uncertain process that involves balancing many competing factors to identify what will improve their lives. This uncertainty applies to parents, carers, child professionals and mental health specialists as well as for the children themselves. The use of measures acts as a rudder in these choppy waters and provide not only indication for a helping system that their approach is working but also the opportunity to adjust direction when it is not. Importantly, they place the child or young person at the centre of the helping process, enabling them to play a pivotal role in determining whether the help provided is enhancing or diminishing their quality of life. Although using measures can feel uncomfortable for many professionals, it often resonates more easily with young people, parents and carers. In the longer term, the consistent use of measures has a broader and essential purpose: helping us learn what works best, for whom, and under which circumstances—whether for practitioners, parents or children.

Implications for Good Practice

1 Measurement of change over time is an essential component of effective help.
2 Tracking change enables children, young people and parents to judge what is helpful in the context of their lives.
3 While measures cannot capture the full complexity of helping children and young people, they serve as a core indicator of whether the support offered is improving a child's well-being and overall life.
4 For measures to be practical and effective, they must be simple, low-burden and make use of emerging online technology.

A Child's Life: Ruby

Ruby, aged 13, lived with her dad, Tony. When they came to see me, it felt as though Ruby was bringing her dad rather than the other way around. Ruby missed a lot of school, partly because she struggled with reading and felt ashamed and humiliated by this but also because she worried about her dad. Tony was determined to be a good parent but their home was often chaotic and Tony would sometimes have phases of drinking at home. Ostensibly, they came to the service because her school felt she needed help with managing her feelings and her poor attendance. Tony, meanwhile, was concerned that Ruby might be depressed, a fear rooted in his experience with her mother, whose depression had led to the breakdown of their relationship. He was anxious about his ability as a parent and worried about the possibility of being fined for Ruby's non-attendance. As a family, they seemed isolated, and a sense of passivity and hopelessness pervaded their situation. It was unclear whether their difficulties were primarily a mental health issue or the cumulative impact of multiple life challenges. I could see how easily their situation could get worse. From our meeting, I felt both hopeless and a bit useless as to how best to be helpful to them. They agreed to a second appointment, and I asked both Tony and Ruby to think about what they would most like to change in their lives. Discussions with colleagues helped me recognise how hopeless I had felt during the first session and how much I had adopted a deficit-based view of their situation, focusing on all the things they couldn't do. To counteract this, I invited a colleague to join the second session, and we used a more strengths-based approach. This shift made a significant difference. Together, we listened carefully to their ideas about what they wanted to change and responded to this by collaboratively creating a plan to strengthen their social support. This involved us jointly working with Ruby's school to support her attendance and inviting them to take their own steps about reducing their isolation. Tony and Ruby together agreed to approach a parenting project for parents of teenagers, and Ruby identified some friends she had gradually drifted away from. Ruby seemed particularly pleased that Tony was getting help too.

Notes

1 **Theories of rain.** This is wonderfully described by Knowles Middleton, W. E. (1965). *A history of the theories of rain*. Oldbourne Books.
2 **Predicting outcomes.** Therapists commonly believe that they are in touch with whether their client is improving or deteriorating. Studies which have examined this have tended to show that therapists may be less proficient at this than they anticipate. A recent study showed that therapists were rarely able to identify clients who showed deterioration on measures of their difficulties (Østergård, O. K., Grønnebæk, L., & Nilsson, K. K. (2024). Do therapists know when their clients deteriorate? An investigation of therapists' ability to estimate and predict client change during and after psychotherapy. *Clinical Psychology & Psychotherapy*, *31*(6), e70015). This difficulty may be due to lack of feedback from their clients (Macdonald, J., & Mellor-Clark, J. (2015). Correcting psychotherapists' blindsidedness: Formal feedback as a means of overcoming the natural limitations of therapists. *Clinical Psychology & Psychotherapy*, *22*, 249–257).
3 **Daniel Kahneman.** His work was brilliantly summarised in Kahneman, D. (2011). *Thinking, fast and slow*. Allen Lane books.
4 **Class size and educational outcomes.** Research on factors that influence educational outcomes was summarised by John Hattie in his book Visible Learning. He reviewed 800 meta-analyses of educational outcomes. He concluded that the most salient factor in achieving educational outcomes was the teacher's capacity to see learning from the point of view of the child or learner. One of the factors that had a very limited impact on educational outcomes was class size which is widely believed to be an important influence on educational outcomes (Hattie, J. (2011). *Visible learning*. Routledge.)

5 **The evidence base for mental health treatments of children.** The evidence base for treatments for mental health conditions in children has been comprehensively reviewed by Peter Fonagy and colleagues. (Fonagy, P., Cottrell, D., Phillips, J., Bevington, D., Glasner, D., & Allison, E. (2015). *What works for whom? A critical review of treatments for children and adolescents* (2nd ed.). Guilford Press).

6 **Professor Miranda Wolpert.** Professor Wolpert was one of the key leaders in promoting outcome monitoring in child mental health practice in the UK and internationally. She set up the Child Outcome Research Consortium (CORC) https://www.corc.uk.net which was responsible for extensive research publications and training in outcome monitoring.

7 **The work of Michael Lambert.** Michael Lambert is an eminent American psychologist who carried out extensive research on the use of outcomes in influencing clinical decision-making. He showed that outcomes could be improved in services if clinicians used measures to identify clients who did not show improvement after a set number of sessions and that this would prompt a discussion with the client about possible different options for how the therapist could be helpful (Lambert, M. (2007). Presidential address: What we have learned from a decade of research aimed at improving psychotherapy outcome in routine care. *Psychotherapy Research, 17*(1), 1–14; Michael, J. L. (February 21, 2017). Maximizing psychotherapy outcome beyond evidence-based medicine. *Psychother Psychosom, 86*(2), 80–89).

8 **Outcome monitoring in Islington CAMHS.** A number of initiatives were taken in the Islington service to monitor outcomes. (Fuggle, P. (2015). Clinician ratings of clinical outcomes. *Journal of Evaluation in Clinical Practice, 21*, 626–632; Fuggle, P., & Cleridou, K. (2018). Innovations in practice: Using clinician-rated outcomes to support improved service decision making in a child and adolescent mental health service. *Child and Adolescent Mental Health, 23*, 57–60).

9 **Goal-based outcomes (GBOs).** Goal-based outcomes have been developed and extensively evaluated by the work of Duncan Law and colleagues along with support from the Child Outcome Research Consortium (CORC) (Law, D., & Bradley, J. (2014). Goal Based Outcomes (GBOs). *Guide to using outcomes and feedback tools with children, young people and families.* (2nd ed.). Child Outcomes Research Consortium CORC; Cooper, M., & Law, D. (Eds.). (2018). *Working with goals in psychotherapy and counselling.* Oxford University Press; Jacob, J., Edbrooke-Childs, J., Law, D., & Wolpert, M. (2017). Measuring what matters to patients: Using goal content to inform measure choice and development. *Clinical Child Psychology and Psychiatry, 22*(2), 170–186.)

10 **Selecting measures for different mental health needs.** There are many texts describing the range of measures available for mental health practitioners working with children and young people (Deighton, J., Croudace, T., Fonagy, P., Brown, J., Patalay, P., & Wolpert, M. (2014). Measuring mental health and wellbeing outcomes for children and adolescents to inform practice and policy: A review of child self-report measures. *Child and Adolescent Psychiatry and Mental Health, 8*, 1–14; Batty, M. J., Moldavsky, M., Foroushani, P. S., Pass, S., Marriott, M., Sayal, K., & Hollis, C. (2013). Implementing routine outcome measures in child and adolescent mental health services: From present to future practice. *Child and Adolescent Mental Health, 18*(2), 82–87; Goodman, A., & Goodman, R. (2009). Strengths and difficulties questionnaire as a dimensional measure of child mental health. *Journal of the American Academy of Child & Adolescent Psychiatry, 48*(4), 400–403).

11 **The POD outcome monitoring system.** POD is an online outcomes data collection tool for mental health providers that can be used on any device with internet access. Details about this can be found on the anna Freud website. It can be used in clinical sessions with young people and families or remotely (via client log in) to fill out clinical and feedback questionnaires and track progress over time. Scores

are calculated instantly and can be presented in a variety of easy-to-understand graphs, tables or visualisations to help with interpreting and sharing results (incorporating subscales and clinical cut offs). This instant feedback can inform timely and meaningful discussions about responses and progress in-session and avoid the double entry and delays of using printed measures or inflexible computer-based systems. Sites have control over their data and can use PODs export tools to easily download data at any time into commonly used formats such as Excel and SPSS for analysis. POD is used by a wide variety of organisations including NHS Trusts, Local Authorities, charities, research projects and workforce programmes (such as the Children Wellbeing Practitioner Programme and the Education Mental Health Wellbeing Practitioner Programme in London & Southeast).

Chapter 10

It Takes a Village

Effective helping systems for children and young people involve families and agencies contributing together many aspects of help.

Introduction

The phrase "it takes a village to raise a child" gained prominence through Hilary Clinton's 1996 book about childcare and parenting in the United States.[1] This proverb suggests that a community must provide for and interact positively with children for them to grow in a safe and healthy environment. Similar sentiments are found in African cultures. For instance, a Bunyoro proverb states, "A child does not grow up only in a single home." This concept underscores the chapter's starting point: while not new, the idea of a village requires fresh consideration, particularly as most people in Western countries no longer live in villages or places where children have easy access to multiple homes within a community. Here, the village serves as a metaphor for the networks of relationships surrounding children in their communities and the wider connections of their families. This contrasts with the notion that the nuclear family alone ensures a child's well-being. Adults often form relationships within their neighbourhoods, workplaces, faith groups and leisure activities, while children build connections through neighbours, extended family, schools and recreational activities. These collective relationships influence the care and development of children and young people. Villages, then, are patterns of relationships rooted in a sense of place. While such places may foster affection and loyalty, they can also represent threat and oppression, potentially increasing the risk of mental health challenges. Generally, families and young people with a stronger sense of community connectedness are more likely to feel safe and thrive. However, not all communities provide such positive environments.

Modern relationships are no longer confined to physical communities. Networks now extend to shared interests, such as football, fishing, model building, dancing, green politics and motorbikes, or to those maintained online. Social

DOI: 10.4324/9781003145523-10

media is not merely a supplement to young people's social world; it is a parallel context where emotional and relational needs are explored and experienced. The experience of social acceptance, approval, rejection and friendship loss is deeply impactful, whether occurring face-to-face or online. Consequently, children, young people and parents engage in a mix of in-person and virtual relationships, all of which shape their development and maturation. These diverse connections form the modern 'village' in which today's children grow up.

Contemporary villages include many people with formal responsibilities for ensuring the village functions well. These individuals may not have personal connections to the child or family but hold paid roles that require specific training, including police officers, doctors, refuse collectors, teachers, housing officers, bus drivers and social workers. Modern societies rely on an extensive list of such roles, contrasting sharply with the stereotype of traditional villages where everyone knew everyone else and the tasks were often shared voluntarily and informally. In some towns in the United States, local people still volunteer to support the fire service, exemplifying shared community responsibility. However, such arrangements are exceptions, as most modern villages depend on a complicated array of formal roles and responsibilities. These roles often involve interactions between people who have never met before, reflecting a shift from the personal familiarity of traditional villages.

This network of relationships operates within formal and informal power structures. Democratic systems enable communities to elect leaders, such as local councillors, who provide oversight and address shared challenges. This intricate web of formal working relationships highlights the contrast with the informal connections of traditional villages. Similarly, for children and young people with mental health needs, a network of individuals with formal roles becomes essential. These roles—including headteachers, local community police, park keepers and social work managers—are part of the child mental health village, even if supporting mental health is not their primary responsibility. At this point, the reader might question the relevance of the village metaphor. Its value lies in emphasising that, within a village, most people knew each other, had close and distant relationships and probably had specific people that they trusted. Challenges were addressed within the context of known relationships. This is not to suggest that traditional systems were better, as abuses often occurred in such contexts. Instead, the metaphor highlights that people were interconnected, for better or worse. In modern communities, much of the village operates without prior personal relationships. A teacher, social worker and therapist may have no knowledge of each other before collaborating to support a child. For each case, they must build relationships afresh with other adults involved in the child's life.

In Martin's village, there are many people. He lives with his foster carer Sandra and Sandra's grown-up daughter, Polly. He knows that Sandra regularly meets with someone from social care and they talk about him. He doesn't really understand what social care is but he meets his social worker and he now has one called Matt, whom he has only seen a few times. Before Matt, he met with a woman whose name he can't recall. Martin doesn't know where his mum, Maisie, is living. He sees her occasionally at a place called a contact centre, but these meetings are unpredictable as Maisie's illness often prevents her from attending. He has never met his dad and doesn't think about him. Although Martin no longer takes medication for ADHD, he sees a psychiatrist, Dr Ella Hurst, for meetings called 'reviews' alongside Sandra and Matt. He changed schools a year ago and is now in Year 6. His class teacher, Fatima, sometimes frightens him, although she can also be kind. He has one friend in his class, Max, with whom he shares an interest in computer games. Occasionally, Sandra comes to school, usually after Martin has had an outburst. She also attends school events. At home, Martin gets along with Polly, who is passionate about environmental issues. Polly volunteers at an urban farm and takes Martin with her on Saturdays. There, Martin hangs out with Brian, who cleans the stables and pens. Martin likes Brian, who lets him interact with the animals and playfully teases him, though Brian doesn't ask about Martin's life. Sandra's mother, whom Martin finds intimidating, sometimes visits or is visited by Sandra. Martin feels somewhat safe in this 'village' with Sandra and Polly but misses his mum and is uncertain if this is where he will stay long-term. In Martin's village, individuals like Sandra, Ella, Polly, Maisie, Fatima, Max, Matt and Brian each know one person in the web of relationships that make up Martin's village. And they would perhaps be surprised to think of themselves as a team supporting Martin. Brian, in particular, might be surprised to learn how helpful his interactions with Martin are viewed by others in more formal roles around Martin. All the children in this book have their own 'villages', composed of a mix of family, professionals, teachers, friends and looser connections.

Key Aspects of Working like a Village

Collaboration between the Family and Professionals Takes Place in a Community

Effective help often stems from collaboration among those in a child's village. However, this does not imply all help is of equal value or that everyone is always helpful. Help is selective, occurring when there is mutual comfort and trust between the helper and the helped. Importantly, mental health problems cannot be addressed through kindness alone. Professional expertise, though essential, may sometimes seem at odds with a purely kind approach. For instance, helping children with severe anxiety or eating disorders may involve guiding the village to step back—not reducing kindness but expressing it in ways that empower the child to take an active role in overcoming their difficulties. This can be very challenging for those closest to the child, who may need assistance from less emotionally involved members of the village.

As discussed in Chapter 4, some 'villages' can be abusive, cruel or neglectful. However, effective support for children and young people almost always requires collaboration among multiple individuals, including family members, professionals and teachers. This is rarely straightforward. A significant barrier is disagreement about what constitutes the best approach. Such disagreements often arise from differing perspectives, particularly among parents. Traditionally, approaches to child difficulties have often been categorised as either 'carrot' (supportive encouragement) or 'stick' (enforcing rules). For example, one parent might feel their child needs encouragement to make changes (more carrot) while the other believes they should be required to act differently (more stick). Often parents may start with different ideas and effective help may involve much compromise and pragmatism, which depend on a foundation of trust among the helpers.

Jacqui's parents exemplified this pattern. Her father believed she needed to make more effort and that she was making a bit of a meal of things. Her mother, on the other hand, was more worried, perhaps due to her own unspoken grief over her mother's death. Despite these differences, they agreed on an approach. This pattern of compromise and collaboration is central to effective help for many children and young people. However, there are times when agreement is very hard to achieve. For instance, one parent might believe it is unacceptable for their 15-year-old to stay out after 9:00 p.m., while the other parent thinks it's okay. Or one parent may think their daughter's staying in bed all day stems from depression, while the other attributes it to avoiding homework or household chores. These conflicts can escalate, with the child's problem amplifying tensions within the family. Strong emotions and convictions are aroused, and it may not be easy to collaborate together when these problems are present. Here others from the village may need to step in, if invited, or professional input may become necessary.

With some capacity for compromise and collaboration, the modern 'village' may work together reasonably well but, for more vulnerable and less powerful members, it can feel muddled, lacking in understanding, uncompassionate and bewilderingly opaque. Above all, despite good intentions, it is frequently difficult for the components of this complex system to collaborate effectively around the needs of its most vulnerable members. Among these are children and young people, which is why this is central to this chapter. What barriers prevent those with formal and informal responsibilities in a modern 'village' from working effectively together to meet the needs of children and young people? And what conditions are required to reduce these barriers?

Collaborative Help

As discussed in Chapter 3, mental health treatments can unintentionally devalue the help provided by non-specialists while placing excessive power and expectation on mental health specialists. It is common to hear that someone is on a waiting list for Child Mental Health Services, as though this intervention alone will resolve the child's distress. This hope is understandable, but treatments often require significant contributions from families, schools and others to help the child more effectively. For example, parent-led approaches to childhood anxiety involve guiding parents through structured steps to help the child overcome their fears and anxieties. The extent to which non-specialists play a role varies across treatments, but it is exceedingly rare for them to have no role at all. Even child psychotherapy, which emphasises creating a private space for the child to process their experiences, is typically accompanied by sessions with one or both parents. It is crucial to avoid a false dichotomy that views help as either entirely the domain of mental health specialists or solely the responsibility of family, school and community. The challenge lies in achieving a balance between these contributions, which is rarely straightforward. For example, Martin's emotional regulation and forming reciprocal relationships required both his psychiatrist, Dr Ella, and the support of Brian, a community farm volunteer. Brian offered a low-demand, safe relationship that aligned with Ella's recommendations, though it is not something Ella herself could provide.

Professional and Non-Professional Forms of Help Overlap

Collaboration between professional and community resources makes sense for another important reason: many evidence-based approaches to common mental health needs align with what families and non-professionals may intuitively consider sensible. While mental health expertise is more than just common sense, it often resonates with good parenting practices, particularly for the two most common mental health difficulties for children and young people: anxiety and low mood (depression).

For anxiety, the core mechanism of change is exposure[2]—helping a young person gradually reduce avoidance of feared situations. Though 'exposure' may sound intimidating, it closely mirrors the encouragement that most parents provide at some point, guiding their children to explore and sometimes confront the more daunting aspects of the world. Exposure treatment essentially formalises this process, offering a structured approach to what many adults already practise. Similarly, for low mood, a key therapeutic method is behavioural activation,[3] which involves encouraging engagement with activities that promote a sense of purpose and enjoyment. This aligns with the perspective of many carers and young people: that active engagement with the world often improves mood.

Professional input in such situations is invaluable because it can help reduce conflict between carers and young people as they navigate these challenges together. Professionals provide structure and guidance, helping carers adapt familiar principles in a way that facilitates recovery. Rather than introducing entirely new concepts, professionals can build on existing ideas, modifying and refining them to suit the specific needs of the child or young person. This collaborative effort between mental health expertise and the wider support system is crucial in fostering effective and sustainable help.

Help May Involve Methods That Are Not Complicated but Are Still Hard to Maintain

Many forms of help do not require highly specialised expertise. For instance, what Martin found most supportive and validating were weekly visits to the urban farm with Polly, his foster carer's daughter. Polly was untrained in mental health but was happy to accompany Martin during his time at the farm. Occasionally, Martin became agitated or upset, such as when it was time to leave, and Polly had to manage his emotional state. In these moments, she drew on guidance agreed between Martin's foster carer, Sandra, and his class teacher. Expert advice from professionals thus filtered into everyday interactions with Martin.

The ideas were not complicated, but staying calm and avoiding making empty threats—"If you don't come home now, we won't come next week"—was challenging. With Sandra's encouragement, Polly shifted her approach to focus on Martin's feelings, naming them in a calm, non-blaming way: "Sorry Martin, we need to go. I understand that makes you feel fed up and cross with me. Let's both calm down before we set off." Although Polly wasn't upset herself, speaking this way helped Martin avoid feeling he was the problem. This approach reflected an effort to create consistency across everyone supporting Martin. However, a helping system isn't made of robots, and people inevitably vary in their responses. Polly initially found this way of speaking awkward but trusted Sandra, who had attended a training course for foster carers on helping children regulate emotions and found it useful. Polly, though sceptical of 'mental health stuff', trusted Sandra enough to try it. Trust was the unspoken glue that allowed the system to function effectively. Trust cannot be commanded, but its presence is often the unsung hero, as it was with Martin and Brian.

The Difficulties of Relationships between Professionals

The examples so far have shown how effective help often depends on the relationships surrounding a child or young person. So far, we have primarily focused on the relationships between practitioners and families/carers, but another critical aspect is the relationships between professionals themselves. These, too, present many challenges, perhaps greater than might be first imagined and relate to the differences between the professions themselves. Each profession is trained to address specific problems using well-established methods: psychotherapists provide therapy, social workers offer strength-based support, speech and language therapists teach communication skills and doctors may prescribe medication. These approaches are underpinned by sophisticated understandings of the child's difficulties and are often highly effective when a child faces a single, clear problem, such as difficulty with reading, social anxiety or low mood.

This was the case with Jacqui, who lived in a supportive family and attended a well-functioning school eager to help her. The therapist in the mental health team helped Jacqui gradually improve her mood and re-engage with school. Her progress was further supported by her parents, who initially struggled to acknowledge her depression but accepted advice from both the therapist and the school. The school also played a crucial role, welcoming Jacqui back and assisting her in catching up on missed work. In this case, professional and family collaboration significantly influenced the effectiveness of the helping system.

But as previously described, many young people face multiple, interrelated problems. In such cases, professional training and specialist forms of help may present much greater types of difficulty. One common dilemma is whether there is agreement on the primary problem. For instance, is the child primarily struggling with a mental health problem such as an eating disorder, or with severe family conflicts at home? While family conflicts may have preceded the eating difficulties, these conflicts can be further inflamed by the anxiety surrounding the young person's weight loss. Different professionals often have strong, differing views on the root cause, leading to diverging ideas about the appropriate type of help.[4] Much like parents who disagree on responding to their child's problems, these differing perspectives can escalate into conflicts between agencies and services. This issue is often compounded by constraints on what help services are permitted to offer. These challenges were evident, to varying degrees, in the cases of Martin, Abdul and Simone.

As part of his time in care, Martin underwent a detailed assessment of his overall needs. Concerns about his distractibility and poor attention led to a referral to mental health services. ADHD was considered a possible diagnosis, warranting treatment if confirmed. Social care lacked the expertise to diagnose ADHD, relying on the mental health team for this. The mental health team, however, saw Martin's cognitive and behavioural difficulties primarily through the lens of attachment problems and hesitated to label him with ADHD. Nonetheless, they agreed to an assessment, which confirmed the diagnosis. Medication was offered as the most effective treatment for ADHD. Martin's social worker, while strongly opposed to "medicating children for things that happened to them", accepted the need to provide appropriate help. Ultimately, the helping system collaborated, albeit reluctantly, to try medication. Its impact on Martin's attention and distractibility was monitored in school, but after one term, the treatment was stopped as it showed little benefit in the classroom. However, the process fostered collaboration between

Sandra, his foster carer, and Fatima, his class teacher, around monitoring Martin's behaviour. This cooperation continued even after the medication ended, providing ongoing support for his behaviour in school.

For Abdul, both his family and school strongly advocated for specialist support to help him manage his social relationships at school and home. He attended therapy sessions designed to help him regulate his feelings and behaviour under stress. However, the intervention had little impact on his school relationships, as Abdul struggled to generalise skills learned in therapy to the school setting—a common issue in such cases. Nonetheless, because his mother attended the sessions, she was able to use some of the stress management techniques at home, leading to improvements in his behaviour there. The closure of Abdul's treatment by the mental health team frustrated his school staff, who felt increasingly burdened with supporting all aspects of his life, not just his education. In their view, their primary responsibility was to educate Abdul, not to address his broader mental health needs.

Simone's difficulties settling into primary school involved the early help team, her school staff and the mental health team. Her class teacher, a highly experienced teacher felt she could have successfully supported Simone's transition if left to manage the situation independently. She believed the early help team's approach was too tentative, underestimating how quickly children regulate their emotions once separated from their parents. When Simone's progress remained slow, the early help team sought specialist input from the mental health team, which further frustrated the class teacher. She felt that this additional involvement was complicating matters. The parents, vaguely aware of professional disagreements, became increasingly uncertain about what they should do. The helping system around Simone was conflicted and ineffective. Recognising this, the psychologist from the mental health team visited the family at home to propose a new approach. During the visit, the maternal grandmother, visiting from France, shared her perspective on what she would have done in a similar situation. This led to a new plan: the grandmother would accompany Simone to school. The family, including the class teacher, supported this approach, and Simone made rapid progress.

All three children—Martin, Abdul and Simone—experienced helping systems marked by strain and tension between different parts. These tensions were managed to a degree that allowed the systems to continue providing support, but in all cases, help was something done *to* the children rather than *with* them. The focus was on what each person or agency identified as the problem rather than what the child felt they needed. The 'village' was problem-focused, with conflicting views on the problem itself and how to address it. Different teams also faced constraints on what they were permitted to do, which further complicated collaboration. As discussed earlier in this book, one way to reduce these challenges is to give more attention to the process of help rather than solely the problem. We now return to this theme briefly.

Losing Sight of the Child or Young Person's Perspective

As described, children and young people with multiple problems often find themselves surrounded by people with differing opinions on what they need, what actions they should take and who should help. This common phenomenon, which we term disintegration,[5] is not a criticism of individual practitioners but an acknowledgement of a common pattern in helping systems. Disintegration often sidelines the child or young person's perspective on what they believe would be helpful. Including their views, while not replacing those of adults or professionals, is a crucial component of making the system work more effectively. However, as noted in the previous chapter, asking children and young people what they find helpful is rarely straightforward. For the young people in this book, such an approach introduces dilemmas and challenges. Their views on improving their lives are often complex and cannot be easily distilled into actionable steps. Yet failing to inquire is unhelpful. Even when their answers are unclear, asking the question encourages the child to take an active role and acknowledges that their motivation is central to their well-being. More than this, the process often uncovers valuable information that strengthens the child's trust in those trying to help them.

Key Processes for Creating an Effective Village

Few people disagree with the principle of adopting a whole-systems approach. At an abstract level, this idea garners near-universal support. Yet, in practice, helping systems often struggle to operate effectively in ways consistent with these principles. In this section, we outline key conditions that could address some of the challenges discussed earlier in this chapter.

Taking into Account Who the Child or Parent Trusts

Problems do not exist in isolation from their context. Alongside understanding the nature of a child or young person's mental health needs, it is equally important to examine the helping system around them. This involves identifying who the child or young person feels comfortable with, who they trust and who they have found helpful in the past. While parents or carers often play a central role, they may also recognise that their own stress about the child's problems can inadvertently affect them. The key point is that the person a child trusts most may not always feel they have the expertise—or the time—to help. Nonetheless, routinely factoring in trust can significantly enhance how a helping system functions. Jacqui trusted Monica, her therapist, and eventually began to trust her parents as they supported her through her depression. Martin trusted Brian and Polly because they refrained from telling him what to do, though over time he grew to trust Sandra as well. Abdul's mother,

Aisha, found trust and support in the parents she met at the ASD group. Daniel was reluctant to trust others with his personal anxieties but felt more comfortable sharing them anonymously in a chatroom.

For Simone's mother, Brigitte, trust was particularly complex. She feared leaving Simone in others' care, feeling it was akin to abandonment. However, she trusted Isobel, her own mother, whose support for David's suggestions about Simone's school transition proved vital in overcoming barriers to Simone's progress. Teresa trusted others but only temporarily. She experienced rapid changes in her expectations of others. Molly, her outreach worker, recognised this, anticipating Teresa's shifts in trust and working to help her notice and understand these changes.

The Obligation for Professionals to Collaborate Together and with Families

Nearly all effective mental health interventions for children rely on collaboration among multiple adults, including family members, non-specialist professionals and mental health colleagues. Few treatments can succeed without the active involvement of others in supporting change and improvement. Mental health services, in particular, cannot operate effectively without collaboration with key agencies such as schools and social care. We propose that all child-focused agencies and practitioners have an obligation to collaborate in addressing children's needs. In the UK, this is most explicitly mandated in the context of child protection and safety. However, we suggest that this requirement to collaborate should extend beyond child protection and take precedence over the individual responsibilities of any single agency.

Creating Conditions for Cross-Agency Practice

The detailed implementation of flexible, collaborative help across agencies and involving families will be explored in the following chapters. Chapter 11 will address practitioner-level implementation, Chapter 12 will focus on teams and Chapter 13 will consider service design and funding. For now, this chapter highlights three key conditions necessary for creating effective helping systems around children and young people.

The need for director and managerial support. The first condition may seem straightforward but carries significant implications for professional practice. Emphasising trust and collaboration requires professionals to step beyond their usual approaches. Instead of viewing themselves as starting a new helping process (e.g., a treatment), professionals must see their role as connecting with and enhancing an existing helping process, even if that process is fractured or demoralised. This flexibility demands robust support from directors and managers, who must foster an environment that encourages professionals to adapt and integrate their efforts into the broader system.

The importance of sharing information. Flexible practice depends on the ability to share information among professionals, families and children, as well as across services and teams. Effective collaboration cannot thrive in isolation. However, sharing information can be fraught with challenges, particularly when families and young people are sensitive about who learns private details of their lives. This creates a dilemma that cannot be perfectly resolved. The tradition of medical confidentiality, widely adopted by mental health teams, adds complexity to information sharing. Meanwhile, the modern 'village' is a paradox: it balances stringent information governance with the openness and disclosures common on social media. Over-protecting information limits the capacity of helping systems to provide effective support, a trade-off acknowledged in safeguarding practices. A culture where sharing is the norm—not the exception—must be cultivated. Families should be encouraged to grant permission for their 'village' to access the information necessary to be truly helpful, while professionals remain respectful of privacy. Striking this balance is essential for creating an effective support network.

Organisational Leadership and the Need for a Single Lead Agency for Children

In addition to managerial support and respectful information sharing, clear strategic leadership is crucial. Currently, professional responsibility for children is divided among health, social care and education agencies. While collaboration between these three is universally endorsed, in practice the lack of coordinated strategy remains a significant barrier to achieving flexible, trust-based practice. This issue is not new. In the 1960s, the United States' Head Start programme faced delays as states argued over which agency would receive federal funds. The impasse was resolved only when the federal government mandated that states identify a single lead agency for children to unlock funding. Similarly, in China, overall responsibility for children lies with education, despite significant roles played by health and social care. To implement the proposals in this book effectively, a unified strategic lead for children and young people is essential. Without such leadership, efforts to create collaborative, relationship-based systems will remain fragmented and hindered by competing agency priorities.

Summary and Conclusions

Effective helping systems for children and young people rely on collaboration between families and child-focused agencies. Rarely can a single service provide effective help on its own. Children live within families, attend school and carry their mental health needs into these environments, as Daniel demonstrates in his struggle to leave his anxieties behind. Having multiple helpers can be beneficial, but it introduces challenges, as professionals and carers often hold differing, sometimes conflicting, convictions. While traditional rural villages may also have faced these tensions, the complexities of modern professional responsibilities make the 'modern village' distinct. Relationships are often shaped by formal roles rather than personal connections. Effective mental health support for children cannot rely on one agency, regardless of its expertise. Greater attention must be paid to how collaboration can be achieved, a topic explored in the next three chapters, which focus on practical implementation.

We do not advocate a return to traditional villages, which often perpetuated abusive environments. Instead, the goal is to harness the relational trust that villages can foster and apply it within the evolving 'modern village'. Encouragingly, examples of thriving modern villages already exist, where relationships are central. However, these are often short-lived, project-based and dependent on specific individuals. The challenge is to sustain and mainstream these practices to create lasting impact.

Implications for Practice

1. Effective help for children and young people almost always involves multiple individuals and cannot be achieved by a single professional, regardless of their expertise or experience.
2. Collaboration among mental health specialists, child professionals, family members and community members forms the modern village that must be nurtured and sustained.
3. Recognising and utilising the existing relationships children and young people have with trusted individuals is a critical component of effective support, unlocking the potential of a village.
4. Flexible practice—responding to the ability of helpers to provide the sort of help that young people ask for, cannot be done without unambiguous support from service managers and directors. Creating the conditions for flexible practice is the responsibility of leadership, not frontline practitioners.
5. Collaboration should be a foundational principle. Professionals must understand what others are already doing and ensure their actions align with the views and feelings of the child or young person.

A Parent's Life: Supporting Each Other

Aisha, a single parent with a three-year-old daughter, had left her family to escape domestic violence. Living in a single room in homeless accommodation, she felt constantly stressed in her relationship with her daughter. A community worker at the hostel invited her to come and meet other parents and have tea with them. Very reluctantly, Aisha attended and was surprised by how friendly and supportive the group was. She returned the following week.

The group introduced her to a nearby ten-week parenting course designed for parents feeling stressed about their lives and children. With childcare provided during sessions, Aisha decided to attend. It was the first time since her child was born that she had an opportunity to reflect on her life as a parent while trusting someone else to care for her child. The course, attended by about ten women, followed a set structure each week. Everybody was encouraged to speak, and she listened closely to what the other parents said. Little by little the women opened up, sharing their vulnerabilities, sometimes crying about their struggles as parents. They discussed ideas on parenting, managing children's behaviour and playing with their children without interfering too much. Aisha valued the group leader's guidance but found the greatest comfort in the support and shared experiences of the other mothers. By the end of the course, Aisha felt more connected, optimistic and confident in her relationship with her daughter. Listening to others with similar lives and trying out new approaches together helped her feel less alone and better equipped as a parent.

Notes

1 **Hilary Clinton.** Clinton, H. R. (2006). *It takes a village: And other lessons children teach us*. (2nd ed.). Simon & Schuster. This has been discussed in several papers (Stams, G. J., & van der Helm, P. (2024). It takes a safe village to raise a child—a commentary on Dana McCoy et al. (2023). *Journal of Child Psychology and Psychiatry, 65*(5), 723–725); Chamberlin, R. W. (1996). "It Takes a Whole Village": Working with community coalitions to promote positive parenting and strengthen families. *Pediatrics, 98*(4), 803–807; Swadener, E. B. (1997). Does the village still raise the child? A collaborative study of changing child-rearing and community mobilization in Kenya. *Early Education and Development, 8*(3), 285–306; Reupert, A., Straussner, S. L., Weimand, B., & Maybery, D. (2022). It takes a village to raise a child: Understanding and expanding the concept of the "village". *Frontiers in Public Health, 10*, 756066).

2 **The role of exposure in treatment of anxiety.** This has been covered in many texts (Parker, Z. J., Waller, G., Gonzalez Salas Duhne, P., & Dawson, J. (2018). The role of exposure in treatment of anxiety disorders: A meta-analysis. *International Journal of Psychology and Psychological Therapy, 18*(1), 111–141; Abramowitz, J. S., Deacon, B. J., & Whiteside, S. P. (2019). *Exposure therapy for anxiety: Principles and practice*. Guilford Publications). However, the degree to which this technique may be used in practice may be less prevalent than the evidence would recommend (Whiteside, S. P., Deacon, B. J., Benito, K., & Stewart, E. (2016). Factors associated with practitioners' use of exposure therapy for childhood anxiety disorders. *Journal of Anxiety Disorders, 40*, 29–36).

3 **Behavioural activation in helping children with low mood.** Behavioural activation (BA) is a component of methods of help for children and young people with low mood (Martin, F., & Oliver, T. (2019). Behavioral activation for children and adolescents: A systematic review of progress and promise. *European Child & Adolescent Psychiatry, 28*, 427–441; Shenton, N., Redmond, T., Kroll, L., & Parry, S. (2021): Exploring behavioural activation as a treatment for low mood within CAMHS: An IPA study of adolescent experiences. *Clinical Child Psychology and Psychiatry, 26*(4), 1153–1169). Its superiority over treatments which do not use BA is unclear (Stein, A. T., Carl, E., Cuijpers, P., Karyotaki, E., Smits, & J. A. J.

(2021). Looking beyond depression: A meta-analysis of the effect of behavioral activation on depression, anxiety, and activation. *Psychological Medicine, 51*(9), 1491–1504).

4 **Professional collaboration in helping children and young people.** There are many reports and studies which suggest that professional collaboration across agencies presents many challenges to good practice (Cooper, M., Evans, Y., & Pybis, J. (2016). Interagency collaboration in children and young people's mental health: A systematic review of outcomes, facilitating factors and inhibiting factors. *Child: Care, Health and Development, 42*(3), 325–342; Darlington, Y., & Feeney, J. A. (2008). Collaboration between mental health and child protection services: Professionals' perceptions of best practice. *Children and Youth Services Review, 30*(2), 187–198); White, S., & Featherstone, B. (2005). Communicating misunderstandings: Multi-agency work as social practice. *Child & Family Social Work, 10*, 207–216; Salmon, G., & Rapport, F. (2005). Multi-agency voices: A thematic analysis of multi-agency working practices within the setting of a Child and Adolescent Mental Health Service. *Journal of Interprofessional Care, 19*(5), 429–443).

5 **Disintegration in multi-agency work.** Disintegration is a concept used in the AMBIT Programme as a way of making sense of inter-agency difficulties in a non-blaming way. More details about this can be found in Bevington, D., Fuggle, P., Cracknell, L., & Fonagy, P. (2017). *Adaptive mentalization-based integrative treatment: A guide for teams to develop systems of care*. Oxford University Press; Bevington, D., Fuggle, P., Fonagy, P., Target, M., & Asen, E. (2013). Innovations in practice: Adolescent mentalization-based integrative therapy (AMBIT)–A new integrated approach to working with the hardest to reach adolescents with severe complex mental health needs. *Child and Adolescent Mental Health, 18*(1), 46–51.

Chapter 11

Implications for Direct Help

Introduction

We will now turn to how the six principles apply at the micro level—the direct process of helping children, young people and their families. The micro level refers to what actually happens in practice when supporting children with mental health needs.

The six key principles of good practice are:

1. *Parents and carers play a central role in helping children manage their mental health, often working in collaboration with professionals.*
2. *Mental health professionals must adapt well-tested methods to align with how families and young people wish to be helped.*
3. *Ensuring children's safety is fundamental to supporting their mental health.*
4. *Children and young people must actively participate in designing, understanding and engaging with the help they need.*
5. *Measuring outcomes of help is essential to understanding what leads to improvement or recovery.*
6. *Effective helping systems are collaborative, involving families, professionals, schools and communities in multiple aspects of support.*

The aim is not to establish rigid procedures but to illustrate how these principles connect with practice. The goal is to support professionals in shaping their work in alignment with these principles, recognising that there are multiple ways to apply them in real-world settings.

Parents/Carers Have a Key Role in the Helping System

One of the first tasks for professionals is to sustain or begin to restore parents' confidence in their ability to help their child. This begins with an interest in their views on what is likely to be helpful and a curiosity about their

DOI: 10.4324/9781003145523-11

strengths as parents and as a family. This is often far from straightforward to achieve. A first appointment with Jenny illustrates this. She burst into the office uninvited, shouting that she was fed up with having to see professionals and answer the same questions she had already answered hundreds of times. She remained standing, towering over me, expressing her frustration at how useless these meetings were. Jenny's children had been temporarily in care but were now back home. I encouraged her to sit down and agreed that it must be frustrating to go through the same conversations repeatedly. I thought she might walk out at any moment. I told her I would try to ask her something she hadn't been asked before—though I had no idea what that would be. Then I said, *"Tell me something you all enjoy doing as a family."*

She sank back into her chair, looked at me and said no one had ever asked her that before. I was relieved, though I doubted it was true. Encouraged, she began to talk about how they kept ferrets for catching rabbits. I knew nothing about ferreting and asked her to explain. She described how it was like hunting, with each of her children having a role in the expedition. The whole family would go into the fields behind their house and later prepare supper with the rabbits they caught. We spoke for half an hour about this experience, something she had never told anyone before. I had learned something invaluable, something I would return to later.

From there, I moved on to asking about her current *helping system*. I acknowledged that there were times when things worked well with her children, but perhaps not always. When things were more difficult, who helped her? She bristled at the question. *"No one helps me. I don't need help."* But she didn't shut me down completely. We spent the rest of the session talking about help—what it meant and how it worked in her life. She agreed to return to talk more. We had barely touched on the problems she was facing with her children. That would come next.

Examples like this can be misleading because not every conversation with families is so dramatic or memorable. But the process remains the same—the need for curiosity about what is going well, even when other parts of family life are not. The purpose is to enable a family to *rediscover their strengths* and capacity to support each other, alongside addressing the specific problems that may now be dominating their family life. Such curiosity is not always received well as some families feel irritated when professionals do not immediately focus on the issue at hand, but there is no set formula for these early conversations. The success of the helping process does not rest solely with the professional. Parents are active partners, and this needs to be made explicit. *"If your child is withdrawn and miserable, what can you do to help them cheer up?"* or *"If I am not being helpful, how will you let me know?"* These questions reinforce their role in finding solutions, rather than positioning them as passive recipients of expert advice.

The task for the professional is to communicate from the outset that parents and family members are central to the helping system around a child. Unlike professionals, who are only temporarily involved, families have a long-term, often 24/7 role in their child's life. However, this reality needs to be held in mind with some caution for two key reasons. First, professionals know that this positive framing does not apply to all children and families. While it is true for most, some children experience abuse or harm at home. Such experiences are rarely visible and almost always hidden. Professionals have learned to be cautious in their assumptions, keeping in mind that a child's difficulties may stem from their home environment. They have a duty to remain open to this possibility, which means that, for professionals, the earlier enthusiastic statement of the positive role of families is always tempered by uncertainty, by an appropriate level of doubt as to what may be the case for an individual child or young person. Secondly, parents seek professional help at a time when their confidence as caregivers is often at its lowest. Their belief in their ability to support their child may be deeply undermined, whether by recent struggles or long-term difficulties. They rarely come to mental health services confident of their own parenting; they often arrive exhausted, demoralised and frightened, hoping that professionals will sort their children out. They may bring their child in the hope that someone will *talk to them, provide therapy, teach them how to behave, get them to pull themselves together, listen to instructions* or *simply do what they are told.* In these moments, they may feel entirely incapable of coping and long for someone else to take over the responsibility of care. Suggesting that they are the main source of help for their child can go down badly at this point. They already know this, but they may not want to hear it at this point in the helping process. Teresa's parents felt this, as did Brigitte and Patrick when struggling with Simone's school refusal.

Other parents arrive just wanting to make sure their child gets the right help. They are doing their best but worry they are missing something. They don't fully understand their child's feelings or behaviour but want to support them better. Their child refuses to go to school, and they have tried everything. *What should we do?* Kande and Chisomo felt this when trying to support Jacqui. They had been through periods of frustration, anger and confusion. At the beginning they did not recognise her behaviour as depression, but once they understood it in this way, their perception of her changed. They wanted guidance on how to help their child navigate this experience. Some parents seek help because they may be concerned about whether their child may be neurodivergent, such as having autistic spectrum disorder (ASD) or attention deficit hyperactivity disorder (ADHD). A diagnosis can have significant implications, particularly in securing additional support in school. This was Aisha's motivation for bringing Abdul for an assessment, even though her husband Ali disagreed with her concerns. She sensed that something was different about Abdul and wanted to understand whether this was the case.

Parents may also seek help because they feel frustrated, even angry, with their child. They may see their child as the problem, believing their behaviour is unreasonable or incomprehensible. Often, they don't want to feel this way, but they struggle to understand why their child acts as they do. They want professionals to tell their child to behave differently, to change how they interact with them. Some parents express a longing to *"get their old child back"*, wanting to parent the child they once knew rather than the one they see now. In the most severe cases, where this pattern has been present for a long time, this way of thinking can be part of a persistent dynamic of emotional neglect or abuse. However, for many, it is more complicated—they both love and resent their child, care for them but also blame them. Often, parents in this situation struggle to see the problem as something within their relationship with their child. It is difficult for them to consider their own role in the difficulties they are experiencing. Teresa's parents fit this pattern. They believed she needed to *face the consequences of her actions*, that others were too soft on her, and that she was simply *going through a phase*—one she would either *grow out of* or learn *the hard way*, eventually realising they had been right.

The first meetings between professionals and parents can take many different forms. Some parents are eager to be involved in the helping process, while others hope it can happen without them. The professional's task is to consider how best to engage the parent to feel part of the helping system. Whether they recognise it at that moment or not, their involvement will be crucial in the long run. All well-tested mental health interventions include a role for parents, although this varies widely. Some approaches place parents at the centre from the outset. For example, in one structured intervention for childhood anxiety, parents are trained to follow a step-by-step method to help their child overcome fears, often without the child needing direct contact with a mental health practitioner.[1] Family-based approaches, such as those used in eating disorder treatment, offer another model where parents are central. As discussed earlier, parents are often key in helping their child apply what they learn in therapy across different situations in daily life. In Chapter 5, we described parents as *practicers*, highlighting their role in supporting their child to apply new ways of coping in real-world settings.

In summary, professionals need to approach their work with the expectation that effective support for children and young people requires the *active* participation of parents and families. Parents' perspectives and experiences are essential in shaping the help that is offered. The examples in this chapter have focused on the early stages of building this collaborative process. Over time, parental involvement must also adapt to the principles of flexibility, safety, agency, measurement and shared support. There is no fixed formula for how parents should take on this role, but success is marked by the development of trust between professionals, children and parents in this endeavour. The six young people in this book illustrate how this process varies in practice. At some point, professional involvement will end, and the responsibility for supporting the child will once again rest with the family, the school and the wider community. This transition can be unsettling for both parents and the young person, but recognising the central role of families in the helping system is key to ensuring sustainable support for the child.

Adapting Well-Tested Methods of Help

Adapting evidence-based methods supports the creation of a therapeutic alliance between the child, parents and professionals. This process takes into account parental states of mind and the views of children and young people, ensuring that the helping process is both collaborative and responsive. A strong therapeutic alliance[2] is essential but often far from straightforward to achieve, as it must include both the child and the parents—who may not always agree on what is needed or what would be helpful. Professionals can find themselves caught between strongly conflicting expectations, where balancing the perspectives of both parents and children is extremely difficult while at the same time maintaining their own clinical knowledge and expertise.

A successful alliance is a two-way street relying not just on the sensitivity of professionals towards families but also on the ability of parents and children to engage with professionals. This aspect is often overlooked, but it is frequently the child's ability to manage the professional relationship that enables a positive relationship to be established. Children who already have trusting relationships with adults, with some encouragement from those they know, are often able to make use of help even when provided by a professional who is a stranger to them. Jacqui is an example of this. Others, like Teresa, may bring distrust, impulsivity or a lack of emotional control into their relationship with professionals, making the process far more challenging. These difficulties are common among young people with mental health needs and highlight the complexities of creating effective helping systems that involve both professionals and family members.

Professionals do not simply adapt their approach to match a child or parent's preferences. Their job is to balance their knowledge of what works with the perspectives of parents and children in order to provide effective individualised care. The Thrive framework (as described in Chapter 4) provides some categories for different types of help. **Advice and Signposting** is for children and families who prefer to manage difficulties independently, seeking guidance rather than ongoing professional involvement. Many children, young people and parents prefer this approach. Daniel is an example of this. Others, like Jacqui, after some persuasion, engaged in **Help** from professionals. Some, like Teresa, required more intensive, long-term intervention due to the severity of their difficulties, requiring **More Help.** Others, like Martin, had ongoing vulnerabilities but did not wish to engage with services, benefiting instead from **Risk Support**—a structured, multi-agency approach aimed at minimising risks without requiring ongoing therapeutic intervention. The key point is that support should be tailored to the type of help that children and families seek, rather than assuming that a one-size-fits-all treatment approach will work for everyone.

Professionals frequently find themselves caught between contradictory expectations. On one hand, they are required to deliver evidence-based interventions within tight organisational constraints, leaving little flexibility to adapt their approach. On the other hand, they are encouraged to place the child at the centre, working collaboratively to co-create goals based on what the child and family feel would be most helpful. For many families, these two perspectives align reasonably well—what the service offers is broadly what they expect. However, for others, their preferences may differ significantly from what is typically available, leaving professionals with little room to manoeuvre. When this happens, professionals must think creatively with families about what might improve their lives, even when it feels like resources are too limited to provide the level of adaptation that families need. This tension between service limitations and individual needs is a persistent challenge in mental health support.

A community youth project referred Jason, a 15-year-old, to a local child mental health service due to concerns about self-harm. He had multiple scars on his arms and legs, was not attending school, had a highly conflicted relationship with his single-parent mother and there were concerns about heavy cannabis use. There was no indication that Jason wanted help and the referral information suggested that Jason was unlikely to engage with services. However, one exception stood out—he regularly attended football training at the youth project, was highly skilled at the sport and had a strong and trusting relationship with his coach, Danny. Rather than offering the standard first appointment at the mental health clinic, the referrer and the mental health team contacted Danny. He was anxious about Jason's self-harm and was supported by the professional to begin conversations with Jason about his well-being. After several weeks, Jason and Danny met one of the mental health team in a local park. The meeting was structured so that Jason could listen to Danny expressing his concerns, without the expectation that Jason would discuss them himself. Later Jason attended a few appointments at the clinic and agreed to a joint session with his mother. However, due to strict service protocols and high pressure of waiting cases, the number of sessions that could be offered was limited. Despite this, a positive connection with professional help was made, and the foundations of a helping system were established. Jason was reported to be having fewer rows at home, though his self-harm continued, albeit less severely. He remained out of school.

Individualised care[3] requires adapting well-tested methods to align with the views of children, young people and their parents on what would be most helpful for them. Few people actively disagree with this but frontline professionals often work in systems that do not fully support their efforts to provide such help. Intense pressure on practitioners to meet very high levels of referral demand has led services to adopt tightly structured care pathways that dictate the amount of professional time allocated to a child or family, regardless of the complexity of their needs. While this approach is rational from a service perspective, it has unintended consequences, which we will explore in the next chapter on teams. For now, it is important to recognise that the adaptation of evidence-based treatments is often constrained by standardised treatment protocols. These protocols determine the length of intervention based on allocated professional time rather than progress made towards shared goals. This can feel like a difficult conundrum to address, a clear choice between resource limitations and effectiveness. However, services may have more wriggle room than is immediately apparent. The assumption is that the system is already operating at maximum efficiency, but this is rarely the case. System inefficiencies occur when valuable professional resources are spent on activities that do not directly improve outcomes for children. Examples include time spent processing referrals for families who are unlikely to engage, missed appointments and repeatedly responding to young people who are frequently referred but not successfully engaged. More individualised treatment protocols may, in fact, lead to greater efficiency by reducing wasted resources elsewhere in the system. The most effective measure of efficiency[4] is not simply the number of appointments delivered but whether children and young people achieve reliable improvement in their desired goals. In summary, effective help involves tailoring evidence-based methods to fit the specific needs and perspectives of children and their families. While service constraints may limit flexibility, this challenge needs to be addressed at the meso level, which we will explore in the next chapter.

Supporting Safety

Effective help for children involves fostering a sense of safety in their lives and relationships. Feeling *safe enough* is fundamental to functioning well and is a core component of all forms of effective support. For mental health professionals, safety has both organisational and interpersonal aspects. The organisational aspects of safety involve responding when a child or others disclose that they feel unsafe or that the world around them is hostile or threatening. This means being vigilant to situations where children are being abused, and/or neglected or when they are exposed to negative social environments in which they may be being bullied or be the targets of racism and personal discrimination. These factors can have a profound impact on mental health. The interpersonal aspects of safety are equally crucial. Children need to feel safe enough in their relationships to communicate about their anxieties, low mood, self-harm or other difficulties. If a child does not feel secure in their connection with a professional or trusted adult, they are unlikely to share their experiences in a way that allows for meaningful support.

Organisational Aspects of Supporting Safety

Child mental health practitioners have a duty of care to report disclosed or suspected abuse and neglect to social care. This is a well-established practice in the UK. Stopping the abuse and neglect of children is not only a moral obligation but also one of the most significant mental health interventions available.

When concerns arise, information should usually be shared with parents and the child before sharing information, unless doing so would increase the risk of harm. The sharing of such information may result in the loss of relationship between professionals and families, as parents may feel betrayed or angry. While maintaining a working alliance with families is important, this should never come at the cost of failing to act on concerns about a child's safety. Reporting abuse is just the first step. Mental health professionals must continue to contribute to ongoing safety planning through child protection meetings and by supporting and monitoring child protection plans. Child safety is not solely the responsibility of social care—it is a shared responsibility across health, education and social services. Addressing safety concerns is a key part of supporting a child's mental health, not a separate issue.

Safety beyond Safeguarding: Addressing Discrimination and Exclusion

Not all threats to a child's safety meet formal safeguarding criteria, but they can still seriously impact mental health. The Equality Act (2010) protects children and young people from discrimination based on nine protected characteristics, several of which—disability, gender reassignment, race, religion and sexual orientation—are particularly relevant in childhood. Acts of discrimination frequently involve bullying, exclusion and the passive tolerance of harm by adults—whether parents, teachers or professionals. Failing to act on racism, homophobia, transphobia or ableism undermines a child's safety and contributes to poor mental health outcomes. However, children and young people may feel anxious about adults intervening, fearing social consequences or retaliation from peers. Knowing how to act on this type of information may be less than straightforward, requiring sensitivity and an understanding of the child's wishes.

Parental involvement is often key to taking meaningful steps to support safety. Professionals should work with children and their families to balance action with the child's sense of security. In addition to individual support, mental health professionals should actively engage with wider efforts to promote inclusion and safety. Anti-bullying, anti-racist and LGBTQ+ inclusion campaigns should be seen as essential parts of mental health practice, not as optional extras. Professionals should be able to link children and young people with organisations and initiatives addressing these vulnerabilities, in the same way that recognising and reporting abuse is already an established part of child protection practice.

Supporting safety is not only about stopping abuse but also addressing its lasting impact on children and young people. This requires services to provide post-abuse support[5] and therapeutic help for both children and their parents or carers once abuse has been identified and acknowledged. Such support may take the form of individual therapy, group sessions for children and parents or family-based interventions. The aim is to help children understand that they are not alone in their experiences, process the emotional aftermath and challenge any beliefs that they were responsible for the abuse itself. Restoring a sense of safety is a necessary condition for children to move forward from these devastating experiences. This is not a separate responsibility of social care; it is an integral part of mental health provision, shared with other teams, services and schools. Ensuring safety is central to the helping system that mental health professionals work to support and sustain.

Supporting Interpersonal Safety

Beyond addressing abuse, mental health professionals also play a crucial role in creating a sense of interpersonal safety that allows mental health concerns to be explored openly. Many children and parents are afraid to talk about their difficulties—whether due to social stigma, shame or because they lie outside what is generally discussed in a family. One of the necessary conditions for most types of treatment is to create sufficient safety for issues that have previously been avoided to be brought into the open.

For Jacqui, progress was made when it became safe to speak about her low mood with her parents. Aisha, too, found that joining the parent support group provided a space where she could express her fears about Abdul's ASD diagnosis. For many families, simply creating a safe space for conversations between parents and children can be one of the most transformative contributions of professional involvement. Sarah's case illustrates this. At 15, she was depressed, withdrawn and hopeless, spending long hours in bed, missing school and avoiding communication with her parents. Her parents, frustrated and angry, saw her behaviour as being 'a difficult teenager' and came to the service wanting professionals to *fix* her. Her father was particularly intolerant of what he saw as her emotional weakness. He believed she *just needed a good talking to.* Sarah was timid and deeply sad. Individual therapy helped to a degree, but the most significant change occurred within her family. As her parents, particularly her father, began to understand her experience as depression rather than defiance, they shifted from frustration to support. Instead of criticising her, they became her advocates. The most important transformation was that it became safe for Sarah to talk about her depression with her parents which both reduced family conflict and improved her mood.

The Role of Safety in the Helping System

Creating psychological and emotional safety for children and young people is a key task for both parents and professionals. Many families seek professional help when safety at home has been lost—either due to longstanding difficulties or the strain caused by their child's mental health challenges. Parents of children engaged in self-harm or disordered eating often arrive at services exasperated by their inability to communicate with their child. Restoring safety in these circumstances is often the first step in establishing an effective helping system and where professionals and families must work to find ways to draw on both professional expertise and lived experience in order to collaborate together. This is a delicate task—one that requires careful listening, understanding and mutual trust between all those involved in a child's care.

Taking an Active Part: Asking Children How They Wish to Be Helped

Encouraging children and young people to take an active role in the help they need should be central to professional practice and shape how professionals collaborate with families. This is not a new idea, but the extent to which it is applied varies widely. It is crucial because having a sense of agency is fundamental to well-being, and fostering this sense of agency is an important aspect of effective support. To illustrate this principle, we will focus on two keyways of supporting agency: asking children what effective help looks like to them and using shared decision-making approaches that involve both children and professionals.

Asking Children about Help

Current good practice encourages professionals to seek a child's consent before offering help. For example, CBT for anxiety is carefully explained, and children are asked if they are comfortable with this treatment. While this is a respectful approach, it is not the same as asking a child or young person what they think would actually help them. This is a much broader, more open question and is essential in encouraging children to play an active role in their own support. Exploring with a child or young person what they believe would make things better is not always easy. Often, children do not have immediate answers, and professionals may feel anxious about what to do if a child suggests something they cannot provide. Open-ended questions, such as *"What would be the most helpful thing to happen for you or your family?"* invite responses that may go beyond the standard support on offer. This approach allows children to express a wider range of needs and wishes, many of which might extend beyond traditional mental health interventions.

For example, one young person struggling with depression was asked what would help most, and she replied, *"I just want my parents to stop arguing."* Another child with anxiety said, *"I wish my anxiety was the same as everyone else's, not this terrifying feeling I have to go through."* A young person with severe social anxiety said, *"I just want to be excused from PE at school because I hate getting changed in front of people."* Another said, *"I want the bullying to stop, but adults don't have a clue how to do that, so there's no point in talking about it."* One young person simply wanted her mother to be at home in the morning before she went to school, rather than having to leave for work at 5.00 in the morning because she needed to do two jobs in order to pay the rent.

Understanding Children's Perspectives

The responses of children and young people highlight that while they are concerned about how they feel, the social conditions of their lives are just as important in how they make sense of the particular suffering that they endure. Asking what would help opens a window into this reality. Yet, this kind of inquiry may happen less often than might be expected because services are often structured around identifying the problem rather than asking about the help that would be valued.

Children need encouragement to express their own ideas about support, even if they raise issues that are difficult to fix—such as poverty, family conflict or feeling unsafe in their neighbourhood. Solutions may not be obvious, but these difficulties may be fundamental in having a real understanding of how a child experiences the world. Understanding their perspective is essential, even when their requests seem beyond the scope of mental health services.

Unexpected Solutions

Curiosity about what would help a child can sometimes lead to unexpected but meaningful solutions. For example, arranging for a young person to attend a dance class might not seem like a core therapeutic intervention, but for that child, it could make a significant difference. A parent wanted to take a computer course to improve her job prospects. Despite encouragement, she had not contacted the local adult education college. During a session, they decided to make the call together. The college informed her that the computer course was full but that there were spaces in a trapeze class. The client responded, *"I don't think there are many jobs for trapeze artists these days."* It was a rare moment of warmth and humour in a challenging situation. They laughed, and then they tried another college. These moments remind us that while structured interventions have their place, helping systems must remain flexible and responsive to individual needs. Asking children and parents what would make a difference to them—however small or unexpected creates an experience of recognition—so can be one of the most powerful ways of creating real, meaningful support.

Asking a child what kind of help they want is often a difficult and unfamiliar question. Many children have little sense of what is possible or what help could look like. At the start, Jacqui would have said she didn't want help, didn't want to be seen as having problems and just wanted to be left alone. She felt ashamed of needing support and only agreed to attend sessions because of her relationship with her mother. It was only after a few sessions that she began to like Monica, her therapist, and found it useful to talk about how she felt and try things out between sessions. But she didn't see it that way in the beginning.

Martin, too, would have found being asked about what would help humiliating, as it meant being questioned about things he hated about himself. But when asked about what he enjoyed, rather than what was wrong with him, he said he liked animals and wanted a pet snake. His foster carer was not keen on this, but Polly agreed to help him look after whatever they chose. At first glance, this might not seem like help for Martin—how would this do anything for his rages or his feelings of being useless and stupid? But what mattered was that the adults around him were starting to focus on things *he* cared about, rather than just on what *they* thought was important. And he appreciated that.

A 12-year-old who was out of school and considered at risk of offending had a good relationship with his social worker who asked him what he thought would be most helpful to him. After thinking about it, the young person said he wanted help with reading because he hated being asked to read at school. His social worker agreed to see if he could have some home tuition, but the young person rejected this—he didn't want a teacher he didn't know; he wanted his social worker to help him. The social worker initially was adamant that he couldn't do this and didn't know how to teach reading. But after taking advice from a specialist teacher attached to the team, he incorporated reading into his home visits. The young person was surprised that his opinion had shaped the support he received. This mattered more than the practice of reading itself—it strengthened their trust and built a far stronger alliance than before. It also reinforced his sense of agency. Asking children, young people and parents what they think would help is not just about gathering information—it is about positioning them as active participants in the helping process. It may not always be possible to do exactly what the child would like but there is almost always a way to incorporate something of their wishes into how support is provided. This shift—from *telling* children what they need to *asking* them—can be one of the most powerful ways to build meaningful and effective help.

Shared Decision-Making

Another way of promoting agency in children and young people is through shared decision-making, which involves collaboratively exploring treatment options and involving the child or young person in choosing the approach that works best for them. Most parents, carers and professionals—particularly those working in specialist child mental health services—believe they share decision-making with children in ways appropriate to their age and understanding. However, feedback from children and young people suggests they often do not experience it this way. As discussed earlier, the level of autonomy a child has in decision-making is often ambiguous. In cases where there are serious concerns about a child's mental health, it is especially important to have explicit processes to ensure their views are included and respected in shaping their support.

Shared decision-making is recognised as best practice in healthcare and is a core principle in the treatment of major health conditions such as cancer, heart disease and in the management of long-term conditions. Adult patients are typically presented with different treatment options, including the possibility of no treatment at all, with the pros and cons of each clearly outlined. Patients, often with input from close family members, are then encouraged to choose the option that aligns best with their needs and values. This process is more complex for vulnerable populations, such as individuals with dementia or those receiving end-of-life care, where autonomy is reduced. Similarly, children and young people depend on others to make key decisions, and the views of parents and carers must also be considered.

Structured shared decision-making methods have been carefully developed for children and young people and are widely documented.[6] These approaches allow children to participate in choosing the type of therapy they feel most comfortable with. Some may prefer a non-directive, exploratory approach, such as counselling or psychotherapy, while others may feel more at ease with a structured, skills-based approach, such as cognitive behavioural therapy (CBT). Different treatments also require different levels of commitment, in terms of time and effort, and children should be given a chance to express their preferences. However, shared decision-making should extend beyond simply choosing a therapy model. It should be a general approach to all aspects of help, including who the child feels comfortable receiving support from, what goals they prioritise and how trust and safety are built into their support.

Agency in Practice: Jacqui, Martin, Abdul, Simone, Daniel and Teresa

Each of the six young people in this book participated in shaping their support in different ways. Jacqui discussed her options first with her mother, Chisomo, and then with her therapist, Monica. She felt her views were respected, and it was agreed that what she shared in therapy would not be passed to Chisomo without her knowledge. She understood that Monica would encourage her to actively try things to improve her mood and motivation—therapy was not something done *to* her, but *with* her.

For Martin, fostering a sense of agency was far more challenging. When he got into trouble, he tended to blame others rather than see himself as having any control over what happened. A key moment in his experience of agency came when Sandra, his foster carer, allowed him to get a pet snake, despite her personal reluctance. This seemingly small decision was a turning point, as it showed Martin that his wishes could be taken seriously, even when they did not align with the preferences of the adults around him. Simone's agency was developed through small but significant choices. She was encouraged to take part in planning how she would get to school, eventually agreeing to go with her grandmother, someone she trusted deeply. This gave her a sense of control over a process that had initially felt overwhelming. For Teresa, agency was elusive. She had little sense of herself as a person and often felt dissociated and empty. However, over time, she began to experience her relationship with Molly, her outreach worker, as different from what she had expected. She slowly learned that she could contact Molly when she was feeling vulnerable or unsafe. While this was a small step, it was a significant shift—from passively enduring her distress to actively seeking help. Daniel maintained strong personal agency, but in a way that resisted outside support. He was reluctant to invite others into his struggles, but he found online chat rooms where he discovered new ways of managing his distress. While this was not the kind of help his parents or professionals might have envisioned, it was an approach that felt right for him and allowed him to take ownership of how he coped.

Fostering Agency as a Continuous Process

Promoting agency in children and young people is a core part of effective support, even when it is incomplete or difficult to establish. In many areas of their lives, children experience the world as something that happens to them, rather than something they can influence. Encouraging a child to see that they can play a role in shaping their help—whether through choosing how therapy is structured, setting their own goals or simply deciding who they feel comfortable talking to—can be transformative. Developing agency is not a single conversation but an ongoing process of finding age-appropriate and family-appropriate ways to shift children from passive positions to active participants. Whether it is helping them cope more effectively, recover from distressing experiences or simply feel more in control of their lives, agency is a key ingredient in making mental health support both meaningful and effective.

Measuring Outcomes: Being Curious about Progress

Monitoring progress and measuring outcomes is a fundamental part of effective help, not an add-on or a separate task from the helping process itself. It plays a crucial role in shaping support, allowing a child or young person to assess whether things are improving. If monitoring suggests that little or no change is happening, it should prompt reflection on whether adjustments are needed in the approach being taken. Change can be difficult to recognise, especially in mental health, where progress is often gradual rather than immediate. It is easy for both professionals and families to feel discouraged when improvements are hard to see. Some changes are clear, such as when Jacqui started attending school regularly after a long period of absence. However, in most cases, progress happens in smaller, less noticeable steps.

For Martin, his meltdowns still occurred, and when they did, they were distressing for both Sandra and Fatima, his class teacher. It was easy for them to feel that things were not improving much for Martin. However, by keeping simple records of how often these outbursts happened, they were able to see that they were occurring less frequently over time. This helped them recognise progress, even when it didn't always feel like things were getting better. For Simone, beyond monitoring her school attendance and her reduction in distress at separation, another important shift was in Brigitte's anxiety. Through her own sessions Brigitte gained insight into her own worries about Simone, which in turn influenced her conversations with her own mother. As Brigitte's anxiety lessened, the helping system itself became less dominated by fear, creating a more contained environment for Simone. Seeing these changes helped the family recognise the progress they were making.

For Abdul, there was no clear outcome measure to track how he was managing at school, making it difficult to gauge the impact of support. In contrast, Teresa and Molly had a shared goal of reducing Teresa's reliance on crisis care—whether through police involvement following fights or visits to A&E due to alcohol excess, suicidality or self-harm threats. For Molly, recording both incidents of crisis care and situations where escalation was avoided allowed them to track progress. Each event provided opportunities for learning and strengthening self-regulation, helping Teresa move towards seeking support earlier rather than relying on others to take control. Again, monitoring showed a clear reduction in both frequency and severity of crisis episodes, offering evidence that things were improving.

Making Measurement Meaningful

Effective measurement works best when it is simple to record and when the helping system is motivated by achieving change that aligns with what is being measured. Standard questionnaires may not always meet this need, but for Jacqui, self-report measures helped her reflect on her progress. Over time, she noticed differences in her responses, acting as a mirror to her experience. Given her fluctuating shame and hopelessness, long-term improvement was difficult for her to recognise. However, tracking her responses helped her see that at times she was feeling better, and that this was partly due to her own efforts to change. For Martin, monitoring his restlessness in school provided valuable information about his medication. The records showed that the medication did not improve his symptoms, leading to the decision to stop a treatment that was not making a difference and explore other approaches. Monitoring progress is not just about tracking outcomes—it is about creating a sense of direction for the child, family and professionals involved. It helps everyone see whether help is making a difference, when adjustments are needed, and, most importantly, when a child's own efforts are contributing to change. Recognising small improvements, even when difficulties remain, can be hugely motivating and is an essential part of effective mental health support.

The need to stop interventions that are not working was a key part of the support offered to Gillian. She was 15 and living with her grandmother after the breakdown of her relationship with her mother, who lived a few streets away with her younger brother. Family relationships were tense, with frequent criticism exchanged between Gillian's grandmother and mother about each other's care of her. Gillian was angry and, at times, violent towards both of them. More recently, she had begun engaging in self-harm, cutting herself with increasing frequency. She attended a Pupil Referral Unit, but her attendance was irregular. Gillian was referred to the mental health team by social care and developed a strong relationship with Angela, a clinical psychologist. The initial aim of therapy was to help Gillian manage her anger, and Angela used an adapted CBT approach to support her in regulating her emotions. Although Gillian actively engaged in the sessions and appeared to enjoy working with Angela, after ten weeks, her behaviour had not changed. A simple diary record showed no significant reduction in her angry outbursts.

Rather than continuing with an approach that was not leading to change, Angela suggested shifting to a more systemic approach, involving both her mother and grandmother. Gillian agreed. At first, they were seen separately, and later, they joined structured joint sessions designed to anticipate and manage high levels of emotion and conflict. Over the next three to four months, monitoring showed a gradual reduction in Gillian's angry behaviour. The change in approach was not due to problems in Angela's relationship with Gillian, which remained positive, but because a different method was needed to achieve progress. The shift also resulted in improved relationships with her grandmother and, to a lesser extent, her mother.

This example highlights the importance of distinguishing between engagement in therapy and actual outcomes. Treatment was changed despite good engagement between Gillian and Angela. Recognising this required active use of progress measures, which enabled a course correction when the initial approach was not effective. Angela also recruited a colleague to co-facilitate the family sessions, recognising that a different skill set was needed to manage the new approach. Good engagement does not always mean that an intervention is working. Therapists and professionals may continue treatment even when little or no change is happening, simply because they have built a positive relationship with the child, young person or family. Using structured measures aligned with agreed goals helps professionals and young people recognise when an approach is not leading to meaningful change. Sometimes, these decisions are difficult for a therapist to make alone. Reviewing progress with a supervisor can help professionals reflect on whether to continue, adapt or shift to a different approach. This will be explored further in the next chapter on supervision and professional development.

In summary, ongoing measurement of progress allows for a systematic review of whether help is leading to meaningful improvement or whether a change in approach is needed. It ensures that discussions about shifting treatment can take place with the young person involved, rather than decisions being based solely on professional judgment. This perspective prevents help from being judged only by the quality of the relationship between the child and the professional. While a strong therapeutic relationship is essential, it is not sufficient on its own to ensure progress. Measuring change provides an additional, objective perspective—one that keeps the focus on whether support is truly helping a child cope better with their mental health needs.

It Takes a Village

Throughout this book, we have emphasised the crucial role of parents and families working alongside mental health professionals in creating an effective helping system for children with mental health needs. Now, we want to widen the scope to include others beyond this core group. Children and young people have multiple relationships, and it is not always obvious who is most significant in supporting them.

A helping system does not separate treatment from support, nor does it assign treatment a privileged, active role while viewing support as secondary. Like an orchestra, where the second violins may not receive the spotlight but are essential to the music, a helping system should recognise and include all those involved in a child's support. As we have discussed, many child mental health treatments rely on parents and carers for their effectiveness. The degree to which those involved are able to play a similar tune often determines success. Here, we expand this idea further—beyond the immediate family—to include a larger choir of support.

Identifying the Helping System

The first step is to ask the child who helps them. Who do they feel close to? Who do they spend time with? This might include teachers, sports coaches, dance instructors, scout leaders, faith leaders or care staff. What matters is the child's perspective, rather than assuming someone is helpful simply because it is their job to be so. The purpose of this sort of inquiry is to make sure that important figures in a child's life are not overlooked. Often, people with key roles are discounted by other adults. This might include separated parents who see the child less frequently but still provide emotional support, or residential care staff, whose understanding of the young people they support is often undervalued.

Sometimes, the most significant people are those who do not take on a traditional helping role at all. Brian, in Martin's story, had a relationship with Martin that was not about mental health support but nevertheless is someone who Martin felt very comfortable with. In a training session with an inpatient mental health team, staff were asked who the young people talked to most. The answer was the unit cook. In the evenings, young people would wander into her kitchen, and she would give them cakes and just be friendly. She was not interested in their problems—just their lives.

These examples do not suggest that figures like Brian or the unit cook replace professional help. Not at all. This would not be a helping system, but a collection of disconnected individuals acting in different ways. As discussed in Chapter 10, it is common for helpers to have very different ideas about what a young person needs, which can create muddle rather than support. The challenge is to encourage supportive figures to appreciate each other's contribution and to avoid pulling in different directions.

Mapping the Helping System

To help with this, it can be helpful to explicitly map out an individual helping system to ensure that all those who are helping the young person are included. This does not require complex techniques. In the AMBIT approach, a simple tool called a Pro-gram is used, where a practitioner and young person create a diagram of who is in their life and how they support them.

A Pro-gram might include:

- Family members (e.g. grandparents, siblings, separated parents)
- Professionals (e.g. teachers, social workers, therapists, doctors)
- Community members (e.g. faith leaders, sports coaches, dance teachers)
- Peers (e.g. best friends, romantic partners)

The diagram is practical and flexible. People who are closer to the young person are placed nearer the centre, and connections between helpers are also shown. The goal is not to create an exact model, but to include all key figures in the child's support network. By recognising and organising these relationships, professionals can ensure that all sources of support are considered, and that helping systems are built around the child, rather than forcing the child to fit into a rigid service structure.

Martin's Pro-gram

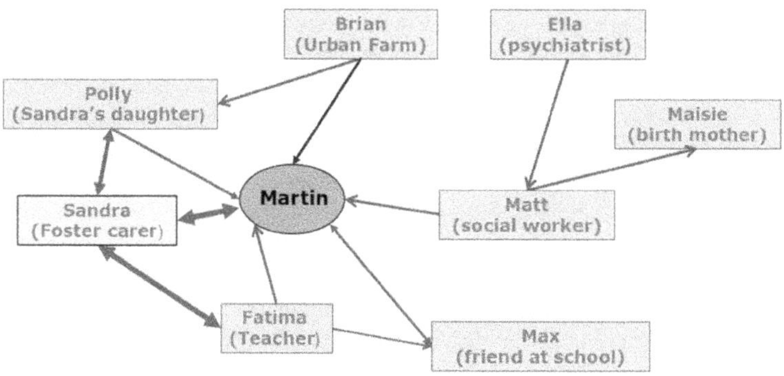

For Jacqui, moving house, changing schools and losing her grandmother meant that, in many ways, she lost her village. A key part of her recovery was rebuilding these wider connections. She maintained a link through social media with a close friend from primary school, texting her when she felt low and confiding in her about her struggles with her parents. However, when mapping out Jacqui's helping system, it became clear that her once rich network of relationships had significantly shrunk. Much of her work with Monica focused on strengthening her relationship with her parents as sources of support, reducing her avoidance of social situations and encouraging her to form friendships in her new school. Reconnecting with a peer group was an essential part of restoring her mood and sociability.

This pattern of a diminished, disrupted or thin support network was present in all the other young people in this book, though for different reasons. For Abdul, his way of relating to others was shaped by his ASD, making reciprocal interactions difficult. In play, he preferred to be in full control, struggling when others tried to change the focus of the game. His helping system was not absent, but it was structured differently.

Simone's village was still her family, and separation from them triggered distress and fear. However, when she felt secure, she was able to enjoy playing with other children. A key figure in Simone's village was her maternal grandmother, whose presence was crucial in helping her settle into primary school. Her grandmother stayed with the family for a month, taking Simone to school each morning, making the transition feel like part of a special time together rather than a distressing separation.

Daniel did not have a helping system around his struggles because he kept them private. He knew his mother was there for him and felt cared for and safe, but he did not share his internal distress with her. He functioned okay in school, participated in activities and had a group of friends, but he kept his village at a distance. This isolation often left him feeling deeply lonely and depressed. His hatred of his physical appearance led to self-harm, though he had no suicidal thoughts. Daniel's support system was found in anonymous chat rooms, where he could engage without revealing his identity. This eventually led to a turning point when his mother agreed to let him join a gym, recognising his strong interest in intensive exercise. He began attending regularly, self-harmed less and made new connections there. His participation in extreme fitness communities gave him a new sense of belonging, altering how he felt about himself. While this was not the traditional form of help his mother had hoped for, it was fortuitous—his interests led him to find others and enter a social world where he felt understood.

Teresa's village reflected the instability in her life and the way she experienced herself. She had many passing acquaintances, but her helping system was almost entirely composed of professionals. She was impulsive and uncontained, using multiple substances, particularly cannabis, as a way to manage her emotional volatility. She was sexually active, at times engaging in paid sex with older men. Her connections were mainly with others whose lives were chaotic and self-destructive. Yet, alongside this, she made some efforts to attend college and maintained irregular contact with Molly, both by phone and in person.

Molly's approach was shaped by Teresa's reality. As part of keeping her safe, she supported her in attending the sexual health clinic and, to sustain some constructive part of her 'village', worked to ensure she did not lose her place at college. Teresa's parents felt powerless, and their relationship with her had completely broken down. If they spoke with her, it was filled with hostility and resentment. In many ways, Teresa's life was shaped by the challenge of managing her own emotional impulsivity while lacking a stable, supportive village. In this situation, the professional part of her helping system was nearly all she had. With her agreement, Teresa was referred to the adult personality disorder team, where she was waiting to start individual and group therapy. For about a year, this was to be the key part of her village of support.

The Role of Schools

Schools are a major part of the village around a child or young person. For all the young people we have followed, schools played an important role in their helping system, even when attendance was a struggle, as with Simone and Teresa. Schools have multiple functions in supporting children with mental health needs. First and foremost, they provide a place where children are with other children and where the needs of children are the purpose for the whole institution, where their development is what matters and where they begin to learn how to navigate relationships beyond their family. School is a child's village in which they learn to study, play, face challenges and form friendships. It is where they develop the ability to function in a broader social world.

This aspect of school is perhaps as important as formal education. Both matter. Pupils who perform well academically tend to be less vulnerable to the impact of mental health difficulties. Feeling competent as a learner can be particularly significant for children dealing with anxiety, low mood, poor self-image or low self-worth. This was true for Daniel, who functioned relatively well in school. His academic success and ability to make friends meant that school was not an aversive experience for him. Despite his private struggles with severe self-doubt and body image distress, he felt safe within his friendship group.

However, schools do more than provide a place for learning and social relationships; they also actively support pupils with mental health needs in various ways. Teachers can be significant sources of emotional support, even when they are not formally part of a child's treatment. This was the case for Jacqui, who was quietly surprised by the effort her teachers made to welcome her back after her long absence. She particularly appreciated Mr Smith, her head of year, who, along with her other teachers, helped her reintegrate into lessons, ensuring she could catch up on missed work without overwhelming pressure. They did not ask her directly about her depression or mental health difficulties, nor did they play a role in her treatment in a clinical sense. Yet they were crucial in helping her reconnect with her village and this had an important impact on her mood and well-being.

Some teachers had a more explicit role in a child's helping system, as seen with Martin and Abdul. For Martin, his class teacher, Fatima, was a key figure in his support network, even though she could not attend joint agency meetings. She was at the heart of his week-to-week support, helping him manage the challenges of school without getting into fights with other pupils and by managing his feelings as well as he could. Alongside Sandra, she implemented a shared approach to managing Martin's emotional outbursts, focusing on calming him rather than confronting him. They recorded incidents of conflict and tracked his progress, ensuring that Martin received consistent feedback when he managed to control his emotions and avoid trouble. Fatima often resented how much extra work Martin required on top of her already demanding role as a teacher. But she was also committed to doing the best for him, as well as for the rest of her class. Most importantly, because they measured his progress, they could see that Martin was gradually settling into school and avoiding serious difficulties. He was also beginning to form friendships, a sign that his village was slowly taking shape around him.

Because he had a diagnosis of ASD, Abdul had an individual education plan that provided him with additional support. His sessions with Rachel, the psychologist from the mental health team, were part of a shared health and education support plan designed to help him cope with the social demands of school while recognising his strengths and vulnerabilities. However, Fenulla, his class teacher, was sceptical about how useful this was for Abdul and would have preferred more teaching assistant support in the classroom. The support plan had been developed through his education and health assessments rather than from the experience of those working directly with Abdul day to day. While it was multi-agency help, the different parts were not well-connected. This contrasted with the collaboration between Sandra and Fatima in supporting Martin. They felt they shared the same lived experience—caring for, teaching and supporting Martin daily—and their ideas for helping him emerged directly from this experience. The key factor in their approach was not just multi-agency input but genuine collaboration and trust in each other.

Teresa's college had a strong commitment to supporting students to engage in their courses, many of whom had struggled with mainstream education. This included young people with disabilities, literacy difficulties, mental health needs and those from highly disadvantaged backgrounds, such as asylum seekers and young carers. Her course tutor was supportive and tried to adapt the requirements to accommodate her infrequent attendance. However, the college lacked the professional resources and expertise needed to fully meet Teresa's additional needs they were working with. Teresa remained on the course, partly due to Molly's efforts in keeping communication open with her tutor and reassuring the college that Teresa was under the care of the young people's outreach team. This small but crucial link between the college and the outreach team helped the college feel that they had a contact point if Teresa faced difficulties beyond what they could manage. Too often, different parts of a young person's professional village remain unaware of each other's efforts, leaving professionals feeling isolated and overwhelmed. For Teresa, maintaining this connection between services was essential in keeping her engaged. Alongside this, Molly continued to support her in making sense of her behaviour and experiences.

Schools are increasingly becoming places where this type of support is provided. For many years, schools have employed counsellors to offer additional help to students in need. Over the past 15 years, mental health support in UK schools has expanded significantly, with plans for every school to be linked to a mental health support team.[7] Currently, around half of all schools in the UK are covered by this programme. This development has allowed children and young people to receive therapeutic support within schools, reducing the need for external referrals. Children struggling with anxiety, low mood or behaviour difficulties can now access help from trained mental health professionals in an environment closely integrated with their education. Jacqui's school was part of this programme, so when she completed her CBT treatment with Monica and was attending school regularly, she was referred to the mental health support team for ongoing support. While this reassured her initially, in practice, she did not feel a connection with the person she was introduced to, and the support did not prove particularly helpful for her.

In summary, children with mental health needs exist within a broader network of relationships—friends, classmates, teachers, community members and family—all of whom play a role alongside mental health professionals. The importance of this wider village in supporting young people through their difficulties is often undervalued. Schools, in particular, are key to providing integrated support. Professionals need to be aware of the individual strengths within a young person's support network and actively engage with them when offering help. However, recognising the power of the wider community does not mean assuming that all influences are positive. As discussed earlier, some figures in a child's environment—such as gang leaders, pimps or drug dealers—can be destructive and exploitative, preying on vulnerability. Supporting a village to help a child must always be combined with a concern for safety, ensuring that those involved in a young person's life are offering genuine support rather than harm.

Conclusions

Effective direct help for children and young people relies on collaboration between parents, professionals and a wider network of support, including family, schools and the wider community. While specialist mental health services can play a key role in helping systems around a child or young person, their role is not always central. Sometimes, their greatest contribution is in supporting the help provided by others whom the young person trusts. A significant number of children and young people with mental health needs do not engage with specialist services. This may be due to waiting times and resource limitations, but also because children, families and schools may have different ideas about how best to manage the difficulties they face. Daniel is an example of this—he found ways to cope without seeking professional help.

When professional and non-professional support systems work together, there are many possible ways to provide effective help. However, what does not work is when different parts of the helping system are in conflict or when one service believes that the problem does not belong to them. Collaboration with schools is often crucial, as school attendance is a key factor in social development and learning for all children and young people. Mental health support for children and young people is not delivered solely by specialist mental health services, as this is not how help actually works in real life. Instead, services need to support and strengthen collective approaches so that communities, families, schools and inter-agency relationships are recognised for the crucial roles they play in helping children and young people. These issues will be explored further in the next two chapters.

Key Practice Points

1. Receiving help, encouragement and support is a normal and essential part of development into adulthood. The ability to seek and accept help is a sign of healthy adaptation to life challenges. Help-seeking should be encouraged, rather than associated with shame or seen as a sign of weakness. Many highly successful adults are often very good help-seekers.
2. Effective help for children and young people with mental health needs is almost always a collective effort, involving family members, child professionals, community resources and specialist mental health practitioners.
3. Ensuring that children feel safe is a core task for mental health services. Safety includes both physical safety and the psychological safety to express mental health concerns without fear.
4. Children, young people and parents should routinely be asked what they would find helpful in managing the difficulties they are experiencing.
5. It may be more important that a young person is supported by someone they trust, rather than by a specialist whose expertise directly relates to their difficulties. Trust and relationship quality are often key factors in successful help.

A Child's Life: Carlos

Carlos was 12 years old. Before coming to see me, his father, who was separated from his mother, abducted him—taking him straight from school, putting him on a plane and taking him to his home country. This was against the wishes of Mariana, his mother, who strongly opposed it. His father later returned to England, and Carlos was left in the care of his paternal grandparents. However, without his father's knowledge, members of both his mother's and father's families arranged for him to return to England to be with his mother. When Carlos and Mariana came to the clinic, I expected the focus of our meeting to be on how he was coping after his return. Instead, I was surprised by how much Mariana complained about his behaviour at home—how he refused to help, rarely spoke to her and was difficult to live with. She was preoccupied with trying to find him a place in secondary school, which she found highly stressful. While I wanted to work with them together to make sense of what had happened and help Carlos settle back into life in England, Mariana had no intention of attending further sessions. She hoped I could help Carlos behave better at home.

Carlos was eventually offered a school place an hour's bus ride from the clinic. Despite this long journey, he made a huge effort to come every week after school. He talked freely about his life and what had happened to him. He did not like his school, had no friends and was teased and bullied. He hated his father, who he was not allowed to see, and felt angry with his mother, avoiding conversations with her because he felt she was always criticising him. At home, he coped best by staying silent. Over time, he began making friends at school and catching up on the learning he had missed while away. Despite the failures of adults to provide him with security, Carlos sought out someone who would listen while he made sense of the frightening events of his recent life. He did not meet the criteria for trauma symptoms in a formal sense, but he lived with a constant worry that he might be abducted again. He was confused, angry and frightened about his family, but simply having space to talk seemed to help.

More than most children his age, I felt Carlos had chosen me to be the person who listened to him. After about six months, it became clear that he was ready to move on. Our sessions were interfering with his life—he wanted to stay after school for football training, and that now mattered more to him than coming to see me. This felt like a good sign. He had always retained a sense of agency, which gave him a resilience that helped him get back on track. At our last session, which Mariana attended, Carlos thanked me for listening to him in a way that, in my experience, was unusual for a 13-year-old. It seemed that what he needed most was not treatment, but to be heard while he found his own way forward.

Notes

1 **Parent-focused approach to childhood anxiety.** This refers to the approach developed by Professor Cathy Creswell and colleagues in training parents to support their child to overcome their anxieties (Thirlwall, K., Cooper, P. J., Karalus, J.,

Voysey, M., Willetts, L., & Creswell, C. (2013). Treatment of child anxiety disorders via guided parent-delivered cognitive–behavioural therapy: Randomized controlled trial. *The British Journal of Psychiatry, 203*(6), 436–444). Other papers on anxiety by the same author (Creswell, C., Waite, P., & Hudson, J. (2020). Practitioner review: Anxiety disorders in children and young people–assessment and treatment. *Journal of Child Psychology and Psychiatry, 61*(6), 628–643; Creswell, C., Murray, L., Stacey, J., & Cooper, P. (2011). Parenting and child anxiety. *Anxiety Disorders in Children and Adolescents, 2*, 299–322).

2 **The therapeutic alliance.** This is perhaps the most fully researched aspect of mental health practice both for adults and children in which its positive role in relation to treatment outcomes has been clearly established. This has been comprehensively examined in major reviews (e.g. Norcross, J. C. (Ed.). (2011). *Psychotherapy relationships that work: Evidence-based responsiveness.* Oxford University Press; Fonagy, P., Cottrell, D., Phillips, J., Bevington, D., Glaser, D., & Allison, E. (2014). *What works for whom? A critical review of treatments for children and adolescents.* Guilford Press).

3 **Individualised care.** This is also described as personalised care, and detailed information can be found at NHS England (https://www.england.nhs.uk/personalisedcare/). The benefits of personalised approaches for parents with children with conduct problems have been reported (McKay, K., Kennedy, E., Senior, R., Scott, S., Hill, J., Doolan, M.,… & Young, B. (2020). Informing the personalisation of interventions for parents of children with conduct problems: A qualitative study. *BMC Psychiatry, 20*, 1–12). The way that personalisation of care can be reduced in periods of service austerity has also been explored with respect to social care practice (Whitaker, E. M. (2015). Personalisation in children's social work: From family support to "the child's budget". *Journal of Integrated Care, 23*(5), 277–286).

4 **Value-based health care.** Michael Porter advocated a value-based approach to health care rather than simply focusing on activity or outputs. This approach suggested that there needed to be a clear understanding about what the desired and explicit outcomes for a service should be and how this related to the costs of the service. (Porter, M. E. (2008). Value-based health care delivery. *Annals of Surgery, 248*(4), 503–509).

5 **Post abuse support and therapy.** There is not a uniform approach to supporting children and young people who have experienced abuse as not all show traumatic symptoms or because of their own choice. A broad approach is commonly advocated (Gold, S. (2013). *Not trauma alone: Therapy for child abuse survivors in family and social context.* Routledge). Some specific treatments, such as CBT, have been shown to be beneficial for this group of children (Deblinger, E., Steer, R. A., & Lippmann, J. (1999). Two-year follow-up study of cognitive behavioral therapy for sexually abused children suffering post-traumatic stress symptoms. *Child Abuse & Neglect, 23*(12), 1371–1378).

6 **Shared decision-making.** Shared decision-making is a major aspect of healthcare delivery. An overview of this approach has been provided by Edwards, A., & Elwyn, G. (Eds.). (2009). *Shared decision-making in health care: Achieving evidence-based patient choice.* Oxford University Press. For children in paediatric services, a review was carried out by Boland, L., Graham, I. D., Légaré, F., Lewis, K., Jull, J., Shephard, A.,… & Stacey, D. (2019). Barriers and facilitators of pediatric shared decision-making: A systematic review. *Implementation Science, 14*, 1–25. Application of this approach in relation to child safety has been described in Coyne, I., & Harder, M. (2011). Children's participation in decision-making: Balancing protection with shared decision-making using a situational perspective. *Journal of Child Health Care, 15*(4), 312–319.

7 **Mental health support Teams (MHSTs).** Details about the UK government's programme for mental health support in schools can be found NHS England website. The first wave of MHSTs for schools was commissioned by the government in 2018 and consisted of Educational Mental Health Practitioners (EMHPs) supported by either Child Mental Health professionals from CAMHS teams or Senior EMHPs. Each school was encouraged to have a Senior Mental Health Lead within the senior management team of the school and to adopt a whole school's approach to the pupils' mental health needs. By 2025, approximately half the schools in England were supported by these newly created teams.

Chapter 12

Implications for How Services Work

Introduction

To begin this chapter, we must acknowledge that all is not well in the current state of services working to address the mental health needs of children and young people in the UK.[1] This is reflected in high levels of staff burnout, significant mental health difficulties among staff teams, high turnover and ongoing recruitment and retention challenges. An increasing number of highly trained psychologists and therapists are moving into private practice, though overall numbers remain low. In the UK, these workforce issues are linked to wider structural pressures, including unstable funding, continuous service restructures and rising demand for support.

Tragic child protection cases lead to intense media and political pressure on services with government statements demanding that "if there is any evidence, any inkling, any iota of harm to any child, that the child is taken away immediately".[2] These calls are often made without a clear understanding of what would actually be required to reduce risks of such events. Long waiting lists further intensify pressures at a local level, forcing services to juggle both the needs of children currently receiving support and those still waiting. The strain extends into local service discussions, where frustration and blame are common. As one commissioner put it, "*if child mental health services were doing their job properly, we wouldn't have children coming into care*"—an expectation far beyond any realistic assessment of what these services can achieve. In this climate, it is difficult for teams not to become overwhelmed by external pressures. What is needed is a service environment that supports sustainable practice and allows creative flexibility in responding to the high levels of need in the community. Some of these issues depend on national strategic policy, which will be explored in the next chapter, but here we will focus on what can be done at the team and local service level.

We will apply the six principles to the way that professional teams and services work as we did in the previous chapter. The focus will be on how teams are organised, what constraints exist for good practice and how team culture supports or hinders effective help. The key themes remain the same: ensuring

DOI: 10.4324/9781003145523-12

that teams are curious about the best ways to be helpful, that they support families to take an active role, that they feel safe and have a sense of agency in their work, that learning takes place through outcome monitoring and that teams are connected with others to create a village of help. The principles that help children and families are the same ones that help practitioners and teams. For this chapter, the reader is invited to imagine a team of 10–12 practitioners providing support to a specific group of children or young people, such as a social care team, an early year's team, a team for children in care or a service for children experiencing self-harm and suicidality. These ideas can be applied equally to health, social care and specialist education teams, or to integrated teams where staff from different agencies work together.

Parents/Carers Play an Active Part in Helping Their Children

Teams will vary about the way that parents are seen to have an active role in helping children, but this principle is widely accepted in current practice. Even when children express the view that they want to be seen without their parents, and their wishes are respected, most teams aim to maintain a working connection with parents and their role in the helping system. Jacqui's experience illustrates a straightforward example of this. For her first appointment with Monica, her therapist, she was invited to attend with her mother, Chisomo, before having time alone with Monica. The treatment plan was discussed with both Jacqui and Chisomo, with an agreement that Jacqui wanted a private space for therapy while Chisomo would join a couple of sessions near the end. This arrangement ensured that Jacqui had autonomy while also keeping her mother engaged in the process.

While parental involvement is standard practice, there may not always be a strong expectation that both parents should take part directly. This could become a barrier to access, as many families may not be able to meet this requirement or may not feel it is necessary. However, when parents are separated, involving both in the helping system can be particularly beneficial, though often difficult to achieve. In such cases, enabling both parents to collaborate around their child's needs may become the central focus of professional support. Teams promote parental involvement in many ways, from parent training groups and parent support groups to structured roles in treatments such as family therapy, eating disorder interventions or parent-led approaches for anxiety, low mood or oppositional behaviour. The challenge for teams is to foster a culture where parents and carers are recognised as active contributors to the helping system.

Team Support for Individualised Care

One of the main tasks of mental health teams is to provide evidence-based interventions for children and families. However, as Thrive has emphasised, not all children and families wish to be helped in the same way. Many teams may feel constrained in adapting approaches, even if they support the principle, due to the overriding pressure to meet high referral demands and see children within agreed timeframes. In this context, flexible approaches can seem unfeasible, as they are often assumed to require more time and resources. This presents a significant challenge. In setting out standards of good practice, we highlight two ways this can be addressed: applying the Thrive principle of Risk Support and enabling practitioners to step back and reduce their role in the helping system where appropriate.

Risk Support

One of the key ideas in Thrive is that professionals and parents can collaborate in different ways to provide effective help. Some children and families may choose not to engage in treatment for their mental health needs. As previously discussed, this could be due to past experiences of treatment that they did not find helpful, a desire to avoid being associated with a mental health service, a preference to manage their difficulties independently or other reasons. As the term *risk support* suggests, the children and young people in this category are often in situations that remain concerning for professionals. They may have persistent school absences, family difficulties related to alcohol use or fluctuating patterns of self-harm. While they do not meet the criteria for a child protection plan, they have ongoing vulnerabilities that can have a long-term impact on their development.

Mental health services work hard to engage children with these needs in treatment, using evidence-based approaches. However, families may attend appointments inconsistently or disengage entirely. Their views about the help offered are often expressed through their behaviour, particularly in poor attendance. This suggests a disconnection between what families perceive as helpful and the help they are actually offered. Frustration and criticism are common on both sides, and an effective collaborative relationship has not been established. Repeated efforts to engage families in treatment can also consume significant service resources. At one point, the Islington Child Mental Health Service estimated that 80% of its resources were being used to support 20% of referred families. While some children and families clearly have more severe needs and require intensive help, this alone did not explain the high level of resources allocated to this group. A significant proportion of time was being spent offering repeat treatments to families who did not actually want the type of help provided. A different approach was needed—one that focused more on the helping process itself rather than repeatedly offering treatment that was not engaged with.

Rather than describing the full details of Risk Support here, which can be found elsewhere,[3] it is important to emphasise that it aligns fully with the six principles set out in this book. Risk Support requires fewer resources than usual treatment. Instead of offering direct interventions, mental health professionals take on a supportive role within the wider system, forming relationships with social workers, teachers or family members so that they can provide advice and support, without the delay of going through a referral process, when needed. Rather than trying to engage families in treatment that they do not want, professionals become part of the helping system by supporting those who already have a working relationship with the family. For this to be effective, practitioners need support from their managers to classify cases under Risk Support and to include this approach within their caseloads. Services also need to recognise that Risk Support does not have the same level of risk monitoring as treatment. Managers must be willing to take responsibility for practitioners contributing to cases where they are not the sole professionals responsible for managing risk. This requires cohesive, supportive teams. The alternative to this approach is that services close cases because they cannot tolerate the risks involved. This may reduce risk for the service, but it does not reduce risk for the child. In many cases, it leaves them less safe, rather than more so. Risk Support provides a way for mental health professionals to remain involved without offering unwanted treatment, ensuring that some level of guidance and support remains in place for those who need it.

Ella was Martin's psychiatrist and had been involved in treating his ADHD with medication. When it became clear that the medication was not providing noticeable benefits, either to Martin's carers or his school, the treatment was stopped. Martin had taken the medication without resistance but had not reported that it helped him. Under normal circumstances, his case would have been closed, but Ella recognised that Martin had ongoing needs and was likely to be referred back to the mental health team in the future. Instead of discharging him, she continued to be involved using the framework of Risk Support. A clinical psychologist in the Looked After Children (LAC) multi-agency team could have taken over Martin's mental health care, but Ella and the team agreed that she would continue instead. This prioritised the relationships Martin had already built, rather than following standard procedures that could have transferred him to a professional he did not know. His disruptive and angry behaviour remained a significant concern, and at times Sandra felt that his placement was at risk of breaking down. Ella agreed that Martin's social worker, Matt, could contact her for psychiatric advice without making a formal referral. Every couple of months, Matt and Sandra would consult her about Martin's mental state and his relationship with Sandra. Ella classified this case as Risk Support and had a small number of children on her caseload under this model. Her approach was explicitly supported by her service manager, and this activity was included in routine reports to the local commissioner.

In summary, Risk Support allows mental health services to contribute to the helping system around a child or young person without requiring formal treatment. This approach enables professionals to support families, schools and other key adults in a child's life, helping them manage vulnerabilities more effectively. The ability to access mental health advice when needed can be highly containing for those involved in a child's care. But the value of Risk Support is not just procedural—it strengthens relationships and builds trust among professionals, carers and families. Trust is a crucial factor in making a helping system function well. Risk Support provides a way for practitioners to adapt their involvement according to the views and experiences of the child and their family, rather than imposing a one-size-fits-all treatment approach.

Ending Treatment in a Helping System

One of the greatest challenges in treatment work is knowing when to stop.[4] Even when treatment is effective, it rarely leads to complete recovery, and difficulties often persist, though in a less severe form. Additionally, a significant proportion of children show only limited improvement despite receiving evidence-based treatment. These factors make it difficult to determine when a treatment should come to an end. This dilemma is further complicated by the strong attachment practitioners develop with the children and families they support. This attachment is a crucial element of all forms of help—it fuels the therapeutic relationship and underpins the deep commitment that professionals have towards the families they work with. However, this same attachment comes at a cost as it makes ending treatment particularly difficult for practitioners.

The process of ending treatment can be understood differently when viewed as part of an ongoing helping system rather than the sole source of help. In this approach, a key goal of treatment is to ensure that support continues beyond professional intervention. Two examples illustrate this well. In parent-led CBT for child anxiety, treatment involves teaching parents how to help their child overcome fears. By the end of the intervention, the child may still struggle with anxiety, but the parents have acquired the tools to continue supporting them in managing fearful situations. In this way, the treatment strengthens the child's natural helping system, ensuring that progress can continue. The conclusion of the parent training sessions is clearly not the end of the helping process. The second example comes from Interpersonal Psychotherapy for depression, which is structured as a fixed-length treatment of 16 sessions. During the treatment, the young person is encouraged to create a *backup team*—a network of peers and adults who commit to providing ongoing support after the treatment ends. This might include specific, agreed actions such as calling the young person back, meeting up or going to the gym together.

Both examples highlight the importance of actively creating a helping system as part of the therapeutic process. In this context, the beginning and ending of treatment is not a rigid transition between *help* and *no help*, but rather a shift in the way support is provided. Different phases of care require different approaches. Hospital admissions may be necessary during periods of acute suicidality, but the key task is ensuring that meaningful support continues when the young person returns to their community. What matters is that the team shares a long-term perspective, fully supported by its leadership and management. Professionals need to see their role as facilitating the development of an ongoing helping system, ensuring that collaboration between family and professionals continues beyond the period of active treatment.

In specialist mental health teams, the language around ending treatment has often been harsh and institutional, with terms such as '*closing the case*' or '*discharging the case*'. This language reflects a rigid, dichotomous framework—either a case is *open* or *closed*, either a professional is involved or not. This has been influenced by medical practice, where doctors need clear boundaries of responsibility, and by psychotherapy, which places great emphasis on the process of *ending* therapy, working through feelings of closure. However, this *all or nothing* approach does not always fit with the way helping systems function more broadly. In non-professional support systems, people often continue to express interest and check in on each other, even after a crisis has passed. Attachment processes work both ways, and sometimes professionals find it difficult to step back, just as young people and families may struggle with the transition. A more graded approach to withdrawal from a helping system is often avoided due to time pressures and resource limitations. However, experience shows that maintaining *light touch* contact after intensive intervention can be highly valuable in preventing relapse. Parents often express this in comments such as, "*I was thinking of going back to the GP for a referral, but being able to talk this through has helped me see that we are still on track—just going through a rough patch.*" A gradual reduction in involvement can contribute to safer and more sustainable practice for professionals while maintaining a sense of security for families.

Jacqui had developed a strong attachment to Monica, her therapist, and was anxious about how she was going to manage after the sessions ended. From the start, she had been aware that therapy would last for 16 sessions, but she had not thought much about this early on. As the final sessions approached, she expressed growing anxiety to Monica about this. Monica suggested that for the last couple of sessions, they include her mother in part of the session to discuss how the family could support Jacqui after therapy ended. This followed a *relapse prevention* framework, aiming to ensure that Jacqui had a plan in place if she began feeling depressed again. The process was about restoring the family's role as Jacqui's primary support system and ensuring a collaborative approach to her needs. Therapy had strengthened her relationship with her mother, and they agreed to schedule a weekly check-in to talk about how Jacqui was feeling and what might help her manage any challenges that came up. Monica also offered a six-month follow-up appointment to see how things were going for her. This structured but flexible plan helped Jacqui feel more prepared for the transition.

In summary, inviting the contribution of parents, adapting practice to the needs of children and families and deciding when or how to reduce or end the level of help for an individual child or young person takes place in the context of teams. Teams provide both the crucial support and supervision that practitioners need if such adaptability and flexibility can be nurtured and sustained. Although help for many children and families may often follow agreed protocols of good practice, all practitioners will be exposed to substantial emotional challenges in their therapeutic decision-making. Team processes are crucial to enable practitioners to navigate these decisions with sensitivity and maintain a sense of agency in their work. These themes will be explored further in the next sections, which highlight the role of teams in providing effective and sustainable mental health support.

Promoting Safety

Children need to feel safe, but this also applies to professionals. Professionals who play a key role in enabling helping systems around young people need working conditions that support their roles in a sustainable way. As described earlier, when young people were asked what they wanted from professional services, the key themes were *kindness, being listened to* and staff *sticking around*. The latter will only happen if staff feel well supported and work in conditions that acknowledge the challenges of their roles. The goal is not to create perfect safety for staff—this would be both unrealistic and unhelpful as professionals need to be open to challenges about their work. However, they also need to feel that their organisation recognises the nature of their work, understands the pressures they face and creates a working culture that provides enough safety for them to do their jobs well. The following sections outline key conditions that help promote safety in teams.

Recognising Practitioner Anxiety

Working with parents, children and young people is highly rewarding for professional staff, but these rewards can be easily lost if the challenges of the work are not fully acknowledged. Because children are vulnerable and dependent, the work frequently evokes anxiety because of the responsibility to manage risks and often face difficulties in finding ways to be helpful when solutions are not clear. Even for the most experienced and skilled practitioners, it is common to feel *useless or lost* when trying to establish a stable helping system around a child. Unfortunately, anxiety in professions is often perceived negatively, closely associated in many people's minds with a sense of incompetence. This association is profoundly unhelpful and, in practice, can increase rather than reduce risks. If a young person expresses suicidal thoughts, it is entirely natural for a professional to feel anxious, no matter how well the safety plan is structured or how robust the helping system appears to be. However, in many teams, anxiety is implicitly seen as the opposite of professional mastery. What is needed is a team culture where anxiety is recognised, discussed openly and managed constructively. This starts with explicit shared non-judgemental recognition of the emotional demands of the work within the team itself.

Martin's social worker, Matt did not feel good about his relationship with Martin and with Martin's foster carer. Due to work pressures, he only saw Martin about once a month, and their meetings felt superficial and disengaged. Matt would ask questions about different aspects of Martin's life, and Martin would respond with short, somewhat dismissive answers. Recently, Matt had worked with another young person who had made a complaint about him to his manager. Matt believed the complaint was unfair, but he did not feel well supported in how it was handled. As a result, his trust in his supervisor was reduced. In supervision, he did not share how he felt about his work with Martin, instead focusing only on decision-making, particularly long-term planning. He kept his anxiety to himself. This understandable response reduced trust and communication, increasing the risk that difficulties would remain unshared in the helping process. What was needed was a positive approach to managing anxiety—one that fosters a help-seeking culture within the team. When practitioners feel safe to discuss their concerns without fear of judgment, they are more likely to seek support, reducing the risks associated with working in isolation.

Creating a Help-Seeking Culture in a Team

Safety is strengthened when teams foster a culture where help-seeking is encouraged and supported[5] Alongside recognising professional anxiety, there needs to be an environment where practitioners feel safe to seek help from colleagues without fear of judgement. Help-seeking can leave a person feeling vulnerable, exposed and potentially ashamed, particularly in professional roles where competence is highly valued. These challenges can be intensified by external pressures on services and by inequalities within a team, such as differences in salary, power or status. Creating a team culture of help-seeking may seem straightforward in a service dedicated to providing help to others, but in reality, it is not. For help-seeking to happen, practitioners must recognise when they need support, feel able to express that need, have access to the right kind of help and be willing to make use of it. These are the same processes promoted within families, yet they do not automatically emerge in professional teams. A culture of help-seeking does not arise simply because team relationships are positive; it requires *explicit leadership and commitment* to embed it into everyday practice.

Brigitte and Simone had been referred to the Early Help team due to Simone's difficulties settling into primary school. The family was allocated to Sarah, a family support worker who was training in family therapy to develop her therapeutic skills further. She was highly motivated and enjoyed her work. The team consisted of six staff, led by Harry, a qualified social worker who had worked in the area for many years. He was committed to supporting his team and had established a weekly problem-solving meeting where staff could bring families who they were struggling to help. Harry encouraged his team to discuss both the *difficulties* of their work and *how they felt about it*, believing this was essential for maintaining team morale. Sarah was struggling with Brigitte and Patrick, who she experienced as inflexible in their approach to supporting Simone attend school. She found it hard to admit this to herself but was becoming frustrated with them. Discussing the case with her team helped her recognise this frustration, which in turn helped her think more clearly about her approach.

Through these discussions, Sarah developed a plan to involve additional support from the mental health team. Initially, she had resisted this idea, fearing that it would be seen as a failure on her part. However, after raising it with the family, they responded positively. The psychologist's consultation altered the dynamics of the helping relationship, and progress began to take shape. Without the support of her team, Sarah might have continued to struggle with the case on her own rather than seeking the additional help that ultimately made a difference.

Reducing Staff Isolation

Practitioners can easily become isolated within teams, keeping concerns to themselves rather than sharing them with colleagues. This can happen at all levels of seniority, with those in leadership roles just as likely (or perhaps even more so) to experience isolation as those in less senior positions. While it is important for managers to have space to think outside the team setting, isolation easily interacts with anxiety to create a pattern of *increasing separateness*, making it harder for individuals to seek support.

A practitioner working with a young person recently felt embarrassed about a session. The young person had attended in a very different state than in previous sessions, and it took the practitioner some time to realise that, for the first time, he was not under the influence of cannabis. She felt foolish for not having recognised this earlier and questioned her competence in assessing his needs. Rather than bringing this to supervision, she kept it to herself, wanting to think it through before discussing it. However, her reluctance to share was not due to a lack of knowledge about the young person's drug use, but rather her own feelings of embarrassment and inadequacy. Isolation can also occur in leadership roles. A team leader was experiencing growing tension with a staff member and felt uncomfortable about how she was handling the situation. She worried that her actions might be interpreted as discriminatory and, rather than seeking guidance from her manager, she avoided discussing it altogether. She knew she had made some insensitive comments but did not want to draw attention to them.

The true test of a help-seeking culture is the degree to which it *supports staff through* their own *feelings of shame and uncertainty*. It is relatively easy to ask for help with challenges that feel manageable, but much harder to do so when one feels vulnerable or incompetent. A strong team culture ensures that professionals can *share their struggles without fear of judgement*, creating a space where trust allows for difficult conversations. Without this, risks can escalate even in teams that generally function well. Promoting open communication and support within teams is crucial in ensuring that both professionals and the children they support receive the best possible help.

Providing Effective Supervision and Reflective Practice

Regular practice supervision is essential for safe and effective professional work, offering a space where practitioners can share anxieties and challenges about the young people they are trying to help.[6] Supervision allows a practitioner to express their own understanding while also gaining an external perspective—one that is not imposed in an authoritarian way but enables the practitioner to see their work from a different angle. This reflective approach is central to effective practice. While reflective practice is generally beneficial, what is helpful for one practitioner may not be for another. To ensure supervision is useful, it is important to regularly check with practitioners about which aspects they find most helpful. Curiosity about what works in supervision is just as important as curiosity in working with children and young people.

An example of this took place in the work with Abdul. Rachel, his psychologist, was highly creative in sessions, and Abdul responded well to practising emotional regulation strategies. However, these skills were not transferring to the school environment as much as hoped. After eight planned therapy sessions, Rachel wanted to continue working with Abdul to address this issue. She had built a strong relationship with both Abdul and his mother, Aisha, and felt invested in supporting him further. But Rachel's supervisor was uncertain about the benefits of extending therapy. She noted that Abdul had developed some capacity to recognise and express feelings and had had a positive experience attending sessions. However, she also felt that Abdul and Aisha needed time to practise these skills outside of the therapy setting. Rachel reflected on her desire to continue helping and recognised that she needed to step back and allow the wider helping system around Abdul to take on a more active role. Trusting her supervisor's perspective, she agreed to pause the work, with a six-month follow-up to check on Abdul's progress.

This example highlights the value of an external perspective in therapeutic work. It is easy for practitioners, having built a relationship with a child, to want to continue treatment. While this can sometimes be beneficial, it is important to reflect on whether extending therapy is truly necessary. Fixed-length treatments were partly introduced to manage this issue, but a more flexible system—one that allows for professional discretion about the length of help and retains some form of light contact after regular sessions—can often be more effective.

Informed Leadership

Organisational safety relies on informed and competent leadership. Many leadership styles exist, but no single model works for all teams and situations.[7] Every team has its own implicit and explicit power structures, but if the goal is to create a culture of help-seeking, this must also apply to those in leadership roles. The ability of leaders to seek help from their teams plays a crucial role in shaping this culture. This is not a rejection of authority or responsibility but a recognition that child mental health work is complex and balanced, authoritative decision-making often benefits from more than one perspective. Leaders need to enable a team to make decisions and then hold them to task to ensure those decisions are followed through and supported. One of their key roles is to understand the importance of helping systems, rather than simply focusing on providing services. The risk is that organisational leaders become entirely focused on the needs of their own service, rather than the needs of the wider helping system of support around children and families. These pressures are difficult to avoid and are a constant challenge for managers and leaders. When faced with a choice between the needs of the broader helping system and the security of their own team's posts, it is nearly impossible to not place the needs of the service before all else.

Summary

Practitioners need to work in teams that promote safety, acknowledge the emotional demands of the work, foster a help-seeking culture and have attuned leadership to support them. These factors are strikingly similar to what children need from their families. Psychological and relational aspects of staff safety are crucial, but so are organisational factors such as stable working conditions and the avoidance of continuous service reorganisation or other unhelpful structural contexts. But it is also important that a team is open to challenge the assumptions that practitioners may have about their work. There needs to be a balance between creating a safe environment for staff and allowing space for different perspectives on what effective help looks like. This challenge can be addressed through increasing the involvement of parents and young people in shaping services and using outcome monitoring to assess what works best for the children the team is designed to support.

Taking an Active Part

Parent and Young People's Participation

Having a sense of agency—being able to take an active role in addressing problems—is a critical aspect of an effective helping system. Just as children and young people benefit from a sense of agency in their own support, teams function better when their members feel that they can actively contribute to the challenges that arise in their complex work. This requires skilled and collaborative leadership, as discussed in the previous section. Here, the focus is on how young people and parents or carers can take an active role in shaping the work of teams, beyond their role in individual helping systems.

Much of this falls under the category of service participation, which remains inconsistent across the UK. Some teams have embedded this into their way of working, while others struggle to prioritise it amid competing demands. However, without meaningful involvement from parents and young people, professionals risk making decisions in isolation, without fully understanding the needs and perspectives of those they serve.

An effective helping system relies on a balanced contribution from both professionals and families. When parents or carers are absent from decision-making at the team level, it becomes harder to achieve genuine collaboration. Teams benefit from having access to the advice and insights of parents and young people, ensuring that services remain responsive to their needs. This can be structured in various ways, such as through a Participation Officer, a young people's support worker, a Parent Advisor role or young people's panels. While the structures may vary, the key issue is the purpose these roles serve.

Professionals need input from parents and young people on many complex issues related to how services collaborate with families. In one service, for example, young people fed back that they expected to be seen alone during their initial contact with the service. This was not the standard practice, and the team was unsure whether to change it. Consulting both parents and young people gave the team greater confidence in their decision to introduce this change. Staff felt that adapting their approach based on direct feedback placed the decision on firmer ground.

Many similar issues arise in team and family communication, such as how appointments are scheduled, whether text reminders are useful, access to case files and how confidentiality is managed within a team. Addressing these organisational and communication issues can be an effective first step in improving parent and young people's involvement. However, the role of parent and young person participation goes beyond these practical improvements. A service once consulted parents and young people about what support would be most helpful while they were waiting for treatment. They asked whether psychoeducational materials about their child's difficulties would be useful or whether this might be confusing if the eventual focus of the work turned out to be different. Involving parents and young people in these kinds of discussions can help avoid frustration and unmet expectations.

Parents and carers can also contribute to shaping how services deliver treatment. At the Anna Freud Centre, a service working with looked-after children established an advisory steering group that included foster carers and care-experienced young people. The service produced reports for court on the needs of the children they assessed, and these reports were reviewed by the steering group. The aim was not to challenge the team's conclusions but to consider how the reports might be experienced by young people and carers. Over time, this group made multiple suggestions that improved the clarity, respectfulness and inclusivity of the reports that the team produced. In another example, parents were included as advisors in the Safeguarding Oversight Group at the Anna Freud Centre. In discussions about safeguarding decisions that had caused distress to parents, the perspectives of parent representatives were included. This provided an opportunity for professionals to hear, not the perspective of the family involved, but the perspective of another parent or carer. This role required parents to undergo training as to how to participate in such a group as there were important matters of confidentiality that needed to be considered with this. The work was not to review specific cases but to reflect on what could be learned for future practice. This type of collaboration is not always easy. There was the potential for the parent advisors to identify too closely with the perspective of parents in specific cases, just as professionals may become defensive about their decisions. The purpose of these groups is not to assign blame but to improve future practice. A useful comparison is often made with the airline industry, where the key question is not "*Who was responsible?*"—which is common in health and social care—but "*How can we try to avoid this happening again?*" This shift in perspective is crucial for making services more effective and responsive to the needs of the children and families they support.

These practical benefits of improved advice are important, but just as valuable is the creation of meaningful connections between professional and non-professional help. This is central to the whole idea of helping systems and extended networks of support. When services are built in collaboration with parents and young people, rather than operating separately from them, they create a rationale for practice that is more grounded and defensible. This protects practitioners from the kinds of relationship difficulties that arise in services that are too detached from those they serve. When practitioners can say that their approach has been shaped through discussion with parents, young people (and possibly representatives of other agencies as well) this provides a solid foundation for practice.

There will inevitably be times when parents and professionals hold very different views about key issues related to helping children and young people. Differences may arise around children's rights and their ability to make independent decisions from those of their parents. There may be differences as to what information should be shared with other agencies such as the police or social care. What is important is that these challenges to team practices take place in structured forums rather than being dealt with in an ad hoc manner around individual cases. Teams will not always reach full agreement on the sensitive and complex issues they encounter, and having an external reference point for some of these decisions allows for collective decision-making and reduces isolation for the service. What needs to be avoided is team insularity and to ensure that services develop and value relationships with all stakeholders in the helping system around children and young people with mental health needs.

Children's Rights in Teams

It is not useful to treat the rights of children as entirely separate from the rights of parents. In any team, there will always be some degree of tension between the two, and the task is to find a balance that is supported by some level of consensus in the wider community. Different countries and cultures take varying approaches to this balance. As described in Chapter 8, Denmark has introduced the Child Law, which legally prioritises children's rights over parental rights. Professionals working with children and young people should always start with the question, *what does the child think about this matter?* If a team is discussing how best to support a young person with an eating disorder or a child whose parent has long-standing, severe substance misuse problems, the discussion should always begin with ensuring that the child's perspective is known and considered.

Anyone who has worked in the UK's child welfare or mental health system—no matter how excellent the service—will recognise the enormous challenge that this seemingly simple proposal presents, both for professionals and for families. However, there is now an opportunity to learn from countries like Denmark, where legal frameworks are evolving to enhance children's rights in ways that directly impact the helping systems around them. Teams should consider working with parents and young people to explore how they might implement a similar principle. A simple but powerful application of children's rights would be for every meeting about a child or young person to begin with the question: *what is known about the child or young person's view on the matter being discussed?* Embedding this practice would be a practical step towards ensuring that children's rights are central to decision-making about their care.

Examples of Participation in Practice

In the UK, work on developing children's rights has been greatly influenced by Laura Lundy's model, as described in Chapter 8. This framework emphasises four key components: *voice*, ensuring children have the opportunity to express their views; *space*, providing an environment where they can form their opinions; *audience*, ensuring they are listened to; and *influence*, meaning their views are acted upon or they are given clear reasons if this is not possible. An excellent example of child participation is the Children's Active Involvement Service (CAIS) in Islington, which enables young people with experience of the care system to develop their views and have an audience for them. One of the key areas young people identified was their desire to have a role in selecting staff for the teams that provided them with support. Young people were trained to take part in the recruitment process, survey the views of other young people and carry out inspections of social care services. Similarly, young people and parents were involved in recruiting staff for mental health teams. While they did not have sole decision-making power, their input was influential. In cases where the panel was undecided about a candidate, the perspectives of young people's views on the chosen candidate could be decisive. Using a helping role through participation also had benefits for young people themselves. Many reported a positive impact on their self-esteem and sense of personal value through engaging in these processes. Surveys conducted as part of these participation efforts also led to changes in practice. As previously described, young people fed back that they expected to have the opportunity to be seen alone during their first contact with a mental health service. This was not routinely the case, and the service was unsure whether it should be. Consulting with young people and parents gave greater confidence in the decision to support this as a standard practice. From the young people's perspective, having a free voice at some stage in the engagement process was essential, aligning with developments in Denmark that prioritise children's rights.

For this kind of work to be embedded into services, dedicated support is needed. In this example, participation was facilitated by a support worker, which ensured young people could engage meaningfully. It is proposed that such a role should be a core requirement in all services, providing young people with opportunities to gain a sense of agency in addressing their own needs and those of their peers. However, routine involvement of young people and parents in the management of specialist mental health services remains inconsistent across the UK. One example of good practice took place in an inpatient unit, where young people attended part of the unit's monthly leadership meeting. Before the meeting, they were supported to draw up issues they wanted to raise. These were often immediate, concrete concerns that affected their stay, such as the quality of food at weekends or broken equipment. However, they also raised issues related to their safety. For instance, they highlighted that they did not feel safe on weekends when there were no permanent staff on duty. In response, the unit made greater efforts to ensure permanent staff were present on every weekend shift. The impact of this involvement went beyond the specific issues raised. The leadership team was held accountable for following up on these concerns, ensuring they were addressed. When young people saw that changes were made as a result of their input, they felt valued and listened to. However, when action was not taken, they often generalised this experience to a broader belief that "*staff don't really care.*" In this way, participation was not just about making improvements but also served as a test of how well the helping system actually worked from the young people's perspective.

While none of the six young people in this book directly participated in service development, participation work still influenced how help was organised and delivered. In Abdul's borough, for example, an active parent group advocated for the needs of children with neurodiverse conditions. Their main focus was supporting parents in navigating the education system to ensure their children received appropriate support. However, they also campaigned for children with ASD to have equal access to mental health services. Through effective lobbying of local mental health service leaders, they secured the expansion of a specialist ASD team that worked closely with education around these needs. This resulted in the availability of the type of specialist psychological therapy that Abdul received—help that may not have been accessible in all areas due to the high demand on mental health services.

A second example has already been described. Following a survey of young people using a mental health service, a decision was made that all secondary school-aged children should have the opportunity to be seen alone during their first appointment. When Jacqui was offered this option, she expressed a preference to stay with her mother for the whole appointment. Adapting services in response to young people's views does not override the importance of respecting an individual child's wishes but ensures that all children have the opportunity to participate in a way that feels right for them.

The Role of Parent Advisors

The role of parent advisors in specialist mental health services is essential to ensuring that all key participants in the helping system around a child are represented in the life and work of the team. However, in practice, these roles often remain marginal to leadership and service planning functions. Despite the vital role that parents and carers play in supporting young people with mental health needs, their influence in decision-making processes is frequently limited or entirely absent. Professional expertise dominates the structures and priorities of services, but this does not have to be the case.

As previously discussed, the safeguarding leadership group at Anna Freud included parents in its oversight team, where they were supported to provide feedback on safeguarding practices within the service. Parents and carers should not be confined to advisory roles at the periphery but should be part of leadership groups in services, developing expertise in the complex challenges that shape priorities and resource allocation. While significant investment is made in developing professionals' leadership and management skills, the same investment in the role of parents in services remains unacceptably low.

A greater integration of family, community and professional perspectives would not only strengthen helping systems but also harness the potential of parents in providing direct support to other parents. Parent-led support groups—such as those for parents of children with eating disorders—can be a vital source of shared understanding, reducing isolation and offering lived-experience guidance that professionals alone cannot provide. Parents can also be trained to take on active helping roles within services. One example is the *Empowering Parents, Empowering Communities (EPEC)* programme,[8] where parents who have benefited from participating in parent support groups are then trained to facilitate similar groups for others. Providing resources and expectations for parents to contribute to service delivery helps prevent an unhelpful division between professional and non-professional support. Too often, the experiences, struggles and resilience of parents remain unheard in the design and implementation of services.

Summary

For teams to achieve a balanced collaboration with parents and young people, they need to actively involve them in how services are designed and delivered. This participation can take many forms, including parent advisors, young people's participation groups and other structured feedback processes. What matters most is that teams do not rely on assumptions about what parents and young people think or feel but instead create clear channels for asking, listening and adapting practice in response to their insights. This shift requires greater power-sharing between professionals and families. The next chapter will explore this further, focusing on the role of parents and young people in the strategic design and leadership of services and wider systems of help.

Measuring

Using Measures in Teams

As part of her sessions with her therapist, Jacqui completed a questionnaire about herself every couple of weeks. It asked her to rate her feelings of low mood, her anxieties and her relationships with others. She had become accustomed to this as part of the way that her therapist worked. Having completed it, her therapist would go through her answers with her, showing genuine interest in how she described her experiences since her last session. Rather than focusing solely on what was on her mind that day, the questionnaire helped Jacqui reflect on things she might not have otherwise considered. It helped her recall both positive and negative experiences, rather than simply following her tendency to focus on the negative. For example, Jacqui's sleep pattern had improved. She was sleeping better, and this was no longer something she thought about. Yet, when she first came for help, her sleep had been very poor. This improvement could have been overlooked. After each session, the therapist manually entered the questionnaire results into the outcome monitoring system. This was annoying and time-consuming, and it was easy to fall behind, leading to a backlog of unentered data. However, when kept up to date, the system summarised the results and provided graphs showing changes over time. The therapist could quickly see whether Jacqui was improving or not. Sometimes, she showed these graphs to Jacqui, inviting her to reflect on them. Such measures can serve as a prompt for therapists—if the scores are not changing, they may need to consider a different approach. They also provide young people with tangible feedback on their progress. For Jacqui, seeing the questionnaire results reinforced the changes she was beginning to feel in herself.

Despite research suggesting that young people generally have a positive attitude towards using such questionnaires, the widespread adoption of routine outcome monitoring in teams over the past 20 years has been disappointingly sketchy. Negative practitioners' attitudes about the use of questionnaires as being crude tools that fail to capture the complexity of mental health and a general reluctance towards using structured forms have played their part in this.[9] Also, and perhaps very significantly, manual entry of questionnaire results into database systems has been time-consuming and inefficient, a task often passed to assistant practitioners, depending on the service's budget and staffing capacity. In a world where AI and digital technologies are transforming data management, manually entering questionnaire responses feels outdated compared to the seamless automation of modern internet and social media platforms. For a team to use measures effectively, there needs to be clear leadership about their value, organisational processes that make them easy to use and a recognition that tracking progress can prevent the continuation of ineffective interventions.

At Anna Freud, an outcome software system called POD (Person Owned Database) has been developed, enabling young people to enter questionnaire responses directly from their phones or laptops.[10] The data is automatically scored and mapped onto graphs, tracking changes over time. Some NHS Trusts are now adopting similar systems, which allow for more comprehensive outcome monitoring across services. These tools provide easily accessible feedback to children, young people and parents, helping them reflect on their progress in relation to their own experiences and life events. Such systems reduce the practical burden on both practitioners and young people. The information can also be shared with others in the young person's helping system, ensuring that progress is recognised beyond the clinical setting.

Outcome monitoring technologies like this have the potential to transform how services track effectiveness, making measurement a more meaningful and integrated part of care rather than an administrative burden.

Using Simple Methods for Outcome Monitoring

Outcome monitoring does not always require multi-item questionnaires. In many cases, a simple record of key events in a young person's life or a basic rating of general well-being can provide valuable insight. As described with Martin, his foster carer and teacher kept a simple diary noting when he had got through the day okay and when he had got into difficulties with his teacher or other pupils. Over time, these records showed that the number of positive days increased steadily although incidents where Martin became angry and upset continued and remained the main preoccupation for Sandra and his teacher. In the earlier phase of his support, this tracking helped inform a key decision about Martin's treatment. It became clear that the medication prescribed for his attentional difficulties was not making a significant difference, so it was discontinued. The decision was based on a pattern of recorded observations rather than relying solely on general impressions or memory. Such diary-keeping requires persistence and can easily lose momentum unless professionals demonstrate interest and value the information being collected. Martin's psychiatrist, Ella, provided Sandra with a simple, tailored spreadsheet that allowed her to log key observations each day. At the end of each month, Sandra sent it to Ella. This straightforward system improved clinical decision-making but relied on professional curiosity and engagement for it to be effective. For outcome monitoring to be meaningful, it needs active support from managers to ensure that practical systems are in place and that it is realistic within busy work schedules. Team discussions about young people's progress should incorporate this information, using it alongside professional judgment rather than treating it as the only measure of success. When balanced effectively, it becomes a vital tool for understanding whether the work is making a difference.

The Challenge of Considering Uncomfortable Outcomes

Routine outcome monitoring offers the opportunity for a team to find out about which young people are benefiting from their work and, more uncomfortably, which are not. It requires a high level of maturity and a safe team culture to engage with this process constructively. One team, for example, used outcome monitoring to track its impact on family relationships and the risk of family breakdown. The data showed that their work had improved family relationships and reduced placement breakdowns, which was validating for the team and reinforced confidence in their approach. However, the same data revealed that their interventions were far less effective in helping young people to attend school regularly. Some of the young people who had been out of school for more than a year did not successfully return to school. The team was invited to reflect on these findings, and the discussion was tense and difficult. It was hard for the team not to feel criticised and blamed for these outcomes. One of the authors, who led the meeting, moved too quickly to discussing alternative ways of supporting a return to work before validating the work the team had done. What was needed was an opportunity for the team to acknowledge the challenges they faced, generate their own ideas about why school attendance remained a problem and explore how they could learn from this feedback rather than feeling that they were '*being learnt at*'.

Summary

The primary value of outcome monitoring is in helping children, young people and families make sense of whether changes are happening as a result of the support they are receiving. It helps them understand their own progress—or lack of progress—within the helping process. For this to work, outcome monitoring needs to be supported both by *team systems*, ensuring that recording measures are simple and practical, and by *team culture*, where measures are seen as a useful way of understanding the help being offered rather than as an administrative burden. Crucially, outcome monitoring also reveals that *not all young people seen by a service improve*. This reality can be difficult to confront, but it provides an opportunity for sensitive discussions about who benefits most from the approaches used and how services might adapt to better meet the needs of those whose lives continue to be burdened by the difficulties that they first came with.

Outcome monitoring is often framed as a way to *prove that a team works*, but its real purpose is to provide insight. It will show that some children improve significantly while others benefit less, and the role of the team is to learn from this variation and adapt its approach accordingly. While external research and academic knowledge can offer valuable guidance, outcome monitoring provides a *real-time, service-specific baseline of effectiveness*. For teams to reflect on this variability requires strong leadership, but the benefits of having a clear picture of how well a service is working—grounded in the actual experiences of children and families—are invaluable.

It Takes a Village: Integrative Practice

Inclusive Help

Integrative practice means that different teams work together in a collaborative way, sharing an understanding of a young person's difficulties and how they would like to be helped. While services play a crucial role in a child's helping system, they are not the whole of it. They need to connect with the child's family, school and local community, as these provide much of the ongoing support for the child or young person.

Except for Daniel, who remained apart from helping services, all the young people in this book had helping systems that involved some degree of connected help between agencies to support their needs. The degree of collaboration and integration varied, and in some cases, relationships between agencies were stronger than in others. For Jacqui, the connection between her school and the mental health team was supported by written communication but also by Chisomo communicating with the school about Jacqui's therapy. Graham, her Head of Year, was initially sceptical about the idea that Jacqui's difficulties were due to depression but was open to supporting a plan that aimed for her to return to full-time education while catching up on missed work. The school agreed that she could leave early to attend weekly therapy appointments and supported her in making a structured plan to complete her schoolwork. Graham considered that Jacqui was an able student and wanted to support her to get back on track with her education. As is often the case, Chisomo played an important role in enabling the agencies involved in supporting Jacqui to act in a relatively integrated way. The combined approach was pragmatic as there was not a fully shared understanding of Jacqui's difficulties—education framed the issue largely in terms of parental passivity, while health focused on her depression. However, despite these differences, both agencies ensured that practical coordination of help was in place. A similar pattern emerged with Abdul, where his mother played a central role in enabling the school and mental health team to provide coordinated but relatively separate support.

Inter-agency collaboration around Martin was more complex and, at the same time, more critical. His helping system involved social care, health and education professionals working together to support Sandra, his foster carer. Sandra had a strong and trusted relationship with Fatima, Martin's class teacher, whom she had known through fostering another child. She deeply valued their collaboration, particularly in navigating how best to respond to Martin's behaviour. She felt that Fatima truly understood what it was like for adults when Martin became angry and distressed, and she appreciated the time she took to compare notes and ensure consistency in how they supported him. Her relationship with Martin's social worker, however, was more strained. She felt that he was part of a group of professionals in Martin's village who *had lots of ideas about Martin but didn't really know him*. She had little trust in the value of his input. Her main concern was Martin's transition to secondary school and how he would cope with a less structured and supportive environment. She felt he needed a health and education support plan but worried that the professional system was not aligned on how best to support his ongoing vulnerabilities.

Sandra was also frustrated that Martin's positive experiences at the urban farm were often overlooked by professionals, even though this was a crucial part of his life. From her perspective, the professionals in Martin's helping system did not fully appreciate the significance of his relationships outside formal services and their role in his sense of stability and well-being. This reflected a broader challenge in integrative practice—ensuring that the helping system values and incorporates all meaningful sources of support, not just those that fit within conventional service structures.

These narratives illustrate the reality of living helping systems—where communication is often imperfect, perspectives on a young person's needs may differ and meeting all aspects of their multiple needs can be a struggle. Yet, despite these challenges, collaboration and a degree of trust in each other's contributions were present. What is being proposed here is not an additional task for mental health teams but a strengthening of the way they support others in the helping systems around the young people they work with. This should be seen as a core part of their role, not something extra. For this to happen in a practical way, teams need to recognise the value that this type of inclusive help brings to their work. Within teams, this includes managers and practitioners; beyond the team (as discussed in Chapter 13), it involves commissioners and collaborating agencies. Awareness of the role of others in the helping system should begin with curiosity—seeking to understand who is involved, including them in the process from the outset and working collaboratively as the helping relationship evolves. Managers and leaders need to support this approach through team protocols and practice frameworks.

For many teams and practitioners, this will not require much change as the collaboration with other agencies is something that they already value and invest in. But they often do it in ways that are not supported by the constraints of the organisation. Instead, they fit it in around the edges of their main tasks. Rather than prescribing fixed protocols, the aim is to offer a principle-led approach, allowing each team to develop its own way of embedding these ideas into their work. The framework should be solving local problems, not simply becoming an imposition from elsewhere, an external directive. If it is this, it will be successfully resisted.

Integrated Teams

Collaborative, integrated practice can be powerfully supported by the creation of integrated teams. These have become a key part of services across the UK, but for this section, we draw on examples that the authors were directly involved in setting up during the early 2000s. In Islington, a range of integrated practice projects placed mental health staff within other agencies. Rather than schools referring children and young people to external mental health services, practitioners were based directly within each primary and secondary school in the borough. This model has since become widely accepted, and mental health teams in schools are now a key element of central government policy. These teams typically include a mix of mental health professionals such as psychologists and psychotherapists, alongside Educational Mental Health Practitioners (EMHPs).

In Islington, the early work of embedding mental health services in schools was based on the principle that the priorities for the service should be set by the school's headteacher. This was not just about integrating resources but also integrating power, a factor that was hugely significant in the project's success. Although the mental health practitioners remained employed by the NHS, they were used differently in each school, depending on the headteacher's priorities. This approach followed a key principle of the helping process: listening to the perspectives of those seeking help.

Organisational barriers often prevent delegated responsibility for resources, which can cause significant frustration for the agencies involved. Integrated practice requires not just strong collaboration between different parts of the helping system but also a clear delegation of authority to one lead agency. This can be difficult to achieve, as it depends on trust between organisations. Without trust, integration is often undermined by competing priorities and struggles over control. Developing truly integrated teams requires a shift in how agencies work together, ensuring that collaboration is not just about co-locating professionals but also about creating shared priorities, decision-making and accountability. This can only succeed when professionals from different services genuinely work as part of a single system, rather than remaining separate entities operating under different management priorities for each agency about what a young person needs.

A similar model was developed for nurseries. Early contract negotiations between health and nursery managers were tense, with nursery heads wanting assurance that mental health practitioners' time in nurseries would be guaranteed each week and used according to their priorities. There was a sense that they felt at risk of being short changed in the relationship. Long discussions took place about whether the service would continue if staff went on maternity leave. Often, they wanted the practitioner to work directly with children or parents rather than providing consultation to staff. This need to control the resource was reduced as trust developed, and a more collaborative approach emerged. A telling example of this shift occurred years into the programme when a nursery head, in a call with the clinical director about the following year's contract, was informed that the same psychologist would continue providing input. Her response was simple: "*If we're having Sarah, then all is fine.*" The fact that the negotiation had moved from detailed discussions about precise time commitments to valuing the relationship with the practitioner reflected the trust that had developed between agencies. The trust was mediated not by project plans or clever strategies but by relationships. As for families, so for services.

Integrated practice was also strengthened through shared locations and joint control of professional resources. There were three areas where this was taken further. The first was the Adolescent Multi-Agency Support Service (AMASS), set up by the Director of Social Care.[11] This service was targeted at young people aged 11 to 16 who were at risk of entering the care system. It was a multi-agency, multi-disciplinary team comprising a social worker, a teacher, a clinical psychologist, a youth worker and an assistant psychologist. Managed within social care, the team integrated professionals from health and education. What made this model unusual was its approach to referrals. The team did not formally take over cases but worked alongside social workers who were already supporting young people at risk of entering care. Instead of transferring cases to a new service, AMASS provided additional help and support to the social worker who retained responsibility for the case. In collaboration with the social worker, the team provided more intensive support than would typically be possible. This included at least two home visits per week and highly structured, goal-based family support. The aim was to support 85% of young people to remain in their birth families, and this target was consistently met each year. The success of the project led to permanent funding after ten years. The model ensured that social work, psychological and educational expertise collaborated to support vulnerable young people without defaulting to onward referrals. Instead, it delivered complex, multi-agency work in an integrated and sustained way.

This principle was extended to another key area of social care practice—decisions about children entering care. Credit for this development must be given to the Director of Social Care at the time, who established a multi-agency panel to review all children being considered for entry into the care system. While social work expertise played the leading role in these decisions, representatives from education and health were also included to explore whether alternative interventions could be provided as an alternative to care. Beyond offering different perspectives, education and health representatives also had a vote in care decisions. This meant that decisions about a child entering care were not made by social care alone but were jointly supported by all three agencies. From a health perspective, this shift was significant—it transformed care planning from a decision made by *others* into one that was *collaborative*. In most cases, all three agencies agreed. However, on one occasion, education and health professionals believed that care was necessary, while the social care manager on the panel did not. In a remarkable example of integrated practice, the case was referred to the Director of Social Care, who supported the majority view of the panel. Statutory responsibility remained with social care who nevertheless invited other agencies to contribute to decision-making around the needs of these young people. Despite its successes this approach also demonstrated the fragility of integrated projects. It was heavily dependent on the personal support of the Director of Social Care, and when a new director took over, this innovation came to an end. The reality of children's services being divided across multiple agencies means that integrated projects often rely on *local champions* who drive them forward. When these champions leave, the projects they have led frequently lose momentum or disappear altogether. This challenge will be explored further in the next chapter, which focuses on integrated planning and commissioning of services.

Integration of support for children at risk of permanent exclusion from school was also developed through a multi-agency team that included health and social care staff, working together to help children return to mainstream education. This team was managed by an education manager who had the authority to direct the work of all staff within the team. As he noted at the time, "*It's not every day that an ex-woodwork teacher manages a Consultant Psychiatrist.*" The psychiatrist, subcontracted to the team for two days a week, fully embraced this unconventional professional structure, which was a large credit to her professional adaptability. The team worked with around 20 to 30 young people with multiple needs, using a service model that placed strong emphasis on family engagement. Creative methods were developed to build relationships with families, including free hairdressing sessions provided by a local salon for parents and staff. These informal interactions significantly reduced barriers between families and professionals, strengthening the helping system around the young people. However, after about two years, the project was closed—not because it was ineffective, but because it did not align closely enough with educational priorities. More attention was given to repairing family relationships, addressing psychological needs and ensuring attendance at the centre than to narrowly defined educational outcomes. Concerns arose that the approach would lead to an unfavourable Ofsted inspection, a high-risk issue for educational leadership. As a result, the decision was made to revert to traditional, single-agency provision with a stronger focus on academic progress.

There were also differences of opinion regarding how far to develop integrated practice. The Clinical Director proposed that the service take on greater responsibility for safeguarding children already on its caseload. Children often developed a degree of trust in their practitioners so that it was not uncommon for children and young people to disclose abuse over time. Following joint agency guidelines, these disclosures were immediately referred to social care. However, this frequently led to a rupture in the helping relationship, as families would often disengage once a referral was made. The helping system was weakened, and in many cases, children were less comfortable in talking with social workers that they did not know and social care investigations concluded that concerns did not meet the safeguarding threshold, leading to case closure. To address this issue, it was proposed that disclosures of abuse be investigated *within* the mental health team by an experienced social worker with child protection expertise. This worker would be jointly accountable to the Clinical Director and the Head of Safeguarding in social care. The aim was to prevent the immediate disruption that often followed a referral and instead allow for a more integrated approach to assessing risk. However, the Director of Social Care judged that this arrangement posed too great an organisational risk. His concern was that mental health teams, due to their therapeutic relationship with families, might become overly identified with them and fail to act decisively when change was necessary. As a result, the formal referral process remained in place. Examples of integrated service teams are now widespread across the UK. One of the most significant developments has been the introduction of centrally funded *Mental Health Support Teams in Schools*, a major step towards embedding mental health support in education. The concept of integrated care is no longer new, but true integration requires more than just professional collaboration—it also requires shared decision-making and delegated power and authority, and this is one of the greatest challenges in integrated care. Agencies responsible for specific aspects of a child's well-being—education, social care and health—have legal obligations that can make them wary of shared accountability. Education is responsible for ensuring children are educated, social care must ensure their safety and health services must provide medical care. Agencies under pressure from public scrutiny are understandably often reluctant to engage in integrated practices where their individual accountability becomes unclear.

As a result, many integrated teams remain temporary or experimental, even when they follow sound principles of care. They are particularly vulnerable when one of the agencies involved faces budget constraints or the risk of public criticism. Often, these teams are not a central priority for any one agency, making them more susceptible to being dismantled when circumstances change. The challenge of having specialist child professionals divided across three separate agencies—health, social care and education—remains a profound problem. This will be explored further in the next chapter, which focuses on integrated planning and commissioning. However, integrated teams provide an effective model for building strong helping systems around young people with mental health needs, even though they often face structural barriers that make their sustainability uncertain.

Mental Health Support Teams in Schools

The national rollout of Mental Health Support Teams (MHSTs) represents one of the most significant developments in the integration of child mental health and education services in England. First introduced in 2019, these teams are now operating in more than half of schools and colleges across the country, with the aim of supporting children and young people with mild to moderate mental health difficulties and promoting a whole-school approach to well-being. MHSTs are built around the role of EMHPs, a new workforce trained to deliver brief, evidence-based interventions for anxiety, low mood and behavioural difficulties. Working alongside more experienced clinicians and embedded within schools, EMHPs offer both direct work with pupils and consultation to staff. In this way, MHSTs strengthen not just individual outcomes but the school's wider capacity to promote mental health. Their work sits well with the principles of integrative practice—local, relational and responsive to the everyday environments in which young people live and learn.

The strategic development of MHSTs has also involved the introduction of Senior Mental Health Leads (SMHLs) in schools—a role designed to ensure there is someone with responsibility and training to coordinate the mental health approach of the school. SMHLs are not mental health professionals themselves, but they bring together staff, families and local services to create a coherent response to pupil well-being. Where MHSTs and SMHLs work together effectively, they help embed mental health into the daily life of the school—not as a separate activity but as part of how children are educated and supported. Early evaluation has shown that MHSTs can achieve meaningful change. Across thousands of cases, recovery rates have been recorded at 59% for anxiety and 49% for low mood—comparable to outcomes in adult NHS Talking Therapies. These teams now reach around 74,000 young people each month, and over 108,000 pupils received direct support during the 2023–2024 academic year. Their contribution extends beyond individual treatment. Staff report increased confidence in responding to pupil mental health, and 85% of schools involved report improved access to support. This reflects not just the impact of EMHPs, but also the wider systems change that occurs when mental health is treated as a shared responsibility across the school community.

Perhaps most important is the potential of MHSTs to offer timely intervention—before difficulties become entrenched in a young person's emotional development or family life. Many mental health problems first emerge during the school years. Schools are where patterns of avoidance, isolation and distress often become visible—long before a referral is made. When emotional needs are picked up early, there is greater scope to respond flexibly, support the family and prevent distress from escalating. MHSTs are not designed to replace specialist services but to act before specialist input is needed—to work upstream in a child's life, not just downstream once problems are severe. In this sense, their role is both preventative and developmental, aiming to support resilience in young people and those around them.

Schools, as the one universal service attended by most children, are a logical and vital place to intervene. They are also one of the few services where staff have day-to-day contact with children and young people over long periods. This makes them ideally placed to notice early changes in mood, behaviour or relationships. MHSTs, working closely with school staff, help translate these observations into structured support—whether through one-to-one interventions, small group work or staff guidance. In doing so, they strengthen the ability of the school to hold and respond to emotional distress, rather than immediately externalising it to other services. However, as with all integrated approaches, MHSTs operate within a system where needs often exceed capacity. There are persistent concerns about children whose difficulties fall between what MHSTs can address and what specialist CAMHS are able to take on. Workforce retention, funding stability and variable local implementation remain challenges. The promise of early intervention can only be realised if systems support sustained collaboration between schools, mental health teams and families. Nevertheless, MHSTs remain a compelling example of what can be achieved when support is located within the relationships and environments that matter most to young people. They are not a full solution, but they are a promising step towards a model of help that is local, preventative and relational qualities that are essential for any service working to support mental health in the early stages of life.

Changing Referral Practices: Supporting the Service Already Involved

Integrative practice can be strengthened by changing referral practices so that they support the team already working with the child and family, rather than shifting responsibility to another agency. Many referrals to specialist services—whether in mental health, social care or education—come from other teams within the same district or region. This is expected, given that many children and young people have multiple rather than single needs. For example, a child receiving social care support due to parent-child relationship difficulties may also struggle with anxiety or school attendance, leading to a referral for specialist mental health support alongside the help that they are providing themselves. This is responsible practice in trying to address all aspects of a child's needs and can work well if the family is open to working with multiple services at once. However, families are often reluctant to engage with a new service, particularly if they are concerned about the stigma of mental health support. Additionally, referrals sometimes happen because an agency has exhausted its allocated resources for a case but remains concerned about the child, leading them to seek involvement from another agency. These circumstances are common, but they often result in the family disengaging from the service they were referred to, while their original service withdraws. The helping system around the child shifts dramatically, leaving them to rely more on their family and school. A better approach is one that supports the existing helping system rather than dividing responsibilities between separate agencies.

The Thrive approach suggests an alternative way of handling referrals. When a team feels that a child's needs would be better met elsewhere, instead of writing a referral letter and transferring responsibility, the current practitioner and the new service should first discuss the child's needs and explore how they could collaborate. If both agree that further involvement would be beneficial, the next step should be a joint meeting with the parent and child to discuss what kind of help would be useful. A crucial part of this process is recognising the existing helping relationship between the practitioner and the family. In many cases, this relationship is an important resource in the helping system and should not be discarded without careful thought. However, there will be situations where the family is ready to move on to a different form of help, and this should also be considered. What should be avoided is the abrupt removal of a trusted professional from the family's support network without properly considering the impact on the child or parent.

To illustrate this, consider the case of Maddy, a social worker who contacted the specialist mental health team to refer a parent, Jasmine, for counselling. Jasmine's ten-year-old daughter, Ruby, had been sexually abused by her ex-partner. Over the past year, Maddy had worked intensively with Jasmine and Ruby to create safety for them and to help them cope with the impact of this abuse on Jasmine and Ruby. The ex-partner was no longer in contact and no longer posed a direct risk to the family. During this time, Maddy had become profoundly trusted by Jasmine. Through her support, the family had regained some level of stability. Ruby had settled into a creative support class in her new school and appeared to be doing well. She was not showing signs of trauma or anxious attachment to her mother, though there was still consideration about whether she needed additional specialist help. The helping system also included Jasmine's mother and the school, both of whom had played key roles in supporting the family.

Maddy's request for counselling for Jasmine was thoughtful and aligned with good professional practice. She saw it as a way to help Jasmine process her experiences and bring some closure to what she had been through. However, the referral raised an important question: should Jasmine start working with a completely new professional, or should counselling be incorporated into the support she was already receiving? Referring Jasmine to another service could undermine the stability she had regained, especially given the depth of trust she had developed with Maddy. This example highlights the importance of rethinking referral processes. Instead of automatically transferring care, services should consider how to work alongside existing support systems, ensuring that help is integrated rather than fragmented. When services collaborate in this way, they are more likely to sustain the helping relationships that have been built, rather than disrupting them through unnecessary transitions.

Jasmine, however, was reluctant to talk with someone new. She disliked discussing her family life outside of her immediate circle and, although she respected Maddy's suggestion, she was not keen on it. The mental health team considered whether she might prefer to talk with Maddy instead, but Maddy felt she lacked counselling experience and that this was outside what her department typically provided. She also found it frustrating that the conversation seemed to be moving towards mental health declining the referral. A compromise was proposed: with the approval of Maddy's manager, she would offer the sessions to Jasmine while being supervised by a mental health practitioner. Jasmine much preferred this idea, and the arrangement was put in place. Rather than being transferred to a new service and practitioner she did not know, Jasmine was able to receive support from the team she already trusted. Although Maddy was initially uncertain, she came to value the experience. Regular supervision helped her to gain new skills which she valued.

Would it have been better for Jasmine to see an experienced counsellor? For some parents, it might have been, but this depends largely on the trust involved in existing relationships and the individual preferences of the parent. These two factors—trust and choice—are often overlooked in the way services operate. While specialist expertise is valuable in theory, it may not be effective in practice as it may well not be taken up. Here lies one of the cornerstone arguments of this book: helping services must consider not only the professional expertise relevant to the problem but also the trusting relationships and preferences of the child, young person and parent or carer too.

This case demonstrates how a helping system that prioritises existing relationships can be more effective than a rigid focus on expertise alone. However, such arrangements can be difficult to establish, and team managers may resist these approaches due to the high pressures on their teams. This is understandable, but in this example, the arrangement did not increase the system's workload—it reduced it. By using an existing trusted relationship, Jasmine did not have to build rapport with a new professional, retell her story or decide whether she could trust someone unfamiliar.

Some might argue that she received a less expert service. Maddy was not a trained therapist or counsellor and tended to focus more on problem-solving than therapeutic exploration. However, she had strong interpersonal skills and was able to learn about a less directive approach through supervision. Despite her initial anxieties, she found the experience professionally fulfilling, and the distinction between high-quality social work practice and counselling skills was not as wide as she had assumed.

This type of practice is a long way from how many services currently operate. There will, of course, be situations where supporting the existing team is not appropriate or is not what the family wants. However, this must be weighed against the large number of referrals between agencies that fail to result in meaningful engagement or help. In many services, non-attendance for first appointments can be as high as 20–30%, representing a significant waste of professional time and resources on referrals that lead nowhere.

Placing the wider helping system at the centre of service delivery may reduce the number of unhelpful referrals. One of the authors was involved in a training programme that included all specialist child teams in a particular city. Practitioners from health, social care and education took part in two days of joint training, funded by service directors across the three services. The training was based on the principles described here. A year later, the joint agency directors reported a **10% reduction** in cross-agency referrals and a noticeable increase in professionals discussing how to support each other with complex cases rather than immediately referring families to another service. This change represented a significant reduction in service costs and workload, demonstrating that a more integrated and relationship-based approach to referrals can lead to more effective support while reducing pressure on overstretched teams.

The Obligation to Assist

To conclude this section, we propose that teams in health, social care and education, when faced with requests to help a particular child or young person, should begin by considering the *existing relationships* in the helping system. The *first obligation should be to assist these relationships* rather than immediately offering separate help. In some ways, this is not different from the current obligations of all child services when it comes to *child protection and safety*, where all teams have a duty to support social care in ensuring a child's safety. Our proposal is that before referring a child or young person to a new service, this should be carefully considered. Helping systems should be prioritised over separate helping services. Rather than defaulting to onward referrals, teams should explore how to *support the professionals, families, and networks already in place* around the child. This approach not only strengthens existing support structures but also helps to *reduce service fragmentation*, which can leave families navigating multiple disconnected services.

Summary

The recognition of the role of the village in supporting children with mental health needs presents some of the greatest challenges to how services currently operate. Applying the six principles to the work of teams requires the support and expertise of team leaders and managers. The scale of this challenge cannot be underestimated, as it runs counter to many of the established principles of structured service design. Current services are well-organised for separate teams and agencies but are not designed for creating effective, integrated helping systems around children and families.

For many managers, introducing these principles could initially feel overwhelming, as it may seem to undermine efforts to provide timely, evidence-based interventions in response to high demand and public concern. We agree! Developing a new way of working will only be possible if strategic and planning changes are made to support children, young people and their families in ways that allow team managers to focus on the effectiveness of help rather than just the delivery of services. This shift requires a broader system-wide approach. The next chapter will explore how strategic planning and commissioning structures need to evolve to create the conditions necessary for teams to build and sustain effective helping systems around vulnerable children and young people.

Conclusions

In this chapter, we have applied the same six principles to professional teams as we did to working with families. The key ingredients that help children and young people are the same ones that can help teams to function well in their demanding roles. These principles are not entirely new or radical, nor are they absent from current practice but they tend to appear in fragments. *Systematically applying them to team structures and interagency collaboration results in a way of working that is significantly different from how many teams currently operate*. The length of this chapter itself reflects the *far-reaching implications of this approach*. Applying these principles requires not just small procedural adjustments but a *fundamental shift in how services conceptualise their role*—moving from a focus on delivering interventions in isolation to actively building helping systems around children and families.

A recent conversation with a senior and experienced mental health commissioner highlighted this shift. At the end of the discussion, he remarked that what was being advocated would require services to work entirely differently from how they do now. To him, these ideas were not minor adjustments but a complete reframing of the nature of help for children and young people with mental health needs.

It is not for us to determine whether this is true. However, we hope that those responsible for leading and managing services can see the potential of these principles to provide a coherent, effective and sustainable framework for supporting vulnerable children and families. The next chapter will turn to strategic and planning changes that would create the conditions needed to enable teams to focus on the effectiveness of help rather than simply the delivery of services.

Key Practice Points

1. Team culture should actively welcome parents as key contributors to effective help for their children. This needs to be communicated clearly from the first point of contact with families.
2. Evidence-based practice is essential, but teams should support practitioners in adapting their approaches to enable children and young people to take an active role in improving their lives and well-being.
3. As advocated by Thrive, teams should have flexible approaches to support families, recognising that not all seek formal treatment. The framework of Risk Support is one way to address this.
4. Teams must create a safe, supportive and affirming environment for professional staff to encourage sustainable and effective practice.
5. Professional teams should include parent advisors and young people's groups to provide consultation and advice on how services are delivered. These should be funded positions rather than relying on volunteers.

6 Teams must foster a help-seeking culture that acknowledges the emotional challenges of the work and the potential for professional shame in the work that they do.
7 A supportive infrastructure for outcome measurement should be in place, allowing teams to learn from and improve their practice.
8 Team managers and leaders should recognise that their team is part of the child's broader village and that relationships with other members of this village are crucial to creating effective helping systems.
9 Professional teams should consider their obligation to assist teams that already have a relationship with the child or young person rather than defaulting to offering separate help that disrupts existing support.

A Child's Life: Sam

Sam was eight years old and lived with his mother, Dana. When Dana and Sam came to see me together, Sam was confident, playful and articulate. He played with the Lego in my room while listening to his mother describe him, interrupting whenever she said something he disagreed with. Dana told me that he had been permanently excluded from his nursery for fighting, but she believed this was due to racism, feeling that he had been treated differently from other children. Sam's primary school referred him to our service because of his aggression towards other children. The school staff were not primarily concerned about the fights themselves—they were experienced in handling conflict—but about Sam's response to them. He always justified his actions, insisting that the other child *deserved it* and showing no remorse. In fact, he seemed to take pride in what he had done. The school wanted Sam to be placed in a Pupil Referral Unit, believing that his aggression was beyond what they could manage. Dana refused to agree to this move but accepted a referral to the child mental health service, though she did not wish to be part of the sessions. I saw Sam for nearly a year, using a broadly CBT-based approach to help him regulate his emotions and problem-solve situations that led to conflict. Together, we created *The Zidane Project*, named after a famous French footballer—Sam's favourite—who had been sent off in the World Cup final for deliberately headbutting an opponent. In our project, we explored why Zidane had reacted in that way, what the consequences were for him and how Sam could *stay on the field* rather than getting sent off. We worked on strategies such as self-control, distraction and alternative ways to respond to provocation.

Sam enjoyed the sessions, and his behaviour at school improved, though it remained unpredictable. Whether his improvement was a direct result of our sessions was unclear, but the school appreciated that he was receiving additional support. I met with his class teacher and class assistant once a month after school to review his progress. While we saw some improvements, none of us was confident whether Sam handled his emotions differently from before. There was increase in self-control probably related to general maturation but there were times when he was still self-justifyingly vindictive to others. He responded well to *positive consequences*, such as being rewarded by his mother if he had a good week at school. Over time, the likelihood of exclusion decreased, and Sam was able to stay in his primary school before successfully transitioning to secondary school. In a team review discussion when finishing this intervention, the general view was that the intervention had enabled the school to become increasingly confident in their ability to manage Sam so that his environment became more contained and safer.

Notes

1 **Child mental health services in the UK.** Multiple media reports have described individual examples where children and families have received poor experience of child mental health services. These reflect public concern although they do not always provide a balanced overview of the way the service is running as a whole. A wider perspective was provided by the Children's Commissioner who reported in March 2024 about her concerns for child mental health services (The Children's Commissioner's office (March 2024) Children's mental health services 2022–2023) particularly focusing on long waiting times for first appointments. A detailed analysis of workforce problems was reported in an NHS Education Benchmarking Report (Children and young people's mental health services workforce: report for Health Education England (2021). *Manchester: NHS Benchmarking Network*).

2 **Ministerial comments on child protection cases.** This example is taken from a comment by Nahim Zahawi, Minister of Education on the case of the murder of Arthur Labinjo-Hughes in 2021.'The father and partner were obviously evil and manipulative, but nevertheless we have to make sure, if there is any evidence, any inkling, any iota of harm to any child, that the child is taken away immediately.' Such comments by political leaders are not uncommon and show a limited understanding of the intrinsic uncertainties of child protection work.

3 **Risk Support.** Information about I-Thrive and risk support can be found at the main IThrive website https://implementingthrive.org/

4 **Ending treatment.** The National I-Thrive Implementation Team runs training for professionals about ending treatment, and details of this can be found at their website. A recent paper on the difficulty of treatment endings in mental health can be found in Moore, I., Archard, P. J., & Simmonds, S. (2024). Clinician perspectives on endings and discharges in community mental health work. *Mental Health Review Journal, 29*(4), 360–373.

5 **Models of help-seeking.** A useful overview on help-seeking is provided by Edgar Schein (Schein, E. (2009). *Helping: How to offer, give and receive help.* Berrett-Koehler Publishers). A more focused description of key factors of help-seeking in the workplace is provided by Van der Rijt and colleagues (Van der Rijt, J., Van den Bossche, P., van de Wiel, M. W., De Maeyer, S., Gijselaers, W. H., … & Segers, M. S. (2013). Asking for help: A relational perspective on help seeking in the workplace. *Vocations and Learning, 6*, 259–279).

6 **Supervision.** A review of studies of supervision in health care suggested that it was associated with improved health outcomes (Snowdon, D. A., Leggat, S. G., & Taylor, N. F. (2017). Does clinical supervision of healthcare professionals improve effectiveness of care and patient experience? A systematic review. *BMC Health Services Research, 17*, 1–11). However, evidence for its value in working with children is more mixed (Carpenter, J., Webb, C. M., & Bostock, L. (2013). The

surprisingly weak evidence base for supervision: Findings from a systematic review of research in child welfare practice (2000–2012). *Children and Youth Services Review, 35*(11), 1843–1853). Its effectiveness may be influenced by methods used in supervision. A recent study showed no difference between clinicians who received expert supervision from those who did not (Weisz, J. R., Thomassin, K., Hersh, J., Santucci, L. C., MacPherson, H. A., Rodriguez, G. M., … & Evans, S. C. (2020). Clinician training, then what? Randomized clinical trial of child STEPs psychotherapy using lower-cost implementation supports with versus without expert consultation. *Journal of Consulting and Clinical Psychology, 88*(12), 1065).

7 **Leadership styles.** Many leadership styles have been described in the literature including transformational, transactional, relational, task-focused, laissez-faire and even destructive styles. These have been examined against a range of key outcomes such as staff well-being, staff mental health, staff retention, task effectiveness and benefits for clients (e.g. Montano, D., Schleu, J. E., & Hüffmeier, J. (2023). A meta-analysis of the relative contribution of leadership styles to followers' mental health. *Journal of Leadership & Organizational Studies, 30*(1), 90–107; Castiglione, S. A. (2020). Implementation leadership: A concept analysis. *Journal of Nursing Management, 28*, 94–101; Votova, K., Laberge, A. M., Grimshaw, J. M., Wilson, B. (November 2019) Implementation science as a leadership capability to improve patient outcomes and value in healthcare. *Health Manage Forum, 32*(6), 307–312. Epub 2019 Aug 25). The effectiveness of leaders is not due to individual attributes of leaders alone but also the organisational context plays a key role in enabling leaders to be able to support implementation of new ways of working. This has been well described in child mental health by Aarons and his team (Aarons, G. A., & Sommerfeld, D. H. (2012). Leadership, innovation climate, and attitudes toward evidence-based practice during statewide implementation. *Journal of the American Academy of Child & Adolescent Psychiatry, 51*(4), 423–431; Aarons, G. A., Ehrhart, M. G., Farahnak, L. R., & Hurlburt, M. S. (2015). Leadership and organizational change for implementation (LOCI): A randomized mixed method pilot study of a leadership and organization development intervention for evidence-based practice implementation. *Implementation Science, 10*(1), 11).

8 **Empowering parents, empowering communities (EPEC).** This impressive programme has been led by Professor Crispin Day at King's College London. It involves training parents to facilitate a structured ten-week group course for parents which draws on key principles of effective childcare. Parent facilitators have all previously completed the course in response to their own needs. Each session has topics for discussion and exercises to enable parents to practice techniques for caring for their offspring. It has been well evaluated in a series of studies (Day, C., Harwood, J., Kendall, N., & Nicoll, J. (2022). Impact of a peer-led, community-based parenting programme delivered at a national scale: An uncontrolled cohort design with benchmarking. *BMC Public Health, 22*(1), 1377; Day, C., Michelson, D., Thomson, S., Penney, C., & Draper, L. (2012). Innovations in practice: Empowering parents, empowering communities: A pilot evaluation of a peer-led parenting programme. *Child and Adolescent Mental Health, 17*(1), 52–57).

9 **Practitioner attitudes to use questionnaires.** Attitudes towards the use of questionnaires in child mental health work have been considered an important part of the uptake of evidence-based practice (Bear, H. A., Dalzell, K., Edbrooke-Childs, J., & Wolpert, M. (2022). Applying behaviour change theory to understand the barriers to implementing routine outcome monitoring. *British Journal of Clinical Psychology, 61*(3), 557–578; Waldron, S. M., Loades, M. E., & Rogers, L. (2018). Routine outcome monitoring in CAMHS: How can we enable implementation in practice? *Child and Adolescent Mental Health, 23*(4), 328–333). A measure of practitioner attitudes

has been developed (Aarons, G. A. (2004). Mental health provider attitudes toward adoption of evidence-based practice: The Evidence-Based Practice Attitude Scale (EBPAS). *Mental Health Services Research, 6*, 61–74; Aarons, G. A. (2005). Measuring provider attitudes toward evidence-based practice: Consideration of organizational context and individual differences. *Child and Adolescent Psychiatric Clinics of North America, 14*(2), 255); (Nakamura, B. J., Higa-McMillan, C. K., Okamura, K. H., & Shimabukuro, S. (2011). Knowledge of and attitudes towards evidence-based practices in community child mental health practitioners. *Administration and Policy in Mental Health and Mental Health Services Research, 38*, 287–300).

10 **POD.** More information about the POD system can be found on the Child Outcomes research Consortium (CORC) website. https://www.corc.uk.net/outcome-experience-measures/pod-mental-health-outcomes-and-feedback-system/

11 **AMASS.** The Adolescent Multi-Agency Support Service (AMASS) was a multi-disciplinary team managed by social care including health, education and youth work staff. The design of the service was to support social workers with families at risk of a young person coming into care. The outcomes of this service were reported. (Talbot, L., Fuggle, P., Foyston, Z., & Lawson, K. (2020). Delivering an integrated adolescent multi-agency specialist service to families with adolescents at risk of care: Outcomes and learning from the first ten years. *The British Journal of Social Work, 50*(5), 1531–1550).

Chapter 13

Implications for Designing and Planning Services

Introduction

In this chapter, we turn to how professional and community services are planned, funded and monitored—the systems that lie behind what families and young people experience when seeking help. In the Thrive model, this is referred to as the *macro* system. It only indirectly affects practitioners and families, but it shapes the conditions in which much of what we have described in earlier chapters takes place. Over the last 40 years, this macro system has been in a near-constant state of change and reform. It has been buffeted by shifting political and organisational ideas about how to manage the healthcare system, how local authorities should connect with it and how education interfaces with both. The role of schools, their independence from central government and the debate about educational standards in the UK have also been part of this shifting landscape. There was a brief period when these efforts came together under a single structure called the Department of Children, Families and Schools.[1] This promising development lasted three years between 2007 and 2010 but one day after a change of government it reverted to the Department of Education. New structures and proposals have routinely been launched with great optimism, claiming that improved outcomes will follow. However, few structural reforms have lasted longer than a single electoral cycle, making it difficult to assess their real impact over time. Of all the chapters in this book, this one deals with the level of the system most affected by repeated reform. And yet, despite all this change, the fundamental challenge of providing effective help for children like Jacqui, Martin, Abdul, Simone, Daniel and Teresa has remained surprisingly constant. The essential work of being helpful to a distressed child has, in many ways, remained untouched by the almost continuous upheavals at this level of the system.

For many practitioners, parents and young people, the macro system is experienced as complex, contradictory and largely impenetrable. The strategic planning of health, education and social care is filled with jargon, acronyms and its own internal culture. At its core, its function is to determine

DOI: 10.4324/9781003145523-13

what the government—funded mainly through taxation—requires services to provide to their local populations. The term used to describe this is *commissioning*. For instance, the government commissions local mental health services for children and young people and sets standards for how these services should operate. Commissioning takes place at both national (NHS England) and local levels (Integrated Care Boards (ICBs)). In this chapter, we will try to avoid becoming entangled in the technicalities of these systems. However, like visiting a new country, some orientation is helpful. We won't attempt to speak the language, but we will offer broad principles that we believe could improve the macro system's role in supporting effective helping systems for children and young people.

There are a few consistent narratives that shape the macro system, regardless of the specific structures in place. First, there is a shortage of professional resources to meet the mental health needs of children and young people, with not enough staff, teams or resources to meet the scale of need—and that the need keeps increasing. Second, there is a need for more joined-up services, often described as *integrated care*. Third, there is increasing public concern for the well-being of children and young people, to include the effects of social media, youth violence, knife crime, abuse within families and persistent school absence. Many local, professional and national bodies are now expected to respond to these issues and often give rise to highly emotional public debates and campaigns, accompanied by political promises that are frequently unrealistic in the face of the complexity of the challenges involved. We do not want to add to this unhelpful cacophony. Instead, we aim to offer a grounded and practical framework that aligns with the lived experiences of children, families and the professionals who work with them. It is seriously unhelpful, following a child murder, for government ministers to stand up and declare that "this must never happen again". While well-intentioned, such statements diminish the depth and seriousness of the debate. Child abuse, murder, rape and suicide are profoundly uncomfortable realities. They cannot be entirely eliminated, and any suggestion that they can be is not only unrealistic but also profoundly unhelpful in developing public knowledge about these matters. When a murder occurs in a local area, we do not routinely see the police force held responsible for its occurrence, the chief of police dismissed and the whole service reorganised. Yet this is often what may happen in social care in response to high-profile child deaths. These reactions rarely move things forward. Instead, they reveal the extent to which those working in the macro system are disconnected from the everyday realities faced by parents, practitioners and team managers operating at the meso and micro levels. They are painfully familiar with the risks that they face each day and just how complex the work of keeping children safe truly is. Often, the inability of national leaders to manage public anxiety in the aftermath of such events leads to reactive policy making. The priority becomes demonstrating that "something is being done", even if those actions bear little relation to the actual work of helping systems around vulnerable children. This disconnection undermines the confidence of practitioners in those operating at so-called higher levels of the system.

This is not a cry of pessimism. It is entirely possible to reduce the number of children murdered by adults. That claim is on firmer ground than many political statements because it is already supported by the evidence.[2] Over the last 50 years in the UK, the average annual rate of child murders by adults has declined to around 50. Is that enough? No. But it shows that improvement is possible. The role of those at the macro level should be to understand and support the broader picture, rather than making short-term or symbolic decisions in response to public pressure. The lack of recognition of this complexity is deeply unhelpful and undermines confidence in the expertise of those in leadership roles. However, we do not intend to dwell on past failures of macro systems to support effective helping systems for children. We do not believe there are simple solutions to the difficulties we face. Our approach, instead, is to suggest ways the macro system could support a helping systems approach, while also acknowledging the barriers and challenges that would need to be addressed for current commissioning and funding structures to be effective for children, young people and their families.

Planning for the mental health needs of children and young people involves four major government departments: education, health, social care and youth justice. The Department for Education has the universal responsibility for providing education to all children, a huge task because all children are in education for over ten years. The Department of Health is responsible for the prevention of ill health and ensuring that children receive appropriate treatment for medical and mental health needs. Social care is charged with ensuring that children are cared for safely and that their social environment supports their developmental needs. The Department for Justice is responsible for preventing youth crime and supporting young people involved in offending. Each department has a clear political responsibility, supported by legal obligations, a defined budget and detailed plans. Each is supported by substantial knowledge, research, professional skill and commitment. The difficulty arises when the needs of a child or young person overlap across the responsibilities of these different departments. As we have described throughout this book, this is far more common than is often appreciated. Because of the central role of school in a child's life, children with social care or health needs are highly likely to also have overlapping needs related to education. The intersection of responsibilities between agencies is one of the key challenges of commissioning integrated care and collaborative helping systems. It is not a matter of coordination alone, but of recognising that the current system, with its clearly separated responsibilities, does not easily accommodate the complexity of children's lives.

The Challenge of Integrated Planning

The challenge of achieving integrated and effective planning at the macro level cannot be underestimated. It is tempting at this point to list numerous examples that highlight the contradictions and inconsistencies in planning and decision-making at this level. These contradictions are not new, and we do not believe it is necessary to dwell on multiple illustrations. However, we will offer one example that clearly highlights the point.

In healthcare, integrated care is now widely recognised as a key component of effective support. This has led to the creation of ICBs in every locality, with oversight for all health care—not just services for children and young people.[3] Local health planning and funding is now led by these ICBs, which have a specific responsibility to promote greater integration across different aspects of healthcare. Their task is to ensure that services—hospitals, community care, primary and secondary care—are coordinated and work effectively together. This vision of integration within health care makes good sense. However, during the same period, the government commissioned a major review of children's social care,[4] which led to its own set of recommendations. These also emphasised the need for better coordination and integration—but specifically within the social care system. Both health and social care promoted principles of integration, but each did so independently, following their own pathways, developing separate structures and creating distinct processes for local implementation. What emerged was a situation where each agency defined its own priorities first, with collaboration across agencies coming later, if at all. Despite both sectors endorsing the need for integration, their planning and funding processes for supporting children remained largely disconnected. This is especially striking considering that children and families often require support that cuts across health, education and social care. These are not new dilemmas, and we are aware of the considerable variability in how different areas of England have attempted to bring these systems together. In some localities, these efforts have been relatively successful; in others, much less so.

Our focus is on the problem of how the macro system can successfully plan and fund methods of practice that enable helping systems to function effectively around individual children at the meso and micro levels. We acknowledge that the structural division between education, health, social care and justice is likely to remain. It is beyond the scope of this book to propose full structural integration of all services for children and young people. Instead, we argue that we must work within this four-part structure, while recognising that it presents a major barrier to integrated practice. This is not a problem unique to the UK. Many other countries struggle with similar issues, and the fragmentation of responsibility across multiple sectors is a common feature of child service systems around the world.

As with the other chapters, we will apply the six principles to consider how the macro system can create the conditions that support effective helping systems to respond to identified needs by promoting the collaboration of families and professionals; adapting commissioning to focus on the outcomes of children; enhancing the safety for children and young people, including safe environments; empowering communities, especially parents, to take part in decision-making about services; using outcomes to inform local decision-making and addressing barriers to integrated practice. That is the task. Our view is that the current planning and funding system in the UK does not serve children, young people and families well. This view comes from long and direct experience of the problems within the system. While there have been many well-intentioned efforts in the past, we believe they have resulted in relatively little lasting improvement. Because of this, we are prepared to propose some bold ideas—ideas that we believe are necessary if the macro system is to function more effectively and support the kind of helping systems that children and families need.

The Need for Unified Leadership

While the ideal system for planning services for children and young people would bring health, education, social care and youth justice into a single integrated structure, we recognise that this is not a realistic proposal in the current UK context. However, we do believe that a unified leadership structure is needed at the local level—one that holds overall responsibility for meeting the needs of children, young people and their families. This leadership should be determined locally rather than imposed nationally. Local areas often differ significantly in the way services are structured and delivered, and a one-size-fits-all national model would not accommodate this variation.

An instructive example comes from the United States in the 1960s, when the Kennedy administration launched *Head Start*, an early intervention programme for preschool children. While the programme was federally funded, there was disagreement at the state level about which agency should be responsible for delivering it. The federal government addressed this by requiring each state to agree on a lead agency as a condition for receiving funding. In some states, education took the lead; in others, it was health. The result was that implementation occurred locally, with clear leadership and shared responsibility, allowing the programme to be delivered successfully across diverse settings.

We propose that a similar principle could be applied in the UK. Central government could make funding conditional on local areas establishing unified leadership for children and young people's services. This would not mean dismantling the existing structure that divides responsibility among health, education, social care and youth justice. Instead, it would create a single, unified system of accountability for how these services are delivered. Unified leadership would enable local systems to respond to contradictions and tensions between different agency objectives. For instance, the goal of reducing school exclusions due to violent behaviour should be considered alongside programmes aimed at reducing youth violence in the community. Likewise, the need to increase attendance at mental health services should not be treated separately from the goal of maintaining school attendance. These objectives often intersect and, without a unified structure, they are too easily pursued in isolation—sometimes even in conflict. The benefit of unified leadership would be its capacity to consider these different priorities together. It would allow local services to address inconsistencies across agencies so that the achievement of an objective for one agency does not undermine the achievement of objectives for other agencies. This structure would recognise the different priorities and find more coherent, integrated solutions. Importantly, it would not require the structural reorganisation of existing systems. We do recognise, however, that such an arrangement would require statutory and legal support.

Parents and Carers Contribute to Unified Leadership

Crucially, we also believe that unified leadership must include representation from the community and families. Effective services for children and young people cannot be created without involving the voices of those most affected. Local agreements on leadership structures should ensure that parents, carers and other community members have an active role in shaping priorities and holding services to account. This is essential for creating helping systems that reflect the real needs of children and families and not just the internal logic of services.

Families and carers are central to the helping systems that support children and young people. Yet in the planning and funding structures that shape professional services, their role has not been given sufficient recognition or power. When we trace the processes that help children to cope with or recover from the challenges they face, the involvement of parents and carers is clearly essential. Despite this, their influence in setting priorities and shaping decisions is often overshadowed by the interests and authority of professionals and service providers. Parents and carers may already have advisory roles in services, and some contribute directly to support offered by professionals. While this is welcome, it is not enough to fully acknowledge or support their central role in helping systems. We propose that unified leadership structures for planning and delivering services for children, young people and families should include formal representation from parents and carers at the highest local level. All proposals and programmes intended to meet the needs of children and young people should be developed in collaboration with the local community—and this fundamentally means involving parents and carers. Currently, planning and funding for children and young people tends to focus heavily on services delivered by paid staff. This is understandable, as this is where the greatest costs lie, but it reflects a narrow definition of support. At the macro level, we must widen our understanding of what children and young people need, beyond what is provided by professionals alone.

We are not proposing that one parent should be appointed to a unified leadership team, as this would risk being little more than a token gesture. Rather, the parent representative should lead a local parent advisory team with a range of staff and trained community members with the capacity to consult with different local communities. The head of this group would then represent a wider parental perspective within the leadership structure. This would require investment in developing meaningful parental involvement—an area that is currently significantly under-resourced. The purpose of such an investment would be to strengthen collaborative practice between parents and professionals, consistent with the helping systems framework described throughout this book. This approach would help ensure that decisions made at the macro level are genuinely informed by the reality of what happens at the micro level—where help actually takes place. It is a way of ensuring that the planning and delivery of services reflect the lived experience of families, and not only the perspectives of service structures or professional priorities.

Adapting Methods of Commissioning Services

The commissioning of mental health services for children and young people is the responsibility of a local leadership structure, regardless of whether the earlier proposals in this chapter are adopted. These structures are tasked with ensuring that evidence-based methods of help are provided to the local community in a way that is timely and accessible. However, as we have argued throughout this book, helping systems around children must be informed by the experiences of children and families themselves and what they actually find helpful. While it is important to specify what kinds of support should be made available, what matters most is not the nature of the provision, but the degree of help it actually produces. As one eminent colleague[5] once put it, "It doesn't matter whether we are providing evidence-based help or not if the young person's life is improving. What matters is knowing whether it is or not."

Outcomes as Well as Activity

This calls for a fundamental shift in how services are commissioned—from a focus on what is being delivered (the supply side) to a focus on whether it is making a difference (the outcome). Monitoring outcomes is not only helpful for individual children or practitioners; it is also essential for services and systems. Simple methods for this are likely to work best. One example comes from the Islington mental health service. In many large-scale pharmaceutical trials, participant benefit is measured with a straightforward rating system: 'very much improved', 'much improved', 'minimally improved', 'no change', or 'worse'. Taking inspiration from this, a similar measure was used in Islington. At the end of involvement with a child, young person or family, the practitioner would rate the level of change using this simple set of categories. Outcome data were collected for over 90% of children seen,[6] a sample of 1,446 cases. The findings showed that 50–60% were rated as showing improvement. This in itself was valuable, but the data also helped answer broader concerns. For example, it showed no difference in outcomes for children and young people from ethnic minority backgrounds, addressing a worry from managers and commissioners that these children might have poorer outcomes. This was an important reassurance, grounded in local data. These measured outcomes were reported quarterly to local NHS commissioners and showed consistent results over time. At one review meeting, a commissioner asked, "What would it take to improve outcomes by 10%? Could we raise the rate of improvement to 60%?" This was an excellent question, and one that could only be asked because outcomes data were being routinely collected and used in the commissioning process. Without this, such conversations would have taken place in the dark.

Commissioners also wanted to know whether it was possible to see more children and young people more quickly. Staff were understandably concerned that this would lead to worse outcomes. But rather than rejecting the idea, the team agreed to explore how changes in the way they worked might allow them to meet this goal. This shift—from fixed models of delivery to more responsive and outcome-informed practice—was only possible because outcome data were guiding both clinical and commissioning decisions. To improve throughput in the service, a new system for assessing and planning treatments for children and young people was introduced, known as the Choice and Partnership Approach (CAPA).[7] CAPA placed greater emphasis on incorporating the views of families into the assessment process. It offered a structured framework that aligned with the principles of shared decision-making and the core ideas outlined throughout this book. Staff reactions to CAPA were mixed—some welcomed the approach, while others were less enthusiastic—but it was agreed to try it.

Because ongoing outcome data were already being collected, the service was able to test whether the introduction of CAPA would lead to a decline in improvement rates. The implementation of CAPA evoked strong views in the staff team; some liked it, some did not. But it was not possible to know whether it had been beneficial without looking carefully at a series of cases. Staff opinions on the change were strongly held on both sides. However, anecdotes and informal reflections, though influential in shaping views, were insufficient for drawing meaningful conclusions. A formal evaluation was carried out.[8] This showed a 47% increase in the number of cases seen compared to the period before CAPA, and outcomes did not deteriorate. In fact, there was a slight improvement: prior to CAPA, 50% of cases were rated as improved, and after CAPA, this rose to 60%. This was the first time a change in service delivery in that setting had been evaluated in terms of both volume and outcome. These examples are shared to illustrate ways to enable commissioners to shift their focus from activity alone to outcomes.

Commissioning Adaptive Practice

To support adaptive, well-tested methods of practice, commissioners must actively endorse and incorporate these approaches into their contracting and review processes. One example is Risk Support, a component of the Thrive model, which could be included explicitly in service contracts. Commissioners could agree on a target number of cases expected to be supported through Risk Support in a given year. This figure could then be reviewed and adjusted in subsequent years. Risk Support cases should cost less than active treatment cases, as they require fewer direct contacts. Instead, the focus is on supporting those already working closely with the child and family, offering a form of relational help—that is, access to a trusted professional over a longer period of time. At present, commissioning tends to focus on short-term, evidence-based treatments, even for families experiencing long-term difficulties. This over-reliance on treatment as the primary form of help in mental health services creates many of the problems discussed in this book. Most of all, it leads to the loss of the most valuable ingredient in help: the helping relationship. Relationships that have been carefully built during treatment are often discarded at the end of an intervention, even when the family continues to face ongoing needs. This is not only unhelpful, but wasteful of a key resource that has already been created through skilled, sustained work. The solution here is not to extend treatment indefinitely, but to support long-term helping relationships. The value of such relationships can be seen in the informal ways that many experienced mental health professionals continue to keep in touch with families they have worked with. These unofficial contacts are rarely used by families, but they offer a valuable sense of continuity and access. For commissioners and service managers, this idea often raises concerns about creating an unmanageable workload. In practice, however, these ongoing relationships are low-cost and high-value. Families make use of them infrequently, but the option of returning to someone they know and trust can help avoid unnecessary re-referrals. It is important to stress that this is not a call for long-term treatment. If occasional contact develops into something more regular or intensive, it can be reclassified as *Help* (an active treatment) under the Thrive framework.

The real capital of helping services lies in the number of trusting relationships they build with children and families. Current commissioning processes often fail to value or sustain this capital but this could be monitored as part of a shared approach across all services. This may present some operational challenges but better to measure what matters than to consider what matters is what we can measure. Trust is more likely to develop and endure when services are shaped by the preferences of children and parents. This inevitably requires adaptation of evidence-based practice, and commissioners must support this through contracts that allow flexibility, rather than enforcing rigid protocols designed to control resources and costs. That said, relational help must be balanced with the principle of encouraging children and families to take an active role in their own help. Without this balance, there is a risk that services create passivity and dependency, rather than empowerment. We will return to the role of commissioners in fostering agency later in this chapter. For now, we turn to another key principle—how commissioners can support safety.

Supporting Safety

Commissioning for the mental health needs of children and young people is not simply about ensuring access to appropriate treatment. The task is much broader. Mental health problems are more likely to arise in environments where children feel unsafe, under constant stress or threatened. A core responsibility at the macro level is to address these harmful conditions. Put simply, a sense of safety may be the most powerful intervention a community can offer its children. Tackling the full scope of this challenge lies beyond the limits of this chapter, but we want to highlight three areas where safety should be a central focus of effective helping systems: the protection of children experiencing abuse; tackling bullying in schools and communities; actively challenging racism and its impact on young people's lives. We recognise that there are other important areas that could also be included here—such as ensuring accessibility for children with disabilities or addressing the needs of LGBTQ+ young people. However, the three areas selected are intended to demonstrate the broader point: at the macro level, the role of commissioning is to create safer environments in which all children and young people can live, grow and thrive.

Identification and Support for Abused Children and Young People

Perhaps more than in any other area of public life, the abuse of children and young people by adults provokes powerful and deeply felt emotions—both at the level of individuals and entire communities. For many people, the abuse of even one child is entirely unacceptable, and any instance rightly elicits outrage. We respect this view and do not wish to convey any complacency about this harrowing aspect of human experience. However, history suggests that abuse and maltreatment of children have been a far more widespread part of society than we are often willing to acknowledge. While tragic cases of abuse—especially those resulting in the murder of vulnerable children—receive significant public attention, as described earlier, the broader picture reveals that the number of children murdered by adults has steadily declined. In the UK, despite the damaging effects of austerity on local authority services over the past two decades, fewer children now die as a result of the care they receive from adults. It would be inappropriate to describe the current child protection system as a success in any celebratory sense. Nonetheless, by international standards, the UK's child protection services are widely respected. It is difficult to determine how much of the decline in child deaths is directly attributable to these services, but it is reasonable to believe they have played a role. Unfortunately, there are few high-profile public narratives about children whose lives have been successfully safeguarded. These stories remain invisible to the public, in contrast to the intense scrutiny that follows when systems fail. And yet, behind the scenes, a substantial amount of effort has gone into establishing shared systems of protection.

Commissioners have played an important role in embedding the understanding that child protection is not solely the responsibility of social care, but a duty shared by all professionals working with children. While social care continues to hold the lead for accountability and coordination, binding procedures have been introduced that require mental health professionals to share information, attend multi-agency meetings and collaborate fully in situations where harm has occurred—or may occur. This shift did not happen easily but it has contributed to a culture in which collaboration is not just encouraged but expected as part of core professional responsibilities. The legal framework now in place makes clear that the best interests—and safety—of the child are paramount. In many ways, child protection practice has become more developed across the micro, meso and macro levels than in any other area of need. The systems in place demonstrate what is possible when there is both a moral and statutory commitment to integrated, shared responsibilities for the safety of children. This development offers a strong example of how macro-level commissioning and planning can support robust, collaborative helping systems on the ground.

Bullying

When children and young people are asked about the things that concern them most, bullying—either the experience of it or the fear of it—consistently emerges as a primary issue. It is frequently reported as a background factor in cases of self-harm and, in tragic instances, completed suicide. There is little doubt that bullying has a significant impact on children's emotional well-being, often shaping how safe and supported they feel in their daily lives. Many schools work extremely hard to create safe environments and succeed in significantly reducing peer bullying during school hours and in structured activities. However, negative aspects of peer relationships, especially in adolescence, are difficult for adults to influence. The emergence of social media has further intensified this problem, allowing bullying to occur in less visible, less manageable ways beyond the school setting.

Anti-bullying programmes[9] have been developed and refined over many years in the UK, Europe and the United States. These efforts aim to address what is now widely recognised as a serious threat to children's well-being and their ability to thrive both in and out of school. One of the most challenging and often puzzling issues for adults working in this area is the reluctance of many children and young people to report being bullied. Even children who have trusting and secure home environments often do not tell their parents about bullying. A deeply rooted fear that the situation will worsen if they disclose it prevents many from seeking help. In this respect, bullying shares characteristics with child abuse: it is highly damaging, difficult to eliminate entirely and extremely hard to address if those affected do not feel safe to speak up.

At the macro level, two areas of action should be prioritised. First, anti-bullying work would benefit from adopting some of the lessons learnt in child protection. Programmes should be fully supported by all agencies and community services involved with children—not just schools. Anti-bullying efforts and prosocial school-based initiatives should be consistently commissioned as part of a core strategy to address the needs of vulnerable children. This means recognising bullying as a common and persistent threat to well-being and embedding this concern in all parts of the system—health, social care, youth justice and education. One straightforward step would be for commissioners to expect that all children seen in social care and health services are routinely asked about their experience of bullying. Services should be able to report on the number of children exposed to bullying, regardless of which agency they are seen by. This would send a clear message that tackling bullying is not the responsibility of education alone but a shared obligation of all services involved in child well-being.

Second, young people must be engaged directly in efforts to tackle bullying within their own peer communities. A number of successful programmes[10] have shown the value of this approach, which should not be viewed as optional or experimental. Instead, it should be embedded as a structural and permanent aspect of service commissioning for children and young people's mental health. By taking both these routes—multi-agency collaboration and meaningful youth engagement—commissioners can play a critical role in reducing the prevalence and impact of bullying. This, in turn, would support children and young people to feel safer, more supported and more able to thrive.

Racism

While bullying is a significant concern in adult settings such as the workplace or in the care of the elderly, it is most clearly recognised as a public health issue for children and young people. Racism, by contrast, is a systemic problem that affects the whole of society—children and adults alike. However, as with bullying, racism is frequently reported by young people and their families as a major threat to well-being and to future opportunities in life.[11] The impact of racism on those subjected to it can be severe, affecting emotional health, education and long-term life chances. Racism is not limited to overt acts like verbal abuse or physical intimidation. It also operates through the policies, practices and structures of institutions. For example, there are disproportionate rates of school exclusions among some ethnic minority groups, and similarly, higher representation of these groups in the youth justice system compared with white British children.[12] This means that children and young people from minority ethnic backgrounds are not only exposed to individual acts of discrimination but also to institutional processes that reflect and reinforce racial inequity. These issues are often intensified by media and political narratives, both global and local, that heighten tensions and contribute to the normalisation of prejudice. Events such as the conflict in Gaza or the murder of children in Southport can trigger public and private responses that are shaped by racist attitudes or interpretations.

In response, there is already a need for—and in some places, an effort towards—explicit education, training and monitoring of racism across child-facing services. However, at the macro level, communities must be supported to work alongside professional services in directly challenging racist attitudes and behaviours. The effects of racism on children, young people and their families should be recognised as a public health concern, on a par with issues such as obesity, poor nutrition or lack of physical activity. Racism's effects are wide-ranging, long-lasting and potentially devastating. Addressing this requires systemic attention. We believe that the active involvement of communities and parents in the leadership structures of children's services will help ensure that this issue is strengthened as a priority. It is through shared responsibility and public accountability that services can take meaningful action to reduce the impact of racism on the lives of children and young people.

Taking an Active Part: Supporting Community Empowerment

Parents and young people must have an active role in shaping services at the macro level. Earlier in this chapter, we proposed the creation of a Parent Director role within a multi-agency leadership team, as well as the inclusion of parent and young people advisors in the teams and services commissioned by local authorities. These are important structural changes, but active participation requires more than formal roles—it requires a community that is capable, organised and confident in expressing its priorities for children. The experiences of the parents and careers of the six young people we have been following in this book are invaluable in shaping the design of helping systems based on the help they provided for the children they cared for. But in the usual way that services are organised this experience is neither sought nor valued. Chisomo, Kande, Sandra, Aisha, Ali, Patrick and Brigitte, Judith, Bernadette and Eamon may have been asked to complete service satisfaction questionnaires, but they were not asked how the professional contribution to helping their child could have been improved. Every service can be improved; there should be no shame in this question. Sandra wanted services to be more joined up; Chisomo wanted a clearer plan about what to do if Jacqui became depressed again; Brigitte wanted more advice about therapy for herself around her anxiety; Aisha wanted a clearer plan around Abdul's secondary education. They all had experience of professional and family collaboration, but their experience was not used to enrich the wider helping system. What is needed are both effective systems for empowering parents to contribute to service design and also well-developed methods of community engagement. For the latter, Community Organising offers one such approach. It is a way of helping communities to act collectively on their own behalf, to articulate shared concerns and to take part in shaping the systems that affect their lives.

Community Organising

Community organising is a method of collective action developed by Saul Alinsky in the United States,[13] originally designed to enable disadvantaged communities to challenge those in power and address issues of social injustice. It was historically linked to the trade union movement and to campaigns focused on civil rights and fighting discrimination against minority groups. Charismatic leaders in the United States such as Martin Luther King and Barack Obama were both highly influenced by this approach. In the UK, community organising has become an approach for supporting marginalised communities and is now strongly championed by organisations such as Citizens UK.[14] At its core, community organising seeks to build collective power by bringing people together to act on shared concerns. A commonly cited phrase within this approach is the goal of enabling "those who suffer disadvantage or injustice to speak to those in power". Over the past 50 years, the methods developed through community organising have become a valuable framework for empowering underrepresented groups, and these principles could be highly relevant for involving parents and carers in the leadership of local child mental health services and in setting priorities.

A central feature of community organising is the *listening campaign*. This is a process of consultation with local people about the issues that most affect their lives. Rather than beginning with assumptions, organisers begin by asking community members what matters to them. While this book has focused on factors such as bullying and racism as key concerns in children's lives, a local listening campaign might identify different priorities, such as substance misuse, transport difficulties or access to early years education. The goal is not to impose priorities but to *genuinely engage* and recruit from within the community those who are motivated to work on issues of social justice.

Community organisers are trained in how to do this work. We propose that such training should be part of the infrastructure that supports parents and carers to participate in service leadership. At present, parents are structurally disadvantaged in the systems that plan and deliver mental health services for children. They have far less power and influence than professionals or service providers. Community organising offers a way to help correct that imbalance and give parents a stronger, more meaningful role in the systems that support their children. As part of establishing parent and young person leadership at the macro level, commissioners should invest in training and support that builds their capacity to consult with and empower others in their communities. Community organising is one example of how this could be done. However, it is essential that parent and young person leaders are *empowered to decide for themselves* whether this approach suits their work and priorities. The goal is not to prescribe a single method, but to create the conditions in which communities are supported to develop their own voice and influence in the planning and delivery of services.

What Does the Child Think About This?

We have previously expressed our interest in the developments taking place in Denmark, where reforms are being introduced to strengthen children's rights in a way that aligns closely with the aim of providing more effective help for vulnerable children. As described earlier, the broader legal and social changes underway in Denmark will take many years to embed and will no doubt involve significant learning about how children's rights can be implemented in ways that support their well-being and development.

However, one early and practical development from the Danish programme is something we believe could be adopted in the UK without requiring the wider systemic shifts currently taking place in Denmark.[15] In the Danish approach, professional practice is being reshaped around a simple but powerful principle: any meeting or plan concerning a child must include some consideration of the child's own views on the matter in hand. This does not mean that the child's view will necessarily determine the outcome, but it does require that the adults responsible for making decisions about the child's care are aware of what the child thinks. For instance, if a social worker recommends that a child be referred for mental health support, the recommendation should include the views of the child about this. Of course it is likely that some children will be unfamiliar with services and may feel anxious or unsure about what is being suggested. Their views may be shaped by a lack of information or understanding. But that in itself is valuable knowledge. If a child's reluctance is based on fear or misunderstanding, then part of the task is to ensure that they are provided with information in a way that is accessible and meaningful to them.

We believe that greater attention to this part of the helping process—understanding and responding to what the child thinks—could be transformative in encouraging active participation by children and young people in decisions about their own care. We recognise that this would represent a significant change for services in the UK—perhaps even more radical than it appears to those without direct experience of how decisions are currently made within the helping systems for children and young people. While this idea might seem to reflect a simple application of common sense, in reality it would mark a profound shift in how services are commissioned, planned and evaluated. The proposal here is that commissioners could play a key role in embedding this practice by making it an expected standard in all services they fund. In addition to promoting evidence-based practice, commissioners could actively promote children and young people's participation in their own help by requiring services to consider and record the child's view as part of the decision-making process—both at the micro level (with individual children) and at the meso level (within team and service planning). This is a small shift in principle but potentially a very significant change in practice. It would move services towards a more respectful, participatory and ultimately more effective approach to supporting the agency of children and young people in their own treatment, education and care.

Measuring Outcomes

As discussed earlier, measuring outcomes is a vital component of direct work with young people and with the teams that make up the wider helping system. In this chapter, we extend that argument to the macro level, focusing on the role of outcome monitoring in strategic planning, service design and commissioning.

Using Outcome Reporting in Service Planning

Service planning cannot be meaningfully carried out without outcome monitoring and reporting. Without some understanding of the benefits that services provide to local communities, local decision-making is vulnerable to shifting political priorities and budgetary pressures. We propose that integrated decision-making at the macro level requires a shared approach to outcome monitoring across education, social care, youth justice and health services. This does not mean all services must use identical methods. But they should use a common language and approach, including some form of: measuring service satisfaction, identifying the proportion of cases that achieved outcomes aligned with service objectives, and reporting the number of cases requiring support from additional services. The last of these is particularly important. It helps to strengthen the capacity of the service that already has a relationship with the family to bring in additional support where needed—rather than transferring the child to a different agency.

The child mental team used outcome data to identify which group of children benefited least from the service.[16] The results showed that adolescents with multiple problems referred from social care had very low rates of improvement—fewer than 10% showed significant change by the time their cases were closed. This was significantly lower than for other groups. The results were difficult for the team to face. The young people had been given substantial time and skilled effort, yet outcomes were poor. To respond, the leadership team developed a decision-making tool to help explore strategic options. This included discussions with social care and with young people and families in this group. These discussions were not easy. They could easily turn to concerns about the reliability of outcome measures or whether referral practices from other services were appropriate. Managers and frontline staff alike felt overwhelmed by the expectations placed on them—both by commissioners and by families. Outcome data, however, suggested that for some groups of young people attending the service, expectations for outcomes were considerably out of line with what was actually being achieved.

Raising such issues can provoke strong emotional responses. In one meeting with senior directors and commissioners, managers were publicly accused of 'abandoning' children who had not improved with help. This was an unfair and distressing accusation. Nothing could have been further from the truth as what the service was grappling with was reducing the likelihood of offering help which would not be effective. But these are difficult discussions. The value of outcome monitoring is not in *proving* that services work or that certain interventions always succeed. Instead, it allowed the service to stop doing things that were not helping, and to think afresh about what might work better. This is not about choosing between *evidence-based practice or nothing*. It is about placing curiosity at the heart of the helping process—especially when outcomes are uncertain, even for well-tested interventions.

What works for a child may be shaped by a wide range of factors: the young person's beliefs and preferences, the quality of family relationships, support from schools, friendships and peer groups and contextual life events such as bereavement, moving house or parental conflict. The risk of persisting with a method of help that is not working is high. Contrary to the commissioner's claim that staff were *giving up*, the data suggested the opposite—that staff were sometimes continuing for too long. But giving up is not the right frame. What is needed is a willingness to take outcome feedback seriously and to respond with creative, thoughtful adaptation. Outcome data provides a way to ask difficult questions—questions that often carry a heavy emotional weight—and to support a team in engaging with those questions honestly. This is essential if we are to offer the kind of help that truly makes a difference to the children and young people we serve.

Commissioners have a central role to play in creating a culture that is safe enough to explore complex issues honestly and constructively. Reactive decision-making, particularly when driven by narrow metrics such as budget pressures or waiting times, is often profoundly unhelpful in addressing the underlying challenges of building effective helping relationships with vulnerable children and young people like Jacqui and all the others we have met in the earlier parts of this book. What is essential is that commissioners become familiar with the patterns of outcomes within the services they commission and begin to ask informed, reflective questions based on this knowledge. As described earlier, the commissioner who asked whether outcomes could be improved from 50% to 60% was asking exactly the right kind of question—one rooted in a developing understanding of how the service actually worked and what it was achieving. This type of questioning reflects a relationship with outcome data that is not about scrutiny or blame, but about curiosity, improvement and shared responsibility for change.

Investment as Value for Money

Communities take responsibility for raising their children. Services, in this context, are not just mechanisms of care—they are investments made by communities to support this complex and essential task. The central question for local leadership is not only how to deliver services efficiently, but how to deliver services that provide the best value to the community by supporting children and young people to develop into healthy, adaptive and successful adults. This is not a straightforward task. One of the most significant challenges for leadership teams is to understand how different needs and difficulties in childhood intersect with one another. Needs do not often stand alone. Take, for example, concerns about disruptive behaviour in schools. It might seem logical to address this by increasing exclusion rates to improve the school environment for the majority. Within the educational system, this may make sense. But this approach has serious consequences elsewhere. If you are leading a local substance misuse service for young people, you are likely to see school exclusion as a red flag—something that increases the risk of future substance misuse. What is helpful for achieving one service's objectives may be harmful for another. Similarly, in areas where there is concern about rising numbers of children entering the care system, pressure may mount on services to support families with high levels of concern even when they do not meet thresholds for care. This can, in turn, increase the pressure on inpatient mental health services, which may be used as a way of managing significant risks without a child entering care.

A key skill for leadership at the macro level is understanding the interconnectedness and intersectionality of children's needs. Without this awareness, even well-intentioned initiatives can create new problems—often in parts of the system that were not initially the focus of attention. Poorly coordinated investment decisions can result in services working at cross-purposes, undermining one another. Commissioners and leaders need to develop an approach that recognises these interdependencies and works to minimise unintended consequences. Investment in one area must be viewed not only in terms of its direct benefit but also in terms of how it supports—or disrupts—the wider helping system around a child or family. This requires integrated thinking and long-term planning, informed by data, community engagement and a commitment to working across organisational boundaries. Without this, value for money becomes narrowly defined and fails to capture the full picture of what communities actually need to support their children.

There is a second important consideration in how priorities are established in a local setting. This concerns the balance between prevention and early intervention, and intensive or high-cost responses to acute and severe needs later in a child or young person's developmental trajectory. This tension is well-known in service planning. Resources are always finite, and decisions must be made about how much can be allocated to early intervention, while still meeting urgent and complex needs that will inevitably continue to arise.

There is no simple trade-off between investment in early intervention and a reduction in immediate demand for acute services. However, with effective leadership, it is possible to create *virtuous cycles* that gradually rebalance the system. For example, in one locality, the introduction of an Outreach Adolescent Team led to a measurable reduction in the number of children requiring inpatient psychiatric care. By monitoring this outcome, commissioners were able to make a more informed decision about the relationship between preventive work and acute treatment. In that case, it was agreed that savings from the reduced use of inpatient beds would be reinvested in the outreach team to expand its capacity. This decision not only validated the work of the team but served as an incentive—it demonstrated that effective early intervention would be recognised and supported. Importantly, this required a commissioning system that could track the relationship between service costs, such as hospital admissions, and investment in community-based support.

A similar process took place when a team was established to reduce the number of adolescents entering care. The cost of a young person in residential or foster care was significantly higher than the cost of supporting them in the community. As with the mental health outreach example, the decision was not made purely on the basis of cost. There was also recognition that institutional or intensive care does not always produce the best outcomes and that such placements are often driven by heightened anxiety about immediate risk, rather than thoughtful long-term planning. Children who needed inpatient treatment or who could not safely remain with their families were still admitted to hospital or taken into care. But what mattered was that decisions were made with a more balanced, informed perspective. When anxiety dominates, the risk is that services respond in reactive, generalised ways, rather than with careful attention to the specific needs of individual children.

Thirdly, we suggest that value for money must also reflect the views of young people and parents about what they consider most important in professional help. In one rural community, for example, young people and their families identified future employment as their primary concern—not mental health or behaviour, but the fear of having no meaningful work in adulthood. What they asked for was support and advice on how to access jobs, as well as more active involvement from the local authority in creating employment opportunities. This shifted the focus of discussion among the children's leadership team. Employment planning had not been seen as part of children's services, yet it became clear that, in that context, it had everything to do with children's well-being and future outcomes. This led to a broader consideration of other factors, such as improving public transport to link rural areas with potential employment locations. Again, these issues may fall outside the traditional remit of children's services but are nonetheless deeply connected to the lives of young people.

These examples point to the importance of maintaining a local perspective. The needs and priorities of children and families vary greatly across different communities, and such variation cannot be fully captured in national planning frameworks. Local leadership teams, with the support of commissioners, must be empowered to understand and respond to the specific needs of their populations—especially when these do not align neatly with established service categories. Value for money, in this sense, is not just about cost-effectiveness, but about the *relevance* and *impact* of services within their local context.

It Takes a Village

Integrated Helping Systems

This book has been about strengthening the interconnectedness of helping processes around individual children, recognising that effective help almost never comes from a single person or agency. More often, it is the result of many people working together to support a child or young person in managing or overcoming their difficulties. Childhood problems rarely exist in isolation. While services often try to divide them into discrete categories to provide more targeted support, this separation is often more fiction than fact.

At the macro level, we have argued for recognising and respecting this interconnectedness in service planning and funding. Children and young people often seek help in ways that reflect their understanding of how different aspects of their lives are linked. As referenced earlier, when children and young people were asked during the children's social care review what they most wanted from their social workers, they said they wanted *kindness, to be listened to* and *for the helper to stick around.* These responses suggest a holistic sense of their experience, not a neatly divided view of problems and services.

Despite how intuitively this insight resonates, it remains difficult to sustain in practice. A warning sign may be when services become heavily focused on eligibility criteria, waiting lists or rigid definitions of remit. When services become preoccupied with defining exactly which needs they are willing to address, they may lose sight of what effective help actually looks like. Of course, these concerns are understandable. Services and their staff are under significant pressure, and the constraints on capacity and resources are real. As discussed in Chapter 12, the well-being of practitioners must be a core consideration. However, restrictive eligibility criteria can often shift the difficulty elsewhere in the system. Barriers put in place to protect one service frequently create more work for another. This results in a helping system preoccupied with defending its boundaries and often defined by mistrust in which the endeavours of respective services are considered with suspicion and criticism about the work that they are able to carry out. Perhaps a more constructive and courageous way forward is not to start with resources, but with outcomes. The question becomes: *Who are we best able to help?* rather than *Who has a problem that fits our service criteria?*

Joint leadership teams must consider how children are helped by multiple services and what the best arrangements are when this kind of collaboration is necessary. There needs to be a strategic overview of how professional services can work together without requiring every service to be directly involved at all times. The village—comprising professionals, families, schools, community groups and services—needs a clearer picture of the children who are passed between its parts. A deeper understanding of these journeys would improve strategic planning, service coordination and ultimately the capacity of local helping systems to respond effectively to the interconnected needs of children and young people.

The training of multi-agency groups would also benefit significantly from the inclusion of parents and carers, both in general and through the voices of those with lived experience—parents and young people who have directly engaged with services. Our starting point throughout this book has been that effective help involves both families and professionals. This principle should be reflected in the local training culture and in the way investment in professional development is organised. Earlier in this chapter, we proposed the creation of a Parent Director role within the joint leadership group for a local area. This role would be supported by a parent and young person team whose task would include engaging with the local community through community organising approaches. An additional responsibility of this role would be to contribute to the training of both single-agency and multi-agency teams.

To take one example further, joint training around self-harm would be greatly enriched by the involvement of parents and young people with lived experience of self-harm. This behaviour is complex, with multiple contributing factors. There are no simple explanations for why it has become so common, but in many cases, it is a form of communication that is paradoxically very difficult to speak about directly. These conversations often take place between parents and their children, as well as between young people and professionals. The helping system in such cases must include both perspectives, and training for professionals that incorporates the views of parents helps to build a stronger, more collaborative approach to care.

The absence of parents and young people in these kinds of training processes sends a strong message: that the professional system continues to hold disproportionate power and responsibility for addressing children's needs. Commissioners have a key role in rebalancing this dynamic by ensuring that lived experience is included in the systems they fund. The professional contribution to a helping system does not come in one form alone. High levels of specialist expertise are essential in some teams—such as safeguarding knowledge in social care, clinical expertise in mental health services or specialist teaching in education. These forms of expertise can be vital at key points in a helping process. However, they are not always what is needed in the day-to-day work of supporting children and families. Services need to include a balance—a professional workforce that includes both high-level specialists and practitioners with broader experience and relational skills. The aim is not to replace expertise but to complement it with flexible, generalist support that is more likely to match the everyday needs of many children and young people.

At present, workforce development efforts tend to emphasise the need for more specialist professionals. However, recent developments such as the creation of community well-being practitioners and mental health practitioners in schools offer a promising shift. These roles are designed to provide middle-level support, combining generic helping skills with practical interventions for common psychological and social difficulties. One encouraging aspect of these new roles is their social inclusiveness. In many cases, people entering these roles come from more diverse backgrounds than those entering traditional professional pathways, making it more likely that minority groups are represented in the workforce. This helps create services that are more attuned to the lived realities of the communities they serve.

Commissioners have an important role to play in supporting this diversity within teams. Services should be structured so that a helping system around a child or young person includes the right level of expertise for their needs—neither over-relying on specialist intervention nor expecting generalist practitioners to manage complex challenges without the right support. Balancing these different forms of professional input is crucial to creating a system that is responsive, sustainable and rooted in real relationships.

Conclusions

The macro level is critical in setting the conditions within which families, practitioners and managers work. The long and troubled history of repeated reorganisations at this level highlights how difficult it is to establish a structure that functions well. In this book, we have deliberately avoided proposing yet another complete overhaul of the macro system. Instead, we have focused on practical and specific suggestions to improve how complex, multi-agency planning systems can operate more effectively.

We believe that a strong relationship with the local community is essential to making this work. It is the local community—families, schools and peers—that provides the majority of care and support for children. When macro systems lose sight of this, they risk becoming focused on helping *services* rather than helping *systems*. Too often, macro-level decision-making becomes dominated by the professional and organisational voices that know how to describe their own importance. While we agree that services are essential, we believe the current balance between community and professional services is skewed. This imbalance needs to be addressed at the level of service design and commissioning. A truly effective macro system must support helping systems that are centred around the everyday lives of children and families, not just around formal service provision.

Key Action Points

1 Local areas need to establish unified leadership for children's services to better support coherent helping systems.
2 This local leadership must include strong representation from parents and carers in the community.
3 Parents should be trained in community organising methods to help them meet the demands of this role effectively.
4 Local leadership structures should be responsible for identifying harmful environments affecting children and coordinating public health responses to address these.
5 Children's views on the help they need should be routinely and consistently sought, with every meeting or decision about them including their perspective.
6 Outcome reporting using a shared language across health, education, social care and justice is necessary to refocus on helping systems rather than isolated service delivery.
7 Integrated helping systems require services to work together and offer mutual support to avoid fragmentation and over-complication in response to complex needs.
8 Local workforce planning should include not only highly specialised professionals but also skilled support workers and mechanisms to strengthen the contribution of families and carers.

A Child's Life: Jessie

Jessie was 15 when she came to see me, accompanied by her father. She had recently survived a serious suicide attempt using paracetamol, and the hospital had referred her for follow-up support and ongoing risk monitoring. Jessie was articulate, intelligent and reflective. Her father was quietly spoken and respectful, both towards her and towards me.

They both agreed that Jessie would attend sessions on her own and that confidentiality was important to her. I explained that I would only share information with her parents if I believed she was at risk, or if we had first discussed it together. Jessie accepted this arrangement. She told me that naked selfies she had shared with her boyfriend had been circulated on social media. When her parents discovered this, she felt overwhelming shame. It was this event that had triggered her impulsive but dangerous overdose. Jessie no longer felt suicidal, but she was struggling to reconcile her active sexual life with her family's values and expectations. It took time before she felt our sessions were safe enough for her to speak openly. Gradually, she talked about her difficulties with her parents, her anger at the betrayal by her ex-boyfriend and the sense of isolation and confusion that followed. But she also liked to talk about her academic successes. She was highly regarded by her teachers and took genuine pride in her learning.

In one session, Jessie mentioned she was reading *Moby Dick*, the American novel. By chance, I was reading it too. I told her this, and for the next few weeks, a small part of each session was spent talking about the book—about the strange digressions and the philosophical reflections buried in the story of whalers. These conversations became like a small island within our sessions. In that space, I let go of my role a little, and we shared something human, something mutual. I wasn't consciously trying to help her during those moments. Rather, it felt like a moment of connection, a way of sharing a world—not of distress or risk, but of shared interest and intellectual engagement. She got to know me a bit more through these exchanges, just as other young people I've worked with have wanted to know which football team I support so they can tease me when they lose. These moments build familiarity and trust.

Jessie was later accepted at a local sixth form college. For her, I think *Moby Dick* became a way of sharing her strengths, not just the vulnerabilities that had brought her into the room. Her experience of help with me had been, in her words, *okay*. It hadn't been aversive. And when our work came to an end, she told me that what she really wanted now was to speak with a woman about her sexuality—something she didn't feel she could do with her mother. Later, I heard that she had started seeing the female counsellor at the college. Jessie had begun to identify what kind of support she needed, and from whom. She was no longer a passive recipient of help—she was shaping her own helping system. And that, more than anything else, marked a significant step forward.

Notes

1 **Department of Children, Families and Schools.** The Department for Children, Schools and Families (DCSF) was a department of the UK government, between 2007 and 2010, responsible for issues affecting young people in England up to the age of 19, including child protection and education. It was a major initiative to bring greater connectedness in support for children and young people. The department was led by the Secretary of State for Children, Schools and Families. The expenditure, administration and policy of the department were scrutinised by the Children, Schools and Families Select Committee. The DCSF was replaced by the Department for Education after the change of government following the 2010 General Election.

2 **Number of child deaths due to assault, neglect or unexplained.** Sidebotham, P., Atkins, B., & Hutton, J. (2011). Changes in rates of violent child deaths in England and Wales between 1974 and 2008. *Archives of Disease in Childhood, 96* (Suppl 1), A92–A93). These findings were further discussed in a second paper (Sidebotham, P., Fraser, J., Fleming, P., Ward-Platt, M., & Hain, R. (2014). Patterns of child death in England and Wales. *The Lancet, 384*(9946), 904–914.). A helpful overview of trends in homicide reports can be found in Morgan, N. (2020). *Trends and drivers of homicide: Main findings*. Home Office.

3 **Integrated Care Boards.** Integrated Care Boards (ICBs) are strategic decision-making bodies for Integrated Care Systems (ICS), responsible for planning and funding most NHS services in a local area, aiming to improve health outcomes and tackle inequalities. The 42 ICSs in England are local partnerships that bring health and care organisations together to develop shared plans and joined-up services. They are formed by NHS organisations and upper-tier local councils and also include the voluntary sector, social care providers and other partners with a role in improving local health and well-being. ICSs were legally established on 1 July 2022, covering all of England. These new arrangements are built on partnerships that were already in place across the country. Further information can be found at Integrated Care Systems Explained | The King's Fund. Recent government policy (March 2025) announced the abolition of NHS England and that these local structures are to be radically reformed and staffing reduced by half over the next two years.

4 **Review of children's social care.** The UK government review of children's social care was launched in March 2021 and produced its final report in May 2022. https://www.gov.uk/government/publications/independent-review-of-childrens-social-care-final-report (Independent review of Children's Social Care (2022). The independent review of children's social care: Final report). This included the recommendation to create family help services that enable families to have a consistent relationship with a social worker when they need help, that will increase use of family networks in supporting vulnerable children and strengthen the voice of children in decision-making about their lives. Many of its recommendations are consistent with the principles of good practice outlined here. The government response to the recommendations was published in February 2023 in Stable Homes, Built on Love can be found at https://www.gov.uk/government/consultations/childrens-social-care-stable-homes-built-on-love

5 **This quote is from Duncan Law.** Duncan Law has taught and published widely on using outcomes to improve treatment for children and young people (e.g. Jacob, J., Edbrooke-Childs, J., Holley, S., Law, D., & Wolpert, M. (2016). Horses for courses? A qualitative exploration of goals formulated in mental health settings by young people, parents, and clinicians. *Clinical Child Psychology and Psychiatry, 21*(2), 208–223; Law, D. (2022). Tools to make low intensity interventions with children and youth more effective. In S. Bennett, P. Myles-Hooton, J. Schleider, &

R. Shafran (Eds.), *Oxford guide to brief and low intensity interventions for children and young people* (p. 64). He has also been a leading advocate in the UK for the use of goal-based outcome measures. The quote came from a very helpful conversation with him.

6 **Clinician-rated outcomes paper.** This service-based evaluation work was carried out as part of routine monitoring of outcomes in the service (Fuggle, P. (2015). Are clinician ratings useful in evaluating outcomes in Child and Adolescent Mental Health Services (CAMHS)? A study of a continuous series of 1446 cases from an inner city CAMHS. *Journal of Evaluation in Clinical Practice, 21*(4), 626–632).

7 **The Choice and Partnership Approach (CAPA).** More details about the Choice and Partnership Approach can be found at the CAPA website https://www.capa.co.uk/

8 **CAPA evaluation.** The local evaluation of CAPA showed significant benefits in its implementation (Fuggle, P., McHugh, A., Gore, L., Dixon, E., Curran, D., & Cutinha, D. (2016). Can we improve service efficiency in CAMHS using the CAPA approach without reducing treatment effectiveness? *Journal of Child Health Care, 20*(2), 195–204).

9 **Anti-bullying programmes.** A meta-analysis of anti-bullying programmes showed modest effectiveness in reducing frequency of bullying (Jiménez-Barbero, J. A., Ruiz-Hernández, J. A., Llor-Zaragoza, L., Pérez-García, M., & Llor-Esteban, B. (2016). Effectiveness of anti-bullying school programs: A meta-analysis. *Children and Youth Services Review, 61*, 165–175). Programmes showed more effectiveness for children under ten. The most well-developed anti-bullying programme has been developed by Dan Olweus in Norway and its effectiveness was recently re-evaluated as showing long term benefits (Olweus, D., Solberg, M. E., & Breivik, K. (2020). Long-term school-level effects of the Olweus Bullying Prevention Program (OBPP). *Scandinavian Journal of Psychology, 61*(1), 108–116).

10 **Involvement of young people in anti-bullying programmes.** Anti-bullying programmes include the recognition that active involvement of young people in the design and implementation of such programmes is likely to contribute to effectiveness (Ttofi, M., & Farrington, D. (2009). What works in preventing bullying: Effective elements of anti-bullying programmes. *Journal of Aggression, Conflict and Peace Research, 1*(1), 13–24).

11 **Impact of racism on children and young people.** The significant negative impact of racism on children and young people is widely recognised and its importance as a determinant of poor mental health (Berry, O. O., Londoño Tobón, A., & Njoroge, W. F. (2021). Social determinants of health: The impact of racism on early childhood mental health. *Current Psychiatry Reports, 23*, 1–10; Trent, M., Dooley, D. G., Dougé, J., Cavanaugh, R. M., Lacroix, A. E., Fanburg, J., … & Wallace, S. B. (2019). The impact of racism on child and adolescent health. *Pediatrics, 144*(2), e20191765).

12 **Exclusion from school.** Increased rates of school exclusion for Black Caribbean children have been consistently reported (e.g. Timpson, E. (2019). *Timpson review of school exclusion*. Dandy Booksellers Limited; Graham, B., White, C., Edwards, A., Potter, S., & Street, C. (2019). School exclusion: A literature review on the continued disproportionate exclusion of certain. *Department for Education*; Black, A. (2022). 'But what do the statistics say?' An overview of permanent school exclusions in England. *Emotional and Behavioural Difficulties, 27*(3), 199–219.)

13 **Community Organising.** The theory and practice of community organising was first developed by Saul Alinsky (Alinsky, S. D. (1941). Community analysis and organization. *American Journal of Sociology, 46*(6), 797–808; Alinsky, S. D. (2010). *Rules for radicals: A pragmatic primer for realistic radicals*. Knopf Doubleday Publishing Group). Its application to health issues has been found to be promising (Kadariya, S., Ball, L., Chua, D., Ryding, H., Hobby, J., Marsh, J., … &

Parkinson, J. (2023). Community organising frameworks, models, and processes to improve health: A systematic scoping review. *International Journal of Environmental Research and Public Health, 20*(7), 5341.) Its application to the needs of children and families has been demonstrated in the development of community schools (Warren, M. R., & Hong, S. (2009). More than services: Community organising and community schools. In R. Deslandes (Ed.), *International perspectives on contexts, communities and evaluated innovative practices* (pp. 195–206). Routledge.)

14 **Citizens UK.** Information about Citizens UK can be found at https://www.citizensuk.org/. Citizens UK is a grassroots alliance of local communities working together in England and Wales bringing together local institutions, including schools, universities, churches, mosques, synagogues, parent groups, health trusts, charities and unions. They have worked on several campaigns, including the UK Living Wage campaign and ending the detention of children for immigration purposes. In 2023, national campaigns included Climate Change, Homelessness, Housing, anti-Misogyny and school-based counselling.

15 **Children's Rights in Denmark.** The Child's Act in Denmark has been effective from January 1, 2024, and its primary objective is to recognise the child as an independent individual, ensuring that decisions affecting them are made based on their best interests rather than those of parents or authorities. The reform programme is called Children First and the legislation is called the Child Law. The application of this law is primarily focused on social care, and its implementation is for social workers and their practice. The major change is that social workers have to seek the views of children on all matters to do with their care, not just one overarching consent to being in care etc. Every time a new decision is made, the child's view should be known. The government is currently planning an evaluation of the impact of this on child outcomes. It has also been relevant to decisions around children following divorce. Two difficult areas for implementation are around children with disabilities and children under three years of age. Children's views do not prevail unchallenged by parents or other professionals, but they must be known. The children have a right to be consulted but they do not have an obligation to offer their views if they prefer not to. The Handbook on the Law of the Child can be found at https://www.sbst.dk/udgivelser/2023/haandbog-om-barnets-lov

16 **Using outcomes in service decision-making.** As previously described, routine outcome monitoring was established in the Islington service and the results of this were reported (Fuggle, P. (2015). Are clinician ratings useful in evaluating outcomes in Child and Adolescent Mental Health Services (CAMHS)? A study of a continuous series of 1446 cases from an inner city CAMHS. *Journal of Evaluation in Clinical Practice, 21*(4), 626–632). From this case series we identified a group that had less good outcomes and used this information to guide decision-making in the service (Fuggle, P., & Cleridou, K. (2018). Innovations in practice: Using clinician-rated outcomes to support improved service decision making in a Child and Adolescent Mental Health Service. *Child and Adolescent Mental Health, 23*(1), 57–60).

Chapter 14

Summary and Conclusions

Over the last 30 years, child mental health has become an increasingly prominent public health concern. While specialist services for children and young people have expanded substantially, with increased prevalence, major challenges persist. Resources remain inadequate relative to need, and professional help is often difficult to access due to long waiting lists and narrowing eligibility criteria. For managers and frontline practitioners, it can feel as though little has changed for the better over the decades, despite numerous national initiatives aimed at 'transforming' the services they work within. These continuing difficulties highlight the ongoing challenge of supporting children and young people with mental health needs, especially when these intersect with other life problems. This book acknowledges both perspectives: that real progress has been made, but also that significant and enduring problems remain in providing effective support.

Child mental health services and related community resources operate within complex national and local public sector systems. NHS, Education and Social Care services are subject to constant organisational change, creating unstable conditions that make it difficult to sustain even well-designed and adequately resourced initiatives. For those on the front line, it often feels like a cycle of repeated, short-lived reforms, each one replaced by another programme greeted with similar enthusiasm. At a local level, services may seem like a ship repeatedly buffeted by funding cuts and opportunistic projects, with new trends often masking long-standing challenges. Rather than another new initiative, we argue for building on the existing expertise and experience of those already doing the work. The principles of good practice discussed throughout this book are already being applied, in part, by dedicated individuals or teams committed to delivering the best for the children and families they serve. Every idea presented here has its roots in long-standing relationships and conversations with colleagues about how to do this difficult work well. These principles reflect their practice. Yet, while the individual pieces of the puzzle exist, they rarely come together in one place; the jigsaw is incomplete, awaiting integration. Inclusive help is a long-standing idea that has been somewhat lost in the push to develop improved professional treatments. Many

DOI: 10.4324/9781003145523-14

people—including young people themselves—can and do play a vital role in supporting children and young people. This includes mental health professionals, those working in other areas of children's lives such as teachers and social workers, parents and carers and others in the wider community, such as faith leaders. The question is not whether professionals or families help best, but how they work together. We suspect that there is something inherent to the human act of *collaboration* that contributes to the process of 'healing' in cases of psychological distress.

Helping children is a profoundly relational process, whether support comes from therapists and doctors, a cook in an in-patient unit, an outreach nurse, a football coach or a grandparent who sees the family needs help. What they all share is that none can offer comprehensive help alone. Effective support depends on trusting relationships being built between adults, which make sense to the child or young person. It is unhelpful to suggest that the wide range of mental health needs can be met solely by professional services. That is an unrealistic burden. What we have proposed is the greater recognition of the contributions of all those involved in supporting children through their mental health challenges. We have called this inclusive help, a framework which does not exclude non-professionals from playing important roles in responding to the mental health needs of children and young people. The process of change or 'cure' may be made possible through the intervention of a mental health professional, however, to us, it does not follow that the actions of the professional brought about the change. In fact, the active coordination of understanding and concern may be the active agent that removes obstacles (physical, social and psychological) in the way of typical development for children with mental disorders.

While we are calling for greater recognition of these roles, we are not claiming that they are new. The moment we look closely at how support happens for individual children, the importance of parents and carers becomes clear. The stories of Jacqui, Martin, Abdul, Simone, Daniel and Teresa all highlight the active role their parents are already playing. The aim is to rebalance our understanding of the helping system around children so that the contributions of both families and professionals are equally valued as their agreed and shared focus on the child and young person may be the critical ingredient of change. This is not to idealise parents and carers. We have tried throughout the book to represent the realities of parenthood respectfully and honestly, acknowledging the challenges faced by both parents and children in trying to overcome distress. Parents and professionals need each other, and inclusive help sets out how this collaboration should work at the level of individual care, team practice and service planning and funding. Achieving this means parents and young people must have a stronger voice, more influence and formal authority to work alongside the professionals and services designed for them.

Our thinking about the need to rebalance the relationship between professional systems and the community has grown out of our experience of child mental health services. It has been encouraging to find similar thinking in critiques of public sector provision more broadly. While we cannot review these in full, one example stands out[1], advocating a strengths-based approach to improving service effectiveness. Crucially, it focuses not on the strengths of services, but on the strengths of the communities they serve. It also distinguishes between relational help and more instrumental forms. As we have argued throughout this book, effective help for children must be relational, because it is in the linking of minds that generates understanding in all of us. Children and young people will not accept less, nor should they, as learning from trusted others is built into their genetic code. Help that fails to recognise this is unlikely to succeed. This strengths-based approach, rooted in the community, resonates with our emphasis on valuing parents and carers. Parents' understanding of the actions of their children, as well as their understanding of themselves, grows through living in a community that embodies the importance of interpersonal understanding and the concern, trust and commitment which a community endowed with social capital gifts to its members. It offers a starting point for rethinking public sector provision as a partnership between services and the communities they serve. Child mental health services belong to their communities, and they exemplify the need to join community and professional support.

Helping children and young people differs fundamentally from helping adults, largely because children have parents, which changes the nature of both the helping process and the systems around it. Children have a built-in mental health repair system—family—where adult members are expected to provide care and support. For children, seeking help outside the family, particularly for issues they consider private, can provoke complex feelings of loyalty and trust. Unlike children, adults can usually decide for themselves whether they want help and can act on that decision independently. They might choose to see a GP and then decide whether to follow the advice given. Young people can do this too, but more often it happens with the involvement or agreement of parents or carers, who frequently play an active role in the process. Seeking help can be difficult for adults, often involving feelings of shame, vulnerability or humiliation, which can lead to avoidance. These feelings are also present for children and young people but may be intensified by their limited autonomy and power, an absence of agency mental disorder often amplifies. In all these ways, the helping process for children is more precarious than for adults, and this requires far greater attention when thinking about how to support developing agency in vulnerable young people, by giving them control over their navigation of the health system which outcomes measurement and goal-based outcomes monitoring is often able to do.

Some readers may be disappointed that we have placed parents at the centre of the helping process, rather than young people themselves, and that we have not taken a position similar to Denmark's approach to children's rights. This is a fair challenge to the coherence of the principles set out in this book. Our starting point, however, has been to ask how help actually works for children—and how it can work better—both inside and outside the therapy room, in supporting them through the challenges they face. When we look at the helping process in full, parents occupy a central role. Helping children is what parents do—some do it well, some too much, some too little and some not at all. A few, tragically, intentionally or unintentionally, harm their children, removing the inbuilt motivation to trust and join in the transgenerational transmission of knowledge upon which human culture is based. Trauma is only a small part of a much wider picture. There are real dangers in handing over the whole helping process to professional services. These services do not have the resources, capacity or in some cases even the motivation to take on the task of initiating a process of healing alone. Their role is to share the burden—providing essential support during times of crisis or severe need, while enabling families, schools and communities to rebuild their own ability to support the young person. If, in highlighting this, we appear to diminish the position of the child or young person, this is not our intention. Children are not part of the helping system—they are the ones in need of help. We hope it is clear that we are also making a strong and unambiguous call for children and young people to shape the help they receive with their own voice and perspective.

Some may feel that the six key principles carry an anti-professional tone, or that the value of professional help for children is downplayed or even sidelined. That is not our view, nor our intention. Our aim has been to set out the complementary value of both professional and non-professional contributions to the helping process. If the argument is that only professionals can help, and that solutions are found solely in the consulting or treatment room, then we must disagree. We fully accept that some interventions—such as trauma-informed CBT—cannot be carried out by even the most knowledgeable and sensitive parent, and that such treatments may be essential to a young person's recovery. But the wider benefits of treatment depend heavily on the social environment in which the child lives, and even on whether they can access the treatment at all. The professional must be aware of the limitations of their role, and not allow their sense of importance to be a potential obstacle in the way of environmental change. For example, in the case of young people with serious eating difficulties, for example, nursing expertise may be necessary at certain times, but a large part of their progress will depend on the support provided by the family they live with. The expert with humility must understand when to step back so sustainable modes of change have an opportunity to emerge. Earlier in the book, we used the example of how children learn to read to show that both expert teaching and practice support are needed. If we relied entirely on teachers to practise reading, paradoxically, children would learn far less.

We also understand concerns that we may appear to have softened our stance on evidence-based practice—that we suggest anything goes, if it fits the child's preferences, or that effective help is like shopping, with the child picking what they like best. This is not what we are proposing. What matters most is not simply whether a child receives evidence-based treatment, but whether their life improves and the difficulties they face are reduced because of the help offered—or the self-help they adopt, as in Daniel's case with the gym. Improvement is more likely if evidence-based methods are used, and professionals have a responsibility to make these methods accessible to children and young people. What is essential is that the outcomes of help are monitored. With outcome monitoring in place, services can offer a more flexible approach that allows the views of children and parents on what might help to be taken seriously—because it will be clear whether change is happening or not. What we do not support is the idea that evidence-based practice means rigidly delivering treatment protocols that all children and parents must follow. That model may be necessary in research trials, but it should not dictate the way community-based services operate. Services, and above all, children and young people, must be able to respond to the diverse and evolving ways in which modern communities seek help.

We have argued that helping systems rely on collaboration between families, professionals, schools and the wider community, and that children rarely receive help for a particular difficulty from only one person or agency. In most cases, multiple people are involved—and this almost always includes both families and schools. Schools are perhaps the most important of these, and seeing their social function increasingly recognised as a platform for timely delivery of support appears to us to be aligned with the principles espoused here and a welcome development. The challenge for services is to find ways of supporting the broader helping systems around each child, rather than simply delivering the standard interventions they are set up to offer in response to specific referrals. Services often present their processes, procedures, eligibility criteria and treatment lengths as though they are the only element of support. The real challenge is how to work alongside and integrate with the other parts of a child's life in order to form an effective, coherent helping system. This is not just a matter of improving parental or educational participation in service delivery. What is needed is a more radical shift in power, where communities, families and parents have greater influence over decisions about how mental health resources are allocated to meet the needs of children in their community. At present, parents are largely absent from decision-making processes about how services are planned and funded. These decisions are dominated by the power held by services and professionals. We propose a rebalancing of that power. Parents and the communities in which they live need to be equipped with the skills and confidence to take part in decision-making, and this will not happen without deliberate support. Community organising may offer a vital framework to enable parents and communities to speak to those in positions of authority and bring about meaningful change.

For both authors, the memory of childhood is now distant. But trying to be helpful to children has been at the heart of our professional lives. We have worked with and listened to children who have faced severe suffering and adversity. These are difficult stories for adults to hear, often stirring deep feelings of sadness, helplessness and, at times, anger. This book is our attempt to distil those experiences and the reflections they have prompted about the lives too many children lead. We believe that many people have a role to play in supporting children, and we hope this book offers a balanced yet hopeful view of how that support can be achieved.

Note

1 **A strengths-based approach to improving public sector services.** A recent report by Demos in 2024 titled 'The Motivational State: a strengths-based approach to improved public sector productivity' authored by Fox, A., Fox, C., proposed a strengths-based, person-led approach to public sector services, co-produced with individuals, families, and communities. By focusing on building relationships, empowering individuals, and leveraging their strengths and capacities, the authors argue that both outcomes and efficiency can improve. The themes are their approach are very similar to the main arguments of this book although the language of productivity is somewhat different.

Index

Note: Page numbers followed by 'n' refer to notes.

For Product Safety Concerns and Information please contact our EU representative GPSR@taylorandfrancis.com
Taylor & Francis Verlag GmbH, Kaufingerstraße 24, 80331 München, Germany

www.ingramcontent.com/pod-product-compliance
Ingram Content Group UK Ltd.
Pitfield, Milton Keynes, MK11 3LW, UK
UKHW022344190926
475702UK00015B/2098
* 9 7 8 0 3 6 7 7 0 2 9 1 5 *